SHAMING THE DEVIL

Shaming the Devil

ESSAYS IN TRUTHTELLING

Alan Jacobs

William B. Eerdmans Publishing Company

Grand Rapids, Michigan / Cambridge, U.K.

© 2004 Wm. B. Eerdmans Publishing Co.
All rights reserved

Wm. B. Eerdmans Publishing Co.
255 Jefferson Ave. S.E., Grand Rapids, Michigan 49503 /
P.O. Box 163, Cambridge CB3 9PU U.K.
www.eerdmans.com

Printed in the United States of America

09 08 07 06 05 04   7 6 5 4 3 2 1

Library of Congress Cataloging-in-Publication Data

Jacobs, Alan, 1958–
Shaming the devil : essays in truthtelling / Alan Jacobs.
p.   cm.
Includes index.
ISBN 0-8028-4894-X (pbk. : alk. paper)
1. Truth. 2. Truth in literature. 3. Truth — Religious aspects — Christianity.
I. Title.

BD171.J23   2004
177'.3 — dc22

2004050608

The author and publisher gratefully acknowledge permission to reprint the following material:

"At the Aquatic Carnival" by Les Murray. Reprinted by permission of the author.

"Passover" from *Waterborne: Poems* by Linda Gregerson. Copyright © 2002 by Linda Gregerson. Reprinted by permission of Houghton Mifflin Company. All rights reserved.

for the crowd at Café Padre

Contents

CONTENTS

part 3
EXPERIMENT

Acknowledgments

I have been very blessed over the past decade in having a number of skilled and sympathetic editors with whom to work: Jody Bottum, Jim Nuechterlein, and John Wilson. May their tribe increase, or at least hold its own. I am also thankful for the interest, support, and patience of Jon Pott and the other good people at Eerdmans.

"Shame the Devil," "Camus: Wisdom and Courage," "The Only Honest Man," "Wole Soyinka's Outrage," and "The Re-Invention of Love" first appeared, each in somewhat different form than here, in *Books & Culture*. "Computer Control" did too, but spread over three issues. "Auden's Happy Eye" (under the title "Auden and the Limits of Poetry"), "The Genesis of Wisdom," and "Iris Murdoch's Go(o)d" appeared in *First Things*. "The Witness" and "The Devil's Party" (the latter in a much briefer version) were first published in *The Weekly Standard*. I am thankful to the good people of the Trinity Arts Conference in Dallas, Texas, for asking me to come and deliver the lectures that appear here (in print for the first time) as "The Judgment of Grace." The good wine and good food and the summer night sky were mighty fine as well.

I am richly blessed with friends, colleagues, and pastors who, in ways known and unknown to them, have shaped me and therefore my writing. To a very significant group of those folks I dedicate this book.

Introduction

"Tell the truth and shame the devil." It's an imperative familiar to many, though some will have heard it from Shakespeare and others from their elderly relations. As a native Southerner, I never want to admit ignorance of any ancient chunk of folk wisdom, but I confess I never came across the phrase until I read the first Henry IV play in college. A friend of mine, by contrast, learned it from his grandmother and was surprised when I told him that I thought it originated with the Bard. And maybe it did. My worn copy of *Brewer's Dictionary of Phrase and Fable* — the reference book than which no more enjoyable can be conceived — says, merely and unhelpfully, that it is "a very old saying, of obvious meaning." Whether that verdict is incompatible with Shakespearean authorship depends, I guess, on what you mean by "very old." In this book's first essay I implicitly credit Shakespeare for it, but readers should take that with all requisite grains of salt.

Whether the meaning is so obvious, though, I doubt. It seems rather odd, on the face of it, to say that truthtelling *shames* the devil. Angers, frustrates, confutes — yes to all of those. But one does not normally associate the devil with shame; indeed, one could say that shame is precisely what he lacks. After all, when we encounter people who seem impervious to moral censure, and indifferent to the displeasure of authorities, we call them shameless; this is surely an even more fitting description of the Adversary.

Yet the concept of shame has another dimension that may be more appropriate to the devilish context. In Homer's *Odyssey*, Penelope, the despairing wife of long-lost (and presumed dead) Odysseus, decrees a contest for her many suitors: the one who can string the mighty bow of Odysseus will have her hand in marriage. This idea they like. But when she agrees to allow a visiting beggar (whom we know to be Odysseus in disguise) to participate in the competition, they demur. One of their leaders, Eurymakhos, whines,

> . . . Our ears burn at what men might say,
> and women, too. We hear some jackal whispering:
> 'How far inferior to the great husband
> her suitors are! Can't even budge his bow!
> Think of it; and a beggar, our of nowhere,
> strung it quick and made the needle shot!'
> That kind of disrepute we would not care for.

Penelope's reply is a masterpiece of irony:

> Eurymakhos, you have no good repute
> In this realm, nor the faintest hope of it —
> men who abused a prince's house for years,
> consumed his wine and cattle. Shame enough.
> Why hang your heads over a trifle now?

The irony lies in her deliberate misunderstanding of Eurymakhos's complaint: she pretends to believe that he is expressing some *moral* scruple, a fear of disapproving judgment, and consoles him by pointing out that his behavior has been so shameless for so long that he can't do any more damage to his reputation than he has already done. But of course Eurymakhos's concern isn't moral at all: he's afraid simply of being *exposed*, of having some dirty old beggar publicly trounce him in a contest of physical strength. He doesn't want anyone to know how weak he really is.

This is the sense in which the devil can be shamed. When we tell the truth, the proverb affirms, the Father of Lies (as Jesus calls him in John

8:44) is deprived of his children; he may also be the Prince of this world, but his dominion has limits of scope and compulsion. Every time we tell the truth we put him in his place. And because he hates his place, and wants more than anyone has ever wanted anything to assume the place of God, he is deeply grieved and shamed when our truthfulness shows the world just how un-Almighty he is.

Thus the necessity of telling the truth. And yet nothing in the world is more difficult, with the signal exception of loving one's neighbor. That is why the subtitle of this book is *"Essays* in Truthtelling," with the emphasis on the original meaning of the word "essay": a trial, an experiment. As has often been noted, "essay" is etymologically connected with "assay" and "assess." One must remember the old Westerns in which a prospector brings a hunk of rock to the local assayer to find out how much gold is in it, how valuable it truly is (as opposed to how valuable it appears, on first glance, to be); the whole set of terms suggests testing, discerning judgment, critical evaluation. Thus Francis Bacon, the first English practitioner of the essay as a literary form, writes that the "mixture of falsehoods" with truth, especially in public life ("civil business"), "is like alloy in coin of gold and silver, which may make the metal work better, but embaseth it." That is, lies may make "civil business" run more smoothly, but only at the cost of what we would call "debasing" it, reducing its value and making it less reliably strong and sound. Therefore, he suggests, our discourse must be assayed — tested, evaluated, and ultimately purified.

Bacon writes these words in his essay "Of Truth," which begins with a famous sentence: "What is truth? said jesting Pilate, and would not stay for an answer." This refers, of course, to a dramatic moment in the eighteenth chapter of John's Gospel. When Jesus tells Pilate that he has come into the world to bear witness to the truth, and that "everyone who is of the truth listens to my voice," Pilate responds with what we can only read as the flippant rhetorical question of an accomplished scoffer. Bacon writes that Pilate "would not stay for an answer" because, as John tells us, "After he had said this, he went back outside to the Jews and told them, 'I find no guilt in him. But you have a custom that I should release one man for you at the Passover. So do you want me to release to you the King of the Jews?'" In this scene, then, Pilate demonstrates that he is a master of all forms of evasive non-commitment. Having parried Jesus' implicit challenge — "Are you one of those who is of the truth?" — with his quick counter-question and immediate departure, he informs the crowd, not that Jesus is certainly innocent and should be freed, but simply that *he* has found no guilt in Jesus. Then, rather than allowing the debate about Jesus' guilt or innocence to continue — a matter, after all, of what the truth is — he again provides an alternative question, this one not rhetorical but pragmatic. Pilate proposes to exchange a controversy over the truth for a practical consideration of what action to take.

He is, in short, a pragmatist of the kind celebrated, and exemplified, by Richard Rorty. Rorty has spent a quarter-century now — since the publication in 1979 of his book *Philosophy and the Mirror of Nature* — arguing that philosophy needs to stop concerning itself with questions about the way things are and pursue instead ways to help us get what we want. Rorty has repeatedly emphasized that, to those "metaphysicians" (as he calls them) who continue to insist that questions of truth are worth pursuing, pragmatists should reply not by making arguments but by "changing the subject." It's hard to imagine anyone carrying out this philosophical program more smoothly than Tiberias Caesar's procurator in Judea.

In all fairness, one must admit that Pilate is in a difficult situation. What resources does he have, after all, to adjudicate this arcane conflict among a bunch of belligerent and opinionated tribesmen in a troubled corner of Rome's empire? How could *he* possibly say who is the true King of the Jews? How could he even know what facts are relevant to the question? One could argue, then, that Pilate actually exemplifies a commendable humility, a recognition of his limits — perhaps even the limits of human knowledge itself. (In my imagination I project Pilate into our time, and I find that I think of him, not as a politician, but as a bishop in the Episcopal Church. But I digress.)

However, Jesus does not ask Pilate to decide who the true King of the Jews is. Jesus asks him (implicitly, but none the less forcibly) whether he is willing to listen to the voice of the One who has come into this world to bear witness to the truth. And Pilate is not willing. His character is not marked by humility, but by indifference or laziness. This is the point made by Chesterton in a famous outburst:

What we suffer from to-day is humility in the wrong place. Modesty has moved from the organ of ambition. Modesty has settled upon the organ of conviction; where it was never meant to be. A man was meant to be doubtful about himself, but undoubting about the truth; this has been exactly reversed. Nowadays the part of a man that a man does assert is exactly the part he ought not to assert — himself. The part he doubts is exactly the part he ought not to doubt — the Divine Reason. Huxley preached a humility content to learn from Nature. But the new sceptic is so humble that he doubts if he can even learn. . . . The old humility was a spur that prevented a man from stopping; not a nail in his boot that prevented him from going on. For the old humility made a man doubtful about his efforts, which might make him work harder. But the new humility makes a man doubtful about his aims, which will make him stop working altogether.

Pilate, Rorty, and their kind are among those who have stopped working altogether — working, that is, to assay truth. (They have other projects about which they can be quite assiduous.) That "aim" they not only doubt but positively deny. What, after all, *is* truth?

The essays in this book often, though implicitly, ask that question, but in each of them I try to stay for an answer — though there are times when it seems none is forthcoming. The first section is devoted to people whom I believe to be exemplary in their quest for truth. They know how hard it is to find — they know better than the pragmatists of the world can ever know. Seeking the truth is in this respect like resisting temptation: "Only those who try to resist temptation know how strong it is," C. S. Lewis wrote. "A man who gives in to temptation after five minutes simply does not know what it would have been like an hour later." The same applies to truth-seeking and truth-telling: only those who devote their lives to the consistent pursuit of truth are in any position to describe for us the difficulty of the task. Those who have given it up or evaded it have nothing to offer on this subject.

The second section I have called "Explorations" because in its essays I reflect on writers and thinkers who give me pause, whose engagement with major questions seems something less than ideal — who, Pilate-like, evade the challenge posed by Jesus, or perhaps merely flinch before its demands. Yet these figures all possess power, power to disturb or even to compel; they pose strong questions of their own from which I try not to flinch, even when they disconcert. I try, then, to explore — and, yes, assay — my responses of dismay, anger, frustration, or disorientation, as it may be. But even as I contend with these thinkers, I thank them for their provocations.

The third section is different, and not just because it consists of a single lengthy essay — an essay which, moreover, may seem to have nothing to do with the problems of truthfulness. Yet "Computer Control" is a necessary component of the serpentine and attenuated story I am trying to tell in this book. In the last essay of Part 1, "The Genesis of Wisdom," I briefly consider the social institutions (in particular the secular university) that circumscribe our quests for truth. But those quests are also, and perhaps even more decisively, circumscribed by our dominant technologies, and among those none is more dominant than the personal computer. The simplest way to put the question I have in mind in that essay is this: does computer technology help or hinder us in our pursuit of truth? — a pursuit which is, properly and deeply understood, part of a still larger quest, what Jacques Ellul calls "the search for justice before God." If what I write in that essay and in this book moves us an inch or so closer to general truthfulness, and thereby towards the justice of the Lord, my work will have been amply rewarded. And if it brings a discomfited blush, even for an instant, to the face of Old Slewfoot, that would be nice too.

part 1

EXEMPLARS

Shame the Devil

In Shakespeare's first Henry IV play, one of the rebels against the king, a Welshman named Owen Glendower, lays claim to marvelous magical powers and supernatural gifts. His powers have been testified to from his conception; he is both a prophet and the object of prophecy. He begins by telling an assemblage of rebel leaders about the dramatic signs in the heavens that heralded his nativity:

> at my birth
> The front of heaven was full of fiery shapes,
> The goats ran from the mountains, and the herds
> Were strangely clamorous to the frighted fields.
> These signs have mark'd me extraordinary;
> And all the courses of my life do show
> I am not in the roll of common men.
> Where is he living, clipp'd in with the sea
> That chides the banks of England, Scotland, Wales,
> Which calls me pupil, or hath read to me?
> And bring him out that is but woman's son
> Can trace me in the tedious ways of art
> And hold me pace in deep experiments.

With these boasts young Harry Percy — Hotspur — has no patience. When Glendower resonantly proclaims, "I can call spirits from the vasty deep," Hotspur replies, "Why, so can I, or so can any man;/But will they come when you do call for them?" When Glendower in turn replies, "Why, I can teach you, cousin, to command the devil," Hotspur's final answer is decisive:

And I can teach thee, coz, to shame the devil
By telling truth: tell truth and shame the devil.
If thou have power to raise him, bring him hither,
And I'll be sworn I have power to shame him hence.
O, while you live, tell truth and shame the devil!

Hotspur's counsel to Glendower is my counsel to all of us. Let it be my text and my meditation.

IN THE AFTERMATH of the September 11th attacks on the World Trade Center and the Pentagon, a particular poem came again and again to the public's attention — a poem by W. H. Auden called "September 1, 1939." On the Saturday after the attacks, Scott Simon read the poem aloud on National Public Radio; a friend of mine who teaches at the University of Virginia heard it declaimed at an inter-faith prayer meeting; on October 11th, the one-month anniversary of the attacks, *The New Yorker* magazine sponsored a program at New York's Town Hall called "Beyond Words" during which many writers read the work of others on relevant themes, and there the Irish poet Paul Muldoon read "September 1, 1939." (I find it ironic that a program entitled "Beyond Words" would be composed of nothing but words; surely during the course of the evening someone called attention to that irony, but the words kept coming all the same. For *The New Yorker*, nothing is ever truly beyond words.) There was even an article about the phenomenon, by Eric McHenry, posted on the online magazine *Slate*, but we'll get back to that later. And just this week there were conversations all over Chicago about this poem, conducted under the rubric "What Can a Poem Do?"

Such use of this particular poem was almost inevitable, given the presence of the month of September in the title, the poem's concern with

4

a just-arrived world crisis, its association with New York City, and the popularity, among literarily educated Americans, of at least some of the sentiments the poem expresses. The first day of September in 1939 was of course the day on which Nazi Germany invaded Poland, and therefore — thanks to a mutual defense treaty Britain and France had signed with Poland — the beginning of the long-dreaded European war. In January of that year, Auden and his friend Christopher Isherwood had come to America for an indefinite stay. (Both, as it turned out, would become American citizens and would live in this country for at least part of the year for the rest of their lives.) The two friends landed in New York, but Isherwood soon decamped for sunnier California; Auden, though, stayed, and soon found a house in Brooklyn where he lived with one of the most extraordinary assemblages of characters one could imagine: the great English composer Benjamin Britten, his lover the tenor Peter Pears, Thomas Mann's son Golo, the writers Paul and Jane Bowles, the young Southern novelist Carson McCullers, and, for a brief time anyway, the most famous of them all, the stripper Gypsy Rose Lee. But Manhattan, then as now, was where most of the action was, and Auden spent a lot of time there; so his poem about the moment at which the European world collapsed begins with these words:

I sit in one of the dives
On Fifty-Second Street. . . .

Though the events which trouble Auden's spirit occurred across the Atlantic, he receives the news in New York; a certain geographical — and perhaps more than geographical — disconnection from the tragic events is essential to the poem's meditative structure. And, really, this is not wholly different from the situation of those gathered in New York's Town Hall a month ago, brooding on the events that had occurred sixty blocks away, at the southern tip of Manhattan Island, a month before.

Casting his mind across the ocean, then, to the continent he had recently abandoned — largely because of the relentless pressures and expectations it held for him — Auden was moved to consider the question that one always considers in such situations: why did this horrible event happen? And his answer would become one of the two most famous moments in this very famous poem:

> Accurate scholarship can
> Unearth the whole offence
> From Luther until now
> That has driven a culture mad,
> Find what occurred at Linz,
> What huge imago made
> A psychopathic god:
> I and the public know
> What all schoolchildren learn,
> Those to whom evil is done
> Do evil in return.

This is basically the argument of John Maynard Keynes' book of 1919, *The Economic Consequences of the Peace,* only in simplified and moralized form: the countries that had placed such an enormous financial and moral burden on Germany with the Treaty of Versailles were responsible for the events of September 1, and only pedantry or manipulative political rhetoric could mask that responsibility. And Auden emphasizes that he speaks not for himself only: anticipating those pedants and politicians he masses the wisdom of "the public" and "schoolchildren" — the appeal is palpably democratic, but the tone hieratic; the prophetic here wells up from below, rather than descending from on high. And again, one can easily trace the links between this poem and the events of September 11th, events which have caused so many people to ask, "What have we done to these people to make them so angry at us?" As I listened over the Internet to Paul Muldoon reading the poem, and noticed the forceful sonorousness — the slight but audible increase in emphasis — with which he uttered the words "Those to whom evil is done/Do evil in return," I could hear in his voice the confidence of one who knows that that the syllables he speaks carry prophetic force; and I could see in my mind's eye row after row of heads in a half-darkened hall nodding in sobered affirmation.

I said that this stanza constitutes one of the two most famous moments in the poem; the other comes in the penultimate stanza:

All I have is a voice
To undo the folded lie,
The romantic lie in the brain
Of the sensual man-in-the-street
And the lie of Authority
Whose buildings grope the sky:
There is no such thing as the State
And no one exists alone;
Hunger allows no choice
To the citizen or the police;
We must love one another or die.

Once again, I recall Paul Muldoon's voice assuming a certain weight and substance as this stanza came to its resonant close — the weight and substance appropriate to the prophetic utterance. And I imagine those many attentive heads nodding again, or perhaps bowing slightly, burdened by the difficult truth of Auden's charitable imperative.

But it is not clear — and was not even at the time clear to Auden — what power commands and undergirds such charity. A few months earlier Auden had written another famous poem, "In Memory of W. B. Yeats," which had its own memorable conclusion:

In the deserts of the heart
Let the healing fountain start
In the prison of his days
Teach the free man how to praise.

But praise what? And why? Similarly, "September 1, 1939" ends with a plea, almost a prayer:

May I, composed like them,
Of Eros and of dust,

Beleaguered by the same
Negation and despair,
Show an affirming flame.

(Here Muldoon, in his reading, became especially emphatic.) But what should this flame affirm? In both poems the tone, the language itself, are hieratic and prophetic. But there seems to be no content to the message — the tone itself soothes or exhorts or encourages or strengthens, but only so long as we politely refrain from wondering why the verb "praise" has no object, and the "affirming flame" nothing in particular to affirm. On close inspection there is a certain vacuousness to such phrases, as though this brilliant poet were paying something less than full attention to the task before him.

As I noted earlier, "September 1, 1939" has been often read, or at least quoted, in the last two months, and frequently commented on; but only Eric McHenry, in the piece in *Slate* that I referred to earlier — its title, by the way, is "Auden on Bin Laden" — only Eric McHenry, to my knowledge, has emphasized one of the most interesting and significant facts about the poem: that within five years of writing it Auden had completely repudiated it, and eventually excluded it from all collections of his poems over which he had control. Why and how did this happen?

ALAS, THE STORY is too long to tell in full here. Suffice it to say that throughout the year 1940, as the war grew in intensity, as news of its cruelties became more detailed, as the character of the Nazi regime became more unavoidably clear — and, moreover, as his own personal life became richer and, then, more complex — Auden had cause to reconsider his thinking on many subjects, perhaps chief among them what St. Paul named "the mystery of iniquity." The more deeply Auden contemplated the human capacity for evil, the more frivolous his explanation of Nazi aggression seemed — not because it is untrue that "Those to whom evil is done/Do evil in return," but because that is a small portion of the truth masquerading as the whole. The lines are resonant — they sound prophetic — because they are simple, but they are simple because they ignore

8

so much of the truth. The prophetic tone, Auden came to believe, masked an evasion — as, he also came to believe, it so often does. In these years of self examination, in the great turbulent anonymity of New York City, Auden came to recognize his own evasions and to repent of them. He eventually returned, with gratitude and relief, to the Christian faith of his childhood.

As for the other famous line — "We must love one another or die" — Auden came to despise it. When compiling the first edition of his collected poems in 1945 — and, incidentally, it should tell you something about Auden's achievement and his stature as a poet that his publishers asked him to collect his verse when he was still in his mid-thirties — Auden left "September 1, 1939" out of the collection, deeming it a poem not worthy of preservation. When his publishers cried that he couldn't possibly omit his best-known poem, Auden held firm for a while, but ultimately gave in — with the provision, though, that "We must love one another or die" be amended to "We must love one another *and* die." But, as he perfectly well knew, this renders the line meaningless, or at best ineffectual, without any remnant of the prophetic force which he had called forth when he wrote it; and in later editions of his poetry he was adamant about excluding the poem altogether. Once, later in the 1940s, Auden picked up a copy of a book containing "September 1, 1939" in the home of a friend, and wrote in the margin next to the famous line, "This is a lie." A lie because, again, it evades — evades our mortality, evades a recognition that that mortality is the wage we have earned with our sin. "We must love one another or die" holds out the implicit promise that if we love one another we will *not* die. Here, death, as it does so often, gets in the way of a beautiful sentiment — the kind of sentiment we all relish, offering as it does a potential rescue from the most implacable of our enemies: the grave.

Many years later, Auden would write a wise and beautiful poem called "Ode to Terminus" — Terminus, the Latin god of boundaries, of limits, or, as Auden puts it, "of walls, doors, and reticence." Terminus, Auden says, alone can teach us that invaluable lesson: what we *can't* do, what is beyond our reach. The poem concludes with a sly look back at his earlier self, the young and brilliant poet who told us that we must love one another or die:

In this world our colossal immodesty
has plundered and poisoned, it is possible
   You still might save us, who by now have
   learned this:

   . . . that abhorred in the Heav'ns are all
   self-proclaimed poets who, to wow an
   audience, utter some resonant lie.

One could say that, in this poem, Auden is reminding himself of Hotspur's lesson to Glendower: the real task of the poet is not to cultivate the prophetic tone, the oracular utterance, but simply to tell the truth, and thereby shame the devil.

I WANT TO TURN NOW to consider another writer, one who also paid attention to the events that led to what we now call the Second World War, and whose truth-telling I think exemplary. Her name is Rebecca West.

In the spring of 1936, the British Council invited Rebecca West to lecture in Yugoslavia. Thanks to the rise of the Nazis and the ongoing depredations of Stalinism, tensions were rising in the Balkans — as if they had not historically been high enough. She wrote to an official of the Council that the country would inevitably be "overrun either by Germany or, under Russian direction, by communism; which would destroy its character, blot out its inheritance from Byzantium." Soon she would realize, if she did not already, that that "inheritance from Byzantium" was also a tense and complex thing, since the Byzantium of Christian Orthodoxy was also the Istanbul of the Muslim Ottoman Empire. Here was a land whose past, present, and future placed it always at the intersection of immensely powerful states, empires, faiths: at this strange place in southeastern Europe Catholicism, Orthodoxy, and Islam collide. It was a place, West soon learned, of endlessly fascinating complication, and a place utterly endangered.

In the following years she would make two more trips to Yugoslavia, covering every province of the country from Croatia and Dalmatia through Bosnia and Serbia and on to Montenegro. And all the time she was writing an account of what she saw, an account that began as an imagined "short book" but gradually transformed itself into one of the largest, most ambitious, and greatest books of the twentieth century. In *Black Lamb and Grey Falcon* West would combine her three journeys into one, changing names, linking events, amplifying characters — but also spinning marvelous historical cadenzas: no one has written more compellingly than West about the assassination of the Austrian Archduke Ferdinand which sparked what then was called the Great War, or the tragic failure of the Emperor Stephen Dushan, or about the key moment in Serbian history, the crushing defeat of the Serbian people by the Ottoman Turks on the plain of Kossovo in 1389. (In the Vrdnik monastery in the Frushka Gora of Serbia, West saw, still lying in state, the headless body of Prince Lazar, who led the Serbs in that debacle. She touched his blackened and desiccated hand.)

West's story is in at least one respect a classic tale of the modern world: the encounter of the liberal mind with something much older than itself, something alien to it — something fully historical. She begins her narrative with frequent expressions of her disdain for the Croats, whom she believes sold their precious birthright for the cold pottage of the money and power offered them by the Catholic Austro-Hungarian Empire. The Croats she met were proud of their links with the West, links which in West's mind (and especially as German expansionism comes back to terrible life) should have been their greatest shame. Her love is reserved for the Serbs, who remained faithful to their Eastern and Orthodox and Slavic roots; she has a kind of Rousseauian passion for their "primitive" attachment to their own history. But as she goes deeper into Serbia, she sees more and more clearly a side of this attachment dark and inexplicable to her. She thinks of a place called the Sheep's Field in Macedonia, where these people whose "preference for the agreeable over the disagreeable" she has loved meet at an ancient stone to sacrifice animals, in hopes of making women fertile. ("But what they were doing at the rock was abominable.") She thinks above all of the strange fact that Prince Lazar is the greatest hero in Serbian history, not in spite of but *because* he lost the battle: the prophet Elijah in the form of a grey falcon demands that he choose between an earthly and a heavenly kingdom. He selects the latter.

11

To the Serbs this is an act of great courage and piety, since the blood of so many of Lazar's people will therefore be on his hands; to West, it is an abysmal revelation:

> "If this be so," I said to myself, "if it be a law that those who are born into the world with a preference for the agreeable over the disagreeable are born also with an impulse towards defeat, then the whole world is a vast Kossovo, an abominable blood-logged plain, where people who love go out to fight people who hate, and betray their cause to their enemies, so that loving is persecuted for immense tracts of history, far longer than its little periods of victory." I began to weep, for the left-wing people among whom I had lived all my life had in their attitude to foreign politics achieved such a betrayal. They were always right, they never imposed their rightness. "If this disposition to be at once Christ and Judas is inborn," I thought, "we might as well die, and the sooner the better, for the defeat is painful after the lovely promise."

A few years earlier, West had written an angry and sometimes scornful biography of St. Augustine; but here, she comes very close to an Augustinian view of the human order. She does not, I believe, understand all that she sees; but she sees with a clarity almost unparalleled in this century.

And such seeing requires an almost astonishing courage, because again and again West must admit the inadequacy of the convictions that led her to Yugoslavia in the first place. She did not find what she was looking for — the "authentic" culture which had preserved its beautiful ancient ways. Nor did she find its opposite, the Conradian heart of darkness, something almost equally easy to discover. Rather she found a mixed thing, beauty and horror constantly side by side. It is true that near the end of the book it is the horror that seems to dominate, but that is a function of the crushing of her high hopes, and the onrushing tide of world war. What *truly* dominates is an overwhelming sense of the complexity of our social and moral worlds, of the extraordinary entanglements that make us who we are. West learns that telling the truth about this world is arduous, even exhausting, but she has the courage and resourcefulness to continue to try, as best she can, to leave nothing out that would make the story neater, more aesthetically pleasing, simpler and therefore more encouraging — and all this though she loves and craves artistic form above all things:

> Art is not a plaything [she writes], but a necessity, and its essence, form, is not a decorative adjustment, but a cup into which life can be poured and lifted to the lips and be tasted. If one's own existence has no form, if its events do not come handily to mind and disclose their significance, we feel about ourselves as if we were reading a bad book. We can all of us judge the truth of this, for hardly any of us manage to avoid some periods when the main theme of our lives is obscured by details.

But despite this passion for the cup which can contain and shape our lives, she won't *impose* form, she won't deface the truth with false clarification — in her time (as in ours) that is too dangerous. A powerful image of the temptation to impose form and meaning comes late in the book, as West and her companions are driving through Macedonia, and West suddenly calls out to the driver to stop the car:

> I had reason; for on the balcony stood a man dressed in shining grey garments who was announcing his intention to address the plains by a gesture of supreme authority. The proud stance of his body showed that he had dug the truth out of the earth where it lay under the roots of the rock. The force of his right arm showed that he had drawn fire from heaven, so that he might weld this truth into our life, which thus shall not perish with our bodies. The long shadows lay bound to the plains, the mountains' bleakness was explored by the harsh horizontal beams of the falling sun; they, and the men and beasts who labored on them to no clear purpose, would know their deliverance so soon as they had heard him. Nearby there squatted on the grass beside the roadside two wretched veiled women, faceless bundles of dust-colored rags, probably Muslim divorced wives of the sort, more pitiable than the beggars of the towns, who hang about the fields and stretch out their hands to the peasants. It seemed as if they must spring up and throw aside their veils, never to beg again, as soon as he had spoken.

But he would never speak. He was a scarecrow dressed in rags which had been plastered in mud to give them solidity against the winter, and he had been stored on the balcony till it was time to put him out among the fruiting vines. His authority was an exhalation from a bundle of straw.... The soul can be uplifted, it can be seduced into seeing an end to its misery and believing that all has been planned for its good from the beginning, by a chance concatenation of matter that in fact means nothing and explains nothing, that is simply itself. So potent was the argument of the scarecrow to the eye that it made for incredulity regarding all other exaltations.

This episode occurs 775 pages into *Black Lamb and Grey Falcon*. The interpretive confidence with which West began her journey has long since given way to confusion and indecision; but so desperately does she want to hear the definitive prophetic word that she is ready at a moment's notice to give herself over to this Führer of the Macedonian fields — were he but to speak. But he does not speak; and her seemingly pointless quest must continue without benefit of the preternatural authority the hieratic figure had seemed, for that one moment, to embody. The prophet capable of resolving the manifold ambiguities of Yugoslavia had not, she discovered, been commissioned by any deity.

So she trudges on, like Dante in the depths of an ever-ramifying Hell, and at one point, very late in the book, she laments the situation in which she finds herself. She must explain, as part of her historical narration, something that happened on the battlefield of Kaimakshalan, but before proceeding, she pauses:

Of this battlefield, indeed, we need never think, for it is so far away. What is Kaimakshalan? A mountain in Macedonia, but where is Macedonia since the Peace Treaty? This part of it is called South Serbia. And where is that, in Czechoslovakia, or in Bulgaria? And what has happened there? The answer is too long, as long indeed, as this book, which hardly anybody will read by reason of its length. Here is the calamity of our modern life, we cannot know all the things which it is necessary for our survival that we should know.

That places so far away that they could not possibly be relevant to our lives nevertheless are, somehow, intensely relevant — that is an experience with which we are increasingly familiar, are we not? And Rebecca West is the great writer of this predicament. She knew, as the book expanded wildly before her eyes, that she was doing something inexplicable to others, yet absolutely necessary. In letters written while *Black Lamb and Grey Falcon* was in progress, she referred to it as a "wretched, complicated book that won't interest anybody." Later she wrote of it as a "complete explanation of the course of history, but that of course will prevent anyone from having time to read it." Reading proofs (when the book had grown from an essay to its final half-a-million words) she saw what she had done as an "inventory of a country down to its last vest-button, in a form insane from any ordinary artistic or commercial point of view." When she finished her manuscript in early 1941, its length posed a singular problem, because in the midst of the war paper was being strictly rationed. But West's publishers, Macmillan of London, seem not to have hesitated: they were utterly compelled by the narrative. As her editor wrote, "Who would not be [compelled] by a book which demonstrated by its argument that the East End of London would not be lying in ruins if the Balkan Christian powers had not been defeated by the Turks in 1389?"

The path that led from Kossovo to the Battle of Britain — and, in our time, we can now see how the path continued from the Battle of Britain back to Kossovo — was a winding and even tortuous one, and it took a writer with true greatness of character to follow it. I doubt that the artist who wished to prophesy or scandalize would have the resolution to follow it more than a fraction of the way. After all, one purpose of prophetic utterance is to cut through the morasses of complexity — as Auden tried to do when discounting "accurate scholarship" in favor of "what all schoolchildren learn." But have we not historically placed the greatest value on those works of art that do justice to complexity, that even reveal more of it than the ordinary eye can see?

Rebecca West is a great writer, and her book a great book, because she told the whole of the truth that she could see — she told the hard truths, and the long truths. To be sure, she shaped her narrative artfully — the work is a masterpiece of form as it is of truthfulness, only the form is harder to discern because of the size of the book and the subtlety of its design (imagine a cross between *War and Peace* and the Divine Comedy). To a reviewer who had praised the book for its "artlessness" she replied:

> Artlessness! You say 'There is no more system or completeness in it than in the colour-scheme of wild flowers in a field.' How I worked to get that effect. I wanted people, not the great and good, but just people — to learn what the South Slav situation is and its importance to them. They couldn't learn anything about that situation without following a long, complicated story, making many more demands on their powers of concentration than they were accustomed to concede. To get them to go the way I wanted them I deliberately gave the story the loose attractiveness of various pleasant things in life — such as wild flowers in a field. Again and again I broke sequences and relaxed tension to get the lethargic attention of the ordinary reader along the road.

But the art is never false, never forced. At every turn, almost, her story offers her the opportunity to utter "resonant lies," the most useful and reassuring of simplifications; but she always prefers the truth. Her narrative sees no need to observe the specific truth-telling canons of journalism, of course — for instance, *Black Lamb and Grey Falcon* describes a single journey, though "in fact" West made three trips to Yugoslavia, no one of which exactly corresponds to the book's narrative structure. But in the strict sense she invents nothing.

That last sentence echoes one of the great poems of our time, and I want to move towards my conclusion by quoting a chunk of it. It's called "Lying," and it's by Richard Wilbur.

> In the strict sense, of course,
> We invent nothing, merely bearing witness
> To what each morning brings again to light:
> Gold crosses, cornices, astonishment
> Of panes, the turbine-vent which natural law
> Spins on the grill-end of the diner's roof,
> Then grass and grackles or, at the end of town

In sheen-swept pastureland, the horse's neck
Clothed with its usual thunder, and the stones
Beginning now to tug their shadows in
And track the air with glitter.

At the end of this poem Wilbur invokes that faculty of elaboration and connection that, whatever we choose to call it, makes art. "Odd that a thing is most itself when likened," he writes, and to "liken" is to pretend that one thing is another. This pretense leads to what Wilbur calls "the great lies told with the eyes half-shut/That have the truth in view." Those who tell such lies discern in ordinary events the lineaments of the extraordinary; for instance (and here Wilbur ends his poem),

That matter of a baggage-train surprised
By a few Gascons in the Pyrenees
Which, having worked three centuries and more
In the dark caves of France, poured out at last
The blood of Roland, who to Charles his king
And to the dove that hatched the dove-tailed world
Was faithful unto death, and shamed the devil.

(The reference here is to the great medieval epic the *Song of Roland*.) By being faithful unto death, and telling the truth as best we can discern it — even, or perhaps especially, by telling "great lies . . . that have the truth in view" — artists fulfill their role and function in society, and honor their God-given vocation. If God wishes to grant their words a prophetic power (as he most assuredly did with Rebecca West, though she did not believe in him), that's his business. The business of the artist is to be attentive — or, as Flannery O'Connor put it in one of her essays, to be *stupid*. "There's a certain grain of stupidity that the writer of fiction can hardly do without, and this is the quality of having to stare, of not getting the point at once." The stupid artist is one too focused on the "the turbine-vent which natural law/Spins on the grill-end of the diner's roof," or on a mud-plastered scarecrow on a hilltop in Macedonia, even to ask whether her vision is a prophetic one, whether her tale will provoke. Conversely, I wonder if the artist who would be prophetic, or provocative, or scandalous, could maintain the persistence of the attentive watcher, the patience of the faithful listener — could maintain that invaluable stupidity — in the face of the demands of *affect*, the calculating logic of "wowing the audience." I think this is what Auden was getting at when, in his prose version of Wilbur's "merely bearing witness/To what each morning brings again to light," he wrote that "a poem is a witness to man's knowledge of evil as well as good. It is not the duty of a witness to pass moral judgments on the evidence he has to give, but to give it clearly and accurately; the only crime of which a witness can be guilty is perjury." And, as any trial attorney can tell you, it is quite common for a witness to become unreliable because he or she has the vividness of imagination to construct a narrative more compelling than the evidence allows; the court wants from its witnesses a certain, shall we say, *stupidity* that generates no false embellishments.

When I say that we want this stupidity from our artists — that I want it in preference to any conscious determination to provoke or scandalize — I do not mean that art should be amoral or apolitical. To the contrary, any art that faithfully bears witness to what each morning brings to light will be morally charged — not because the intentions of the artist are overtly moral but because the God-made world itself is morally charged.

For instance, in the pivotal poem of Auden's extraordinary verse-sequence "Horae Canonicae," "Nones," the poet describes the aftermath of the Crucifixion — in this case, as it takes place in a small Italian fishing village (which is where Auden lived as he was writing these poems). The event is over, and we are left to meditate on the meaning of the death of "our victim."

> Soon cool tramontana will stir the leaves,
> The shops will re-open at four,
> The empty blue bus in the empty pink square
> Fill up and depart: we have time
> To misrepresent, excuse, deny,
> Mythify, use this event
> While, under a hotel bed, in prison,
> Down wrong turnings, its meaning

Waits for our lives: sooner than we would choose
Bread will melt, water will burn,
And the great quell begin, Abaddon
Set up his triple gallows
At our seven gates, fat Belial make
Our wives waltz naked; meanwhile
It would be best to go home, if we have a home,
In any case good to rest.

And so the customary siesta begins. We sleep; perhaps we dream; perhaps
our dreams are comforting, but more likely they accuse us. Perhaps we
sleep dreamlessly. But in any case, *as* we dream something happens — indeed many things happen, though very few of us are aware of them, and
still fewer understand their meaning:

That, while we are thus away, our own wronged flesh
May work undisturbed, restoring
The order we try to destroy, the rhythm
We spoil out of spite: valves close
And open exactly, glands secrete,
Vessels contract and expand
At the right moment, essential fluids
Flow to renew exhausted cells,
Not knowing quite what has happened, but awed
By death like all the creatures
Now watching this spot, like the hawk looking down
Without blinking, the smug hens
Passing close by in their pecking order,
The bug whose view is balked by grass,
Or the deer who shyly from afar
Peer through chinks in the forest.

Our bodies — our *animal* bodies, working heedless and independent of
our ruined, rebellious wills — bear witness not just to God's creative
power, but to his ever-gracious, universal, ongoing work of healing and

restoration. Whether we suffer righteously, at the hands of evil persecutors, or suffer the inevitable consequences of our own "spite," the restorative work of our flesh continues, a free gift offered to all and, yes, *received* by all — though by most unwittingly.

I WOULD CALL this lovely passage a prophetic word, even (in a certain sense, and especially for a Gnostic culture such as ours) a scandalous word. But it is a word made available to us only by Auden's stupidity, by his attentiveness, by his determination not to commit perjury when he is called to the stand to give his testimony. May every artist, by God's grace, be stupid enough to tell the truth and shame the devil.

Auden's Happy Eye

1.

By the mid-1930s W. H. Auden was the most famous and most widely imitated young poet in England. His verse was brilliant, ironic, often funny, wide-ranging in its reference — equally at home in the worlds of Anglo-Saxon heroic poetry and the technology of mining — and sometimes impenetrably obscure. His poetic voice was from the beginning so distinctive that in 1933, when Auden was just twenty-six years old, Graham Greene could employ the word "Audenesque" in a movie review, confident that readers would know what he meant. The phrase "the Auden age" was in use before the poet turned thirty. But this widely recognized leader of the British intellectual avant-garde was an unhappy and confused young man.

Auden had been unable to believe in God since his adolescence: his loss of faith and his discovery of poetry had come, interestingly enough, at almost the same time. But in the late thirties, as Auden's uncertainty about his role as a poet grew (along with political and social tensions in Europe), some odd things began to happen to him. When in Spain during that country's Civil War, for instance, he was shocked and disturbed to see that supporters of the Republican cause had closed or burned many of Barcelona's churches — but could not account for his reaction. Soon afterward, he met the English writer and editor Charles Williams, and felt himself to be "in the presence of personal sanctity" — though what sanctity meant in a world without God he could not say.

In December of 1939 Auden had his most decisive experience of this kind. He went to a theater in what was then a German-speaking section of Manhattan to see a newsreel about the German invasion of Poland, which had occurred two months before. But it was not the film so much as the audience that Auden later remembered. Whenever the Poles appeared on the screen — as prisoners, of course, in the hands of the Wehrmacht — members of the audience would shout in German, "Kill them! Kill them!" Auden was stunned. "There was no hypocrisy," he recalled many years later: these people were unashamed of their feelings and attempted to put no "civilized" face upon them. "I wondered, then, why I reacted as I did against this denial of every humanistic value." On what grounds did he have a right to demand, or even a reason to expect, a more "humanistic" response? His inability to answer this question, he explained much later, "brought me back to the Church." By the fall of that year (1940) he was going to church again, for the first time since childhood, and would affirm the Christian faith for the rest of his days.

However, the many readers who have rejoiced in the work of Auden's fellow British Christians, the Inklings — Lewis, Tolkien, Charles Williams, and (peripheral to their circle) Dorothy Sayers — have paid little attention to this remarkable man or the extraordinary work that emerged from his embrace of the Christian faith. This is, as we shall see, an understandable but deeply lamentable state of affairs.

2.

Edward Mendelson's extraordinary book *Later Auden* ends with these words: "and his work was done." This conclusion provides the key to understanding Mendelson's project not only in this book but also in its predecessor, 1981's *Early Auden*. In these two rich and resourceful volumes, Mendelson has written the definitive account of one of the greatest poetic careers of our century. The story he tells is not the story of Auden's life, in the usual sense of the word, though all elements of that life naturally enter into the story; rather, he narrates for us the complex and fascinating history of a body of work, the fruit of a calling. Mendelson gives us the biography of Auden's vocation.

Not long after he began writing poetry at age fifteen, Auden came to understand that words were the medium in which he should work. But who or what imposed this "should" upon him? And how should he use the words he was called upon to use? In *Early Auden* — which began with Auden's first adult poems, written in 1927 when he was twenty years old, and ended with his leaving England in January of 1939 — Mendelson traced Auden's oscillations among several divergent and probably irreconcilable descriptions of the poet: conjuror, teacher, servant, prophet, redeemer. *Later Auden* begins with the poet in a new land, a place famous for encouraging new beginnings. When, with his friend Christopher Isherwood, Auden boarded a ship for America, he was the most celebrated young poet in England, but he knew that his career was at an impasse. All of the models for the writing life which he had tried out in the previous decade had come to seem empty, sterile, and in some cases repulsive. But he had no idea what could replace them. The germ of a new understanding, Mendelson shows, can be found in a word which Auden began using just before he left England: he said that the poet had a gift.

The presence of a gift implies the activity of a giver. But who, or what, gives the gift of poetry? Auden's conversion, less than two years later, indicated that he had found an answer to that question. But Auden's conversion did not resolve his puzzlement about his life as a poet: what should he do with the gift that God had given him? During the war years, from his apartment in New York, his pursuit of an answer to that question led him upon a remarkable intellectual and spiritual journey. In reviews and essays commissioned by major American periodicals, he would explore thinkers and ideas that he hoped would help him figure out what he was supposed to do, as a poet and a man: he considered Kierkegaard, Reinhold Niebuhr, and Paul Tillich, along with a host of less well-known figures like the historian Charles Norris Cochrane and, a little later on, the polymathic but odd philosopher-historian Eugen Rosenstock-Huessy.

As Mendelson demonstrates, Auden's essays and reviews consistently depicted these figures as having some significant contribution to make to the interpretation of Western culture at that particular and terrible moment. But in the poems Auden was writing at the same time, Mendelson convincingly argues, he was preoccupied with the questions he could not answer, with the doubts that even the greatest of his intellectual helpers left unassuaged. Among these poems are some of Auden's finest achievements, including the three long poems which he wrote between 1941 and 1947, "For the Time Being: A Christmas Oratorio," "The Sea and the Mirror: A Commentary on *The Tempest*," and *The Age of Anxiety: A Baroque Eclogue*. The first and last of these, Mendelson contends, have brilliant passages but are flawed in either their concept or execution; and even the masterful "The Sea and the Mirror" fails to offer a clear and satisfying account of the problem it sets out to address, namely, whether art can have spiritual significance. (He told his friend Ursula Niebuhr — the wife of Reinhold — that the poem was "really about the Christian conception of art.")

Mendelson fully recognizes the greatness of this poem, and the extraordinarily intelligent ambitions of the other two. His point is not that the poems are less than they could have been, but rather that none of them satisfied its author. In the Thirties, Auden had nurtured hopes that the poet might be a prophet to or even a redeemer of a sick and chaotic society; in the aftermath of his conversion, his thinking dominated by what he later called a "neo-Calvinist (i.e. Barthian) exaggeration of God's transcendence," he found poetry valuable only when it acknowledged its hopeless, incompetent distance from anything true or good that it tried to represent.

One sees this notion vividly illustrated in one of the concluding speeches of "The Sea and the Mirror," when Caliban — the "deformed and salvage slave" of Shakespeare's *The Tempest*, now become, for reasons too complicated to explain here, outrageously loquacious — explains what he thinks to be the only kind of situation in which the artist receives any genuine illumination. He asks us to imagine "the greatest grandest opera rendered by a very provincial touring company indeed." Paradoxically, it is the very poverty and ineptitude of the production that makes it valuable to its actors, for even though "there was not a single aspect of our whole performance, not even the huge stuffed bird of happiness, for which a kind word could, however patronisingly, be said," nevertheless it is "at this very moment [that] we do at last see ourselves as we are." And, more important, "for the first time in our lives we hear . . . the real Word which is our only *raison d'etre*." At the moment when all pretense to aesthetic achievement helplessly falls away, and the actors are confronted with the authentic selves which they had used their performances to escape, they come to see God precisely in their distance from him:

> . . . we are blessed with that Wholly Other Life from which we are separated by an essential emphatic gulf of which our contrived fissures of mirror and proscenium arch — we understand them at last — are feebly figurative signs. . . . it is just here, among the ruins and the bones, that we may rejoice in the perfected Work that is not ours.

Similarly, earlier in the poem Prospero, musing on the kind of life he will live after having given up his magical powers, says "I never suspected the way of truth/Was a way of silence." But if Prospero is right, what can the poet do except stop writing? One suspects that at this point in his career Auden was contemplating just that: making his commentary on *The Tempest* his farewell to poetry, just as *The Tempest* itself has always been read as Shakespeare's (not just Prospero's) farewell to the dramatic arts. Prospero, after all, gave up his "rough magic"; he broke his staff and drowned his book. Yes; but Prospero was an old man, Auden still a young one — thirty-six when he wrote Caliban's discourse — and there remained his sense that poetry was the vocation to which he had been called, not just by his temperament or aptitudes, but by God himself, "the author and giver of all good things" (as he wrote in a 1941 poem). How, then, given the ineptitude of language to encompass the most important things in and beyond this world, could he fulfill that calling?

3.

One of Auden's chief helpers in thinking through this problem was Kierkegaard; he found especially useful the Danish thinker's notion of "indirect communication." (This is a theme which Mendelson makes too little of, but since almost every other critic of Auden has made too much of it, the "fault" is easily pardonable.) Many of Kierkegaard's works — in fact, all of his most famous ones — are not explicitly Christian. Such books are easily identifiable because Kierkegaard did not sign his name to them: they appeared under various pseudonyms. These works approach the questions with which Christianity is most concerned, but they do not offer Christian answers to those questions; indeed, their failure to produce compelling responses is just what leads the reader toward the Christian faith which alone can provide what we need. "An illusion can never be destroyed directly," he wrote, "and only by indirect means can it be radically removed."

Auden adopted this approach, and adapted it to his poetic needs. In the great poems of his maturity, Christianity appears as the missing piece of the puzzle, the answer to a question no one thought to ask. In "The Shield of Achilles," for instance — one of the very greatest poems of our century — the blacksmith god Hephaestos, watched by Achilles's mother Thetis, portrays our world as it appears to the carnal eye, the eye unillumined by faith. He inscribes on the shield "three pale figures" being bound to three posts; the poem indicates their condition:

> The mass and majesty of this world, all
>   That carries weight and always weighs the same
> Lay in the hands of others; they were small
>   And could not hope for help and no help came:
>   What their foes like to do was done, their shame
> Was all the worst could wish; they lost their pride
> And died as men before their bodies died.

A little later we see another figure:

> A ragged urchin, aimless and alone,
>   Loitered about that vacancy; a bird
> Flew up to safety from his well-aimed stone:
>   That girls are raped, that two boys knife a third,
>   Were axioms to him, who'd never heard
> Of any world where promises were kept,
> Or one could weep because another wept.

In the Christian understanding, we indeed live in a world where such events occur. But the cold eye of Hephaestos, while it sees with terrifying clarity, is blind to some things: that one of those three bound figures may be different than the other two; that somewhere promises are kept, and people weep with their brothers and sisters who weep. In Auden's poem the Christian interpretation of history is evoked all the more powerfully by its absence: the indirect communication of "The Shield of Achilles" has a terrible force more overt testimonials often lack.

4.

The Christian faith helped Auden to keep writing in another way as well, by offering him — though not immediately, and not without years of profound study and reflection — a way of comprehending a problem which had obsessed him for many years: the relationship between freedom and necessity. In almost every major poem he wrote after coming to America, says Mendelson, Auden in some way "incorporated the significant events of his life. But he confronted each time a new variation on his inner debate: whether those events were better understood as the product of involuntary necessity or of free choice." Mendelson begins his book by reflecting on this obsession of Auden's, and one of the great achievements of *Later Auden* is the skillful patience and critical tact with which he explores Auden's changing views on this vital subject.

Auden came to formulate the problem in this way: alone among the creatures, human beings live in history as well as in nature. In the natural world all obey the laws which govern their being; only we make choices and live out the consequences of them. That's what history means. In a lovely poem called "Their Lonely Betters," Auden sits in a chair in his garden, listens, and thinks about what he hears:

> A robin with no Christian name ran through
> The Robin-Anthem which was all it knew,
> And rustling flowers for some third party waited
> To say which pairs, if any, should get mated.

Not one of them was capable of lying,
There was not one which knew that it was dying
Or could have with a rhythm or a rhyme
Assumed responsibility for time.

Let them leave language to their lonely betters
Who count some days and long for certain letters;
We, too, make noises when we laugh or weep:
Words are for those with promises to keep.

The robin cannot decide what song to sing; the flowers cannot select their mates. These creatures, living wholly in nature, neither celebrate the wisdom nor lament the folly of their choices, for they have no choices to make; we, on the other hand, must and do choose, and thereby enter into the historical world of accountability ("responsibility for time"). We know what it means to have "promises to keep" — and what it means to break them.

But we are not just historical beings: we are also participants in nature, we are in that sense too part of the Creation. And Mendelson shows, as no other critic of Auden has yet shown, how Auden came to wrestle with and ultimately to accept, with gratitude, the limits and circumscriptions of our natural, our bodily, lives.

I have said that Auden was deeply influenced by Kierkegaard, but he gradually came to understand that there were some valuable things, necessary things, that Kierkegaard didn't understand. Late in his life, Auden would write of Kierkegaard that, "like all heretics, conscious or unconscious, he is a monodist, who can hear with particular acuteness one theme in the New Testament — in his case, the theme of suffering and self-sacrifice — but is deaf to its rich polyphony. . . . The Passion of Christ was to Kierkegaard's taste, the Nativity and Epiphany were not." Auden contends that, while Kierkegaard's consciously held beliefs were scrupulously orthodox, he was "in his sensibility" a Manichee, who felt strongly the evil and degradation of matter, of our bodies. Indeed, Auden wrote in another essay, with pardonable exaggeration, "A planetary visitor might read through the whole of his voluminous works without discovering that human beings are not ghosts but have bodies of flesh and blood." And to have bodies of flesh and blood is to live in the world of nature's necessity as well as in the world of history, of existential choice.

We are therefore, Auden came more and more to reflect, compound beings: subject always to natural laws and yet called upon to "assume responsibility for time" by making decisions — decisions whose inevitable consequences are yet another form of necessity. For Auden, this peculiar situation is above all comic: there is something intrinsically funny about our mixed identity, as we try to exercise Divine powers of decision and yet always find our bodies getting in the way. "A sense of humor develops in a society to the degree that its members are simultaneously conscious of being each a unique person and of being all in common subjection to unalterable laws." And this sense of humor about one's condition is for Auden absolutely necessary to spiritual health: he may have dreamed in his youth of redeeming the world through his poetic power, or being destroyed in the effort, but as an older man he found himself, as he often remarked, just a "martyr to corns," which afflicted his feet and made him comfortable only in carpet slippers.

By the 1950s most of the people who had admired the young Auden had rejected his mature poetry as trivial. But the heart of Mendelson's book, in many respects, is his demonstration that in this later poetry Auden is working "at the height of his powers," though in a poetic idiom that was incomprehensible to those who loved the gnomic and hieratic pronouncements of Auden's earlier verse. In 1948, Mendelson notes, Auden

> began to write poems about the inarticulate human body . . . : the body that never asks to be regimented or idealized, feels no abstract hatred or intellectual envy, believes no theories, and is moved by impulses that, fortunately for us, are not exactly the same as our own. He dedicated to the body some of his most profound poems, works whose depth and breadth have been underestimated because their treatment of their subject matter was novel and unexpected in an age whose writers hesitated to see the body as "simply, publicly, there." And because he learned to value the body as sacred in itself, Auden learned to believe in it as the means and promise of salvation.

"Means" is perhaps not quite right: it is not through the body that we are saved, but we are saved as embodied creatures, and saved for a future of embodiment — Auden came to believe the doctrine of the resurrection of the body a vital one and a necessary corrective to the implicit Gnosticism and Manicheanism of his existentialist influences. But Mendelson's argument is compelling, and if there is any justice in the world will put an end to the ill-informed dismissals of Auden's later verse.

These poems about the body are often poems of gratitude and thanksgiving. In a poem dedicated to his senses, "Precious Five," he concludes by invoking

> That singular command
> I do not understand,
> *Bless what there is for being,*
> Which has to be obeyed, for
> What else am I made for,
> Agreeing or disagreeing?

In one sense this recurrent emphasis on blessing and thankfulness is a correction of the theology which dominated Auden's early years as a Christian. I have already noted how important for Auden was Kierkegaard's statement that "before God we are always in the wrong": in that movie theater in Manhattan Auden confronted his own infinite capacity for sinfulness as well as that of the Germans. One of Auden's friends relates that he taught Sunday School in 1942, and once asked the class, "Do you know what the Devil looks like?" He then answered his own question: "The Devil looks like me." Not too long afterward, he wrote of his conviction that Jesus is Lord: "I believe because He fulfills none of my dreams, because He is in every respect the opposite of what He would be if I could have made Him in my own image." But why not one of the other great teachers, like Buddha or Mohammed? Because, Auden wrote, chillingly, "none of the others arouse all sides of my being to cry 'Crucify Him.'" Auden never rejected this deep conviction of his depravity, but he came to realize that if he tried to build his whole theology around it he would become, like Kierkegaard, a "monodist" and an inadvertent heretic. Thus the necessary poems of praise and thanks-giving.

It is in light of this sought theological balance that we may best under-stand Auden's sequence of poems "Horae Canonicae," based on the "ca-nonical hours" that govern time in monastic communities and many churches. These poems have rarely been given serious attention, but Mendelson points out that they "occupied [Auden's] attention longer than any other" work of his career — seven years, off and on — and believes that they constitute "arguably his greatest work." In these poems, some of which are deceptively casual in tone, Auden attempts to do no less than to encompass self-censure and gratitude, necessity and freedom.

The first poem, "Prime," begins with an awakening: in this first pre-conscious moment of opening eyes Auden is (we all are) an "Adam still previous to any act"; but he is (we all are) "Afraid of our living task, the dy-ing/Which the coming day will ask." In the next poem he speaks of "our victim," the one who will do the dying, the one who "knows that by sun-down/We shall have had a good Friday." Writes Mendelson, "The day in which the events [of this sequence] occur is Good Friday, and also any day; and the place where they occur is Jerusalem with its law court and temple, and also the Italian fishing village where the poems were written, or anywhere." This juxtaposition of times and situations is made possible by the understanding of time embodied in the canonical hours: in them, as in the larger calendar of the church year, unrepeatable events (the pro-nouncement of judgment, the Crucifixion, the deposition from the Cross) are remembered and in a sense re-enacted. But of course this remem-brance is done day after day, year after year, according to the necessary rhythms of the seasons and our bodies: thus the sequence ends, not with the evening prayer of "Compline," but with "Lauds," the song of another morning.

This second morning song not only emphasizes the repetitive nature of bodily actions, including worship, but also indicates, in Mendelson's el-oquent words, the blessed movement "from fatal memory to uncondi-tional hope. This is no transcendent escape from the physical world but an undignified, saving scramble back into it. In imagining it, [Auden] found himself at home not only in both his work and his body — their reconciliation is one of the private achievements of the poem — but also in the double world of nature and history, neither an imaginary past nor a visionary future, but the place he lived now." For only if we live in the world where God has placed us can we fulfill the vocations to which he has called us.

5.

Why are Christians so indifferent to Auden? It is a question made compelling by Mendelson's brilliant and sympathetic analysis. It is certainly true that Auden is not nearly as accessible a writer as Lewis, Tolkien, Sayers, or Charles Williams; however, neither is T. S. Eliot, and yet Eliot continues to hold a totemic status for Christians interested in modern literature, while Auden is almost completely neglected. This state of affairs bears reflection.

The first problem is an obvious one: throughout Auden's life he was a practicing homosexual. After his conversion to Christianity, such sexual activity became problematic for him. His good friend Christopher Isherwood wrote of Auden's attitude toward his homosexuality that "His religion condemned it and he agreed that it was sinful, though he fully intended to go on sinning." This is only partly right. In a letter to Isherwood — a letter which may have been the source of Isherwood's comment — Auden wrote, "Though I believe it sinful to be queer, it has at least saved me from becoming a pillar of the Establishment." The comment is illuminating. Auden tried to resist his sexual temptations, but felt them to be stronger than him: in one poem he ruefully echoes a famous prayer of Augustine's, writing "I am sorry I'm not sorry . . ./Make me chaste, Lord, but not yet." But his determination to "bless what there is for being" led him to seek ways to be grateful to God even for his sins and afflictions, through which he believed God to work for His own purposes: thus his thankfulness not to have become an Establishment figure. He also believed that the homosexual was less likely to engage in the idolatry of eros that is so common among heterosexuals. In his view his sexuality was, therefore, an affliction which bore the seeds of potential blessings.

But however complex Auden's attitude toward these matters, the mere fact that he was homosexual has written him off the books of many Christians — even Christians who are quick to forgive C. S. Lewis's peculiar liaison with Mrs. Moore, or Charles Williams's penchant for spanking and being spanked by young women. The Christian world has its hierarchy of sins, and may be right in its judgments. But it is singularly unfortunate that, even if we have judged Auden's sins rightly, we should allow that judgment to disable us from the wisdom which his writings exhibit and proclaim.

In any case, homosexuality alone is not enough to explain the Christian neglect of Auden. More important, perhaps, is his Kierkegaardian emphasis on indirect communication. This emphasis stemmed from Auden's determination to repent of his, and his fellow poets', prideful assertions of their own importance. But Christian readers, for the most part, don't want their poets to be humble: their tastes are pretty thoroughly Romantic, and they want their poets to be seers, prophets, "unacknowledged legislators of the world" (as Shelley put it) — just as long as they are *Christian* seers, prophets, legislators. As they often say, they like poems that are "redemptive." But Auden understood that nothing and no one is redemptive except Jesus Christ — least of all the poets and their poems: he called Shelley's famous line "the silliest remark ever made about poets." As he wrote to Clio, the mythological Muse of History,

> Approachable as you seem,
>   I dare not ask you if you bless the poets,
> For you do not look as if you ever read them,
>   Nor can I see a reason why you should.

He sent this poem to J. R. R. Tolkien, and in an accompanying letter referred to it as "a hymn to Our Lady." Mary, as the mother of Christ, presides over the world's moments of ultimate significance: what can poetry add to the Incarnation or the Passion of our Lord?

Auden consistently repudiated the notion that poetry has any privileged access to truth, any especially sanctified role to play. Poetry was certainly his vocation, and he loved it: as Mendelson writes, "vocation, for Auden, is the most innocent form of love, a voluntary loss of self in an object." He knew he would be wrong not to love his work, not to achieve what he called "that eye-on-the-object look" characteristic of people who are "forgetting themselves in a function." But he would never claim that his calling was superior to any other: in this sense he was purely Lutheran, emphasizing the dignity of every calling before God. It is not surprising that he wrote a poem based on the medieval legend of *le jongleur de Dieu*, the poor "clown of God" who can offer nothing to the Christ Child but his juggling — and whose offering is received, not because it has special value, but because he gave what he had to give.

As a result of this penitential humility, he came to insist over and over again that one cannot in poetry speak the Truth directly and unequivocally. In one of his most powerful poems, "Friday's Child," he remembers, in a characteristically oblique way, the martyr's death of Dietrich Bonhoeffer. (The title is typical of Auden's approach: he trusts us to remember that "Friday's child is loving and giving," trusts us also to understand that the old Mother Goose rhyme draws on the memory of Good Friday, when God loved and gave most fully.) The poem concludes with an invocation, and a recommendation, of silence in the face of an evil that cannot be comprehended and a faith that, as Kierkegaard said, can be neither explained nor justified:

> Now, did He really break the seal
> And rise again? We dare not say;
> But conscious unbelievers feel
>   Quite sure of Judgement Day.

> Meanwhile, a silence on the cross
> As dead as we shall ever be,
> Speaks of some total gain or loss,
>   And you and I are free

> To guess from the insulted face
> Just what Appearances He saves
> By suffering in a public place
>   A death reserved for slaves. (CP 676)

The key phrase here, I believe, is "We dare not say." It is not the same as "We dare not believe" — though Auden confessed in his later years to dark times of doubt — nor does it mean "We dare not proclaim," since undoubtedly Auden often did proclaim, in church at least, "On the third day he rose again in accordance with the Scriptures." Auden's "we" does not refer to Christians, but to poets, whose tendency (as he writes in another poem) to "utter some resonant lie" makes them unfit bearers of the Gospel proclamation. As Auden said repeatedly, almost obsessively, "Orthodoxy is reticence"; orthodoxy is knowing when to shut up. This is not what Christian readers want to hear from their poets, but Auden knew what poetry can't do, and felt always the need to put himself and other poets in their proper place. Thus the wittily self-deflating question in "Compline": "Can poets (can men in television)/Be saved?"

Late in his life, he said in a lecture that he and his "fellow-citizens of the Republic of Letters" — a phrase coined by Voltaire — had but one "political duty": "to love the Word and defend it against its enemies." And who or what are those enemies? The "principal enemies of the True Word are two: the Idle Word and the Black Magician." On the one hand, he came to see much of his early poetry as intolerably careless not only in its technique but in its disregard for whether it meant what it said. It was full of idle words. But the other enemy was more dangerous still. The Black Magician encourages poets to believe that they can be prophets and redeemers, or, as Auden put it once in a review, tries to make a person try "to do for himself or others by the writing of poetry what can only be done in some other way, by action, or study, or prayer." Auden uses poetry to remind us of what poetry can never give us; but this assigns poetry a genuine and important role, as it points always beyond itself in a strangely mute witness to that of which it is unable definitively to speak. As Auden wrote in one of his later poems,

> We can only
> do what it seems to us we were made for, look at
> this world with a happy eye
> but from a sober perspective.

Camus: Wisdom and Courage

1.

When I think of Albert Camus, two photographic images, distorted no doubt by the tricks of memory, immediately come to mind. The first is of that face, both thoughtful and tough, a cigarette drooping from the lips, the collar of a trench coat showing. The second is of the crushed automobile in which he died early in January, 1960. These images are not important just to me; they may be said to define the dominant impression many readers had (and perhaps still have) of Camus. If Hollywood had invented an existentialist writer, the homely, scholarly Jean-Paul Sartre, with his squat body and thick spectacles, wouldn't have made the cut. No, it would be Camus: he looked like Humphrey Bogart and died like James Dean.

What is ironic about all this is the simple fact that Camus came closest to existentialism at the beginning of his career, in his first published novel, *The Stranger,* and in his first book of philosophy, *The Myth of Sisyphus,* both of which were published in 1942 — and Camus even claimed that the latter book was written as a conscious *repudiation* of existentialism. By the end of his life he had become completely alienated not just from existentialism as a philosophy but also from the whole French intellectual culture within which existentialism was then the dominant force. Perhaps if Camus had remained in lock-step with Sartre and Simone de Beauvoir he would be more popular today. Instead he remains perhaps the most neglected ma-

jor author of the second half of this century — one of the few, along with
W. H. Auden, Czeslaw Milosz, and a handful of others, who represent the
nearly forgotten virtues of wisdom and courage.

Whatever we Christians aver about God's sovereignty over our allot-
ted lifetimes, like everyone else we regret it when it seems to us that lives
are cut short, and we imagine what their possessors might have done with
a few more years in which to work. It is impossible *not* to speculate about
what Keats might have achieved had he been given more than a decade in
which to write; it is hard to believe that Mozart would not have profited by
living at least into his forties, or the sculptor Henri Gaudier-Brezska by
surviving the Great War and making it at least to thirty.

Camus died at forty-six, and the recent publication of *The First Man*,
the novel he was working on when he died, suggests that he would have
made very good use of another five years. *The First Man*, as we have it, is but
a draft fragment, a direct and unedited transcription from Camus' final
notebook — a notebook found, inside a briefcase, in the car in which
Camus died. In the new Knopf edition it comes to over three hundred
pages (albeit rather small ones), but the appended notes and outlines make
it clear that this constitutes perhaps a third of the book as Camus planned
it. Beyond question it would have been the grandest and most ambitious
project of Camus' life, not only in length but in narrational and thematic
scope. One could even say that it would have been the first product of
Camus' full maturity as a writer and thinker, for, though he had won the
Nobel Prize for literature in 1957 (when he was only forty-three!), his political, philosophical, and literary vision was just beginning to achieve something like coherence. It is impossible for anyone who appreciates Camus'
work to read *The First Man* without a sharp pang of regret at what never
came to be.

2.

Though Sartre and Camus are often linked in the public mind, they are
dramatically different figures. There was a brief period when they seemed
on the verge of forming a real friendship: each had reviewed the other's

work positively, and when they met (in 1943) they discovered a mutual interest in the theater. Indeed, Sartre asked Camus to direct and act in a play he had just written, one which would prove to be his most famous: *No Exit*. Throughout the war the two writers found themselves involved, in different ways, in the common cause of the Resistance. But their temperamental differences made a lasting friendship impossible. Sartre distrusted, and perhaps envied, Camus' toughness and flamboyance, what one might call his *Bogartisme*; Camus distrusted, and perhaps envied, Sartre's analytical and philosophical mind.

The breaking point in their tenuous relationship occurred in 1952, after *Les Temps Modernes*, the intellectual journal largely run by Sartre, ran a hostile review by Francis Jeanson of Camus' recent meditation on political philosophy, *The Rebel*. Camus directed his reply to Sartre (whom he thought should at least have done the criticism himself): "I'm getting tired of seeing myself, and particularly seeing old militants who have known all the fights of their times, endlessly chastised by censors who have always tackled history from their armchairs." Sartre retorted by saying that Camus was arrogant — "Tell me, Camus, what is the mystery that prevents people from discussing your books without robbing mankind of its reasons to live?" — and philosophically incompetent: "But I don't dare advise you to consult *Being and Nothingness*. Reading it would seem needlessly arduous to you: you detest the difficulties of thought."

Annie Cohen-Salal, Sartre's biographer, is right to see ideological differences at the roots of this dispute (all of which appeared in the pages of *Les Temps Modernes*): Sartre's attempt to soft-pedal or even evade recognizing the evils of the Stalinist Soviet Union, in hopes of sustaining the socialist vision, against Camus' belief that Soviet Communism and fascism were morally equivalent. On this view, Sartre's philosophical condemnation of *The Rebel* masks his anger at Camus' total repudiation of violence as a means to achieve any political cause, however noble. As Cohen-Salal admits, Sarte's tendency was to be "pragmatic" on such issues.

Pragmatic about means, perhaps; but absolutist about causes. Sartre believed that the French in Algeria, for instance, should all get out, and if they did not, Algerian terrorists were justified in killing them. And it was this issue, not the disagreement over Stalinism — about which Sartre eventually admitted he had been wrong (in 1956, after the Soviet invasion of Hungary) — which insured lasting enmity between Sartre and Camus. And it is this issue which proves central to Camus' plans for *The First Man*.

3.

Politically speaking, one could say that Sartre never overcame the Manichean dichotomies which were arguably appropriate during the war against the Nazis. That the Soviets had stood against fascism placed them firmly on the side of the angels. (Best not to reflect, at least publicly, on the uncomfortable fact that Stalin had signed the Pact of Steel with Hitler, and that Hitler was the one who broke it.) For this reason Sartre could forgive, or at least avert his eyes from, the purges of the '30s and the continuing hell of the Gulag. In Sartre's political world there were only oppressors and oppressed: fascism stood for the former, communism for the latter. Likewise, in Algeria, since the native Algerians were by definition the oppressed, they were incapable of sin; conversely the *pieds noirs*, the French colonists, were reprobate and irredeemable. Thus Sartre endorsed the decision of the Algerian FLN (Front de Libération Nationale) to kill any and all French men, women, and children in Algeria whenever possible; a position he was still taking in 1961 when he wrote a famous and lengthy introduction to *The Wretched of the Earth*, the major work by one of this century's greatest theorists of terrorism, Franz Fanon.

Camus, on the other hand, was himself a *pied noir*; his family's roots in Algeria went back a century and a half. Members of his family, including his mother, still lived in Algeria, and were endangered daily by the FLN's random shootings and bombings. Yet Camus was not, nor had he ever been, indifferent to the abuses which the French had inflicted on the Arabs of Algeria. Indeed, in the 1930s, at the beginning of his career as a writer, Camus had striven ceaselessly to call attention to these abuses, but was generally ignored — by the French left no less than the right. So he was not pleased to have a difficult and morally complex political situation reduced to an opportunity for French intellectuals to strike noble poses: to those who would "point to the French in Algeria as scapegoats ('Go ahead and die; that's what we deserve!')," Camus retorted, "it seems to me revolting to beat one's *mea culpa*, as our judge-penitents do, on someone else's breast." Those who are really so guilt-stricken at the French presence in Algeria should "offer up themselves in expiation." Camus boldly affirmed that his family, "being poor and free of hatred" — and Camus really was raised in abject poverty — "never exploited or oppressed anyone. But three quarters of the French in Algeria resemble them and, if only they are provided reasons rather than insults, will be ready to admit the necessity of a juster and freer order." It should, then, be possible to give the proper rights and freedoms to Algerian Arabs without condemning and destroying the *pieds noirs* indiscriminately, or forcing them out of the only country they had ever known.

But such subtleties were lost on almost everyone involved in this conflict. When Camus received the Nobel Prize in 1957 and gave a press conference in Stockholm, he was bitterly condemned by an Arab student for failing to endorse the FLN. His reply was simple, direct, and forceful: "I have always condemned the use of terror. I must also condemn a terror which is practiced blindly on the Algiers streets and which may any day strike down my mother or my family. I believe in justice but I will defend my mother before justice." Michael Walzer is almost unique among Camus' commentators in seeing the significance of this stand: he identifies Camus as an example of the "connected social critic," that is, the critic who does not stand above the political fray and judge with Olympian disinterest, objectivity, and abstraction. That was the way of Sartre: absolutist, universalizing, committed to a single overriding binary opposition, that between the oppressors and the oppressed. But for Camus the universal could not so easily displace the local; commitment to "Justice" in the abstract could not simply trump his love for and responsibility to his family. "I believe in justice but I will defend my mother before justice."

Walzer points out, with regret, that Camus ceased to write about Algeria after 1958: "the silence of the connected social critic is a grim sign — a sign of defeat, a sign of endings. Though he may not be wrong to be silent, we long to hear his voice." But the draft of The First Man suggests that Camus was not prepared to remain silent; instead, he was seeking a new way to speak about a complex social reality with which the common political discourse of the French intelligentsia could not cope. A fragmentary note makes this clear:

> The *two* Algerian nationalisms. Algeria 39 and 54 (rebellion). What becomes of French values in an Algerian sensibility, that of the first man. The account of the two generations explains the present tragedy.

Jacques Corméry, Camus' alter ego, is "the first man," a kind of Adam in that he represents a new breed of human being: a *pied noir*, yes, a person of "French values in an Algerian sensibility," but one who has been forced to acknowledge the claims of the native Algerians to equality as persons and under the law. In this sense he must support the nationalism of the 1930s, which sought just that, equality; but what can he say to the later nationalism of Ahmed Ben Bella, a leader of the FLN, whose slogan was "Algeria for the Algerians" and who was ready to kill any *pied noir*, however supportive of Algerian independence, who would not leave the country? And what can he say to François Mitterand, then France's Interior Minister, who in 1954 said that with the Algerian rebels "the only possible negotiation is war"? Ben Bella and Mitterand, for all their mutual hatred, share a conception of the political sphere which cannot comprehend the moral imperative to love and defend one's mother.

4.

When Camus died, Sartre responded with a handsome eulogy which reveals that, despite all their enmity, he understood the fundamental character of Camus' work: "Camus represented in this century, and against History, the present heir of that long line of moralists whose works perhaps constitute what is most original in French letters. His stubborn humanism, narrow and pure, austere and sensual, waged a dubious battle against events of these times. . . . He reaffirmed the existence of moral fact . . . against the Machiavellians." I cannot allow that last comment to pass without noting that Sartre was one of the Machiavellians against whom Camus contended. But it is indeed the moralistic tradition, the tradition of

Montaigne and La Rochefoucauld, to which Camus belonged, and it is worth noting that this tradition has always had an ambivalent relationship to Christianity. In a lecture called "The Unbeliever and Christians" which Camus gave in 1948 at a Dominican monastery in France, he spoke in terms which eerily prefigure the Algerian crisis of the next decade: "Between the forces of terror and the forces of dialogue, a great unequal battle has begun. . . . The program for the future is either a permanent dialogue or the solemn and significant putting to death of any who have experienced dialogue." (The primary targets of FLN terrorism, at least at first, were neither *pieds noirs* nor French soldiers but rather Arab and Muslim moderates, that is, would-be compromisers and dialoguers.) And the question that Camus puts to his Christian audience is, Which side will you be on? He is not sure of the answer; he fears that the Roman Catholic Church in particular will choose terror, if only terror by means of the papal encyclical, and argues that if that happens, "Christians will live and Christianity will die."

In Camus' first two novels moral questions occupy the foreground, while Christianity occasionally flickers at the margins of the reader's attention. In *The Stranger*, Camus' first and most popular novel, the protagonist, Meursault, seems to be everything an existentialist antihero should be. He is alienated and confused. He commits a murder which appears to illustrate the existentialist theme of the *acte gratuité*, the gratuitous or utterly unconditioned act which is supposed to indicate the terrible freedom with which we humans are burdened. He is amoral, in the sense of being unable even to understand what others, especially the priest who visits his prison cell, call morality. Camus' later ("admittedly paradoxical") comments on Meursault didn't help those who would like to know how we should evaluate this young man. What did Camus mean when he said that Meursault was condemned because he would not lie, would not "play the game"? Still more puzzling was his claim that Meursault is "the only Christ we deserve." And when he suggested that those unfamiliar with the Algerian culture in which the book is set were likely to misunderstand Meursault, he was simply ignored.

Rieux, the protagonist of *The Plague*, Camus' allegory of fascism and the resistance to it, is a clearly and profoundly moral man — perhaps because (not in spite) of his inability to explain and unwillingness even to think about the sources of his morality. Here religious questions are rigorously suppressed by Rieux's own character, since he is the narrator of the story, though this is not revealed until the end of the book.

The narrator and protagonist of Camus' last completed novel, *The Fall*, is almost as enigmatic as Meursault. But far from being amoral or unreflective about morality, the ex-lawyer Jean-Baptiste Clamence tells a story that concerns little other than his forced confrontation with his own moral failings. Camus' lifelong interest in and reflection upon Christianity seems here on the verge of becoming something more serious: Clamence's "confession" follows traditionally Christian patterns of penitence. One sees this even in the setting of the book, since Clamence, a man who always loved and craved the heights, has exiled himself to the lowlying city of Amsterdam — a city whose concentric circles of canals he compares to the circles of Dante's Hell. Indeed, he describes himself as no longer a legal advocate but a "judge-penitent," who confesses his sins to those whom he thinks might profit by his tale of woe. (As noted above, Camus used the phrase "judge-penitent" in reference to the critics of *The Rebel*; but their penitence was on behalf of others rather than themselves.)

Christian readers, therefore, might be forgiven for hoping that *The First Man* would mark yet further development of Camus' interest in Christianity. But such hopes, it appears, are misplaced. The moral and spiritual introspection, the penitential self-awareness, of Clamence are absent here — or rather, transposed into the key of filial affection, the relationship between a son and his mother. And it is the juxtaposition of this familial theme with the historical crises of modern Algeria that makes *The First Man* a distinctive and potentially powerful work.

This is the most historically and culturally rich of all Camus' books. Unlike Camus' earlier protagonists, Jacques Corméry is fully situated in a social, and more particularly a familial, world. The news of Meursault's mother's death comes in the first line of *The Stranger*; in *The Plague*, Rieux is separated from his wife by a quaratine, and eventually hears of her death in a sanitorium; the judge-penitent Clamence never married and lives alone in his exile. In some respects Corméry is like these men: the ordinary social world seems absurd to him, his friendships are few and awkward, and he constantly seeks a self-understanding which he vaguely feels has been denied him by his father's death when he was only an infant. But it is quite clear that his story is ultimately one of connectedness, emplacement, rootedness. In the main text one sees this in the lush romanticism of Camus' descriptions of Corméry's childhood: his play with friends, especially on the football field, his life with his family, his experiences at school where instruction and religion are mixed, and so on. This romantic language, whose long sentences seem to derive from the fascination with Faulkner which chracterized Camus in the last years of his life, contrasts rather dramatically with Camus' typical narrative austerity. It is so autobiographical that Camus sometimes forgets the fictional names he has assigned the characters and uses the real names of his family members. Moreover, in the notes for uncompleted sections of the book we see emerging with striking clarity a plan to depict not only Corméry's relationship to his mother but his increasing awareness of the centrality of that relationship in his life and of the dignity and strength of his mother's existence. One sees this plan with particular force and eloquence in this passage from the notes:

> I want to write the story of a pair joined by the same blood and every kind of difference. She is similar to the best the world has, and he quietly abominable. He thrown into all the follies of our time; she passing through the same history as if it were that of any time. She silent most of the time, with only a few words at her disposal to express herself; he constantly talking and unable to find in thousands of words what she could say with a single one of her silences . . . Mother and son.

But the apparently timeless intensity of this bond between mother and son is always placed within the context of Algerian history. It appears that Corméry's recognition of the depth of his love for his mother was to emerge in large part from her constant endangerment by the bombs of terrorists, whose beliefs and purposes she never understands, occupied as she is by the difficulties of living with scarce resources in a harsh world. And this attempt to live in peace and with dignity in the midst of violence dominates her experience long before the rebellion of the fifties, since it was in the Great War that she had lost her husband:

A chapter on the war of 14. Incubator of our era. As seen by the mother? Who knows either France, nor Europe, nor the world. Who thinks shells explode of their own volition, etc.

Thus it seems clear that the lyrical nostalgia of the book's drafts — its Edenic character, evident in the book's title, and so reminiscent of the work of Dylan Thomas — was to be contextualized, though not, I think, discredited or ironized, by an ever-deeper immersion in the violent world of modern history. Or so Jacques Corméry, with his education and his experience of Europe in the second of its great wars, might characterize the narrative movement; Camus' greatest narrative challenge, it appears, would have been to allow his mother's experience its full scope: "Alternate chapters would give the mother's voice. Commenting on the same events but with her vocabulary of 400 words." Some people, it seems, are *in* history, however unwittingly or unwillingly; but only Corméry and Camus and readers like us are, strictly speaking, *of* it. But how can this be portrayed in art?

5.

The late literary critic Northrop Frye once reflected on the curious fact that the nineteenth century found it obvious that *Hamlet* was Shakespeare's greatest play, while the twentieth century has, for the most part, bestowed that honor on *King Lear*. For our predecessors the problems of *Hamlet*, which revolve around the nature and stature of the individual human person, were paramount; in our century we have come to contemplate *Lear's* dilemma, which is to find the line (if it exists) which separates the tragic from the absurd. What, Frye mused, will be the essential Shakespearean play of the next century? His admittedly speculative answer was *Antony and Cleopatra*, because that play represents a situation which more and more people in our world will face: the confrontation of deeply personal desires with world-historical events, or, in other words, the potentially tragic consequences of the creation of a global village. To get Frye's point, we need only recall the now-general agreement, which has arisen among warring parties in this century, to disregard old distinctions between combatants and non-combatants, to eliminate the concept of "civilian." But these movements are economic as well as military: I think of a Guatemalan farmer whom my wife once met: he could not get his crops to market because, suddenly, he could no longer afford the necessary gasoline, gasoline which had risen in price because of the Persian Gulf war. So a man who had never heard of George Bush or Saddam Hussein was in danger, because of their actions, of losing the ability to feed his family. That people may find themselves implicated against their will in historical events is nothing new; but the reach of historical (political, economic) movements has gotten so long so quickly that the connections have become strange, and hard for most of us to accept.

It is precisely this bizarre juxtaposition of the personal and the historical, or this erasure of the line between the two, that Camus was seeking to elaborate in *The First Man*. This was to have been his answer to his critics, to those who failed to comprehend, or who found inexcusable, his decision to defend his mother before some abstract notion of Justice. In recent years very similar concerns have emerged in the fiction of V. S. Naipaul, especially his *A Bend in the River*; and in a very different way in the poetry of Czeslaw Milosz. But I think Camus was the first to see the full implications of this massive change in the nature of historical experience.

Camus never wrote a great book, though each of the three novels he published in his lifetime is nearly perfect. His plays, stories, and essays reveal a similarly high level of technical accomplishment and thematic depth. But clearly he had not found the subject which would enable him to fulfill his promise and exercise his abilities to their full — until, perhaps, *The First Man*. Though it would not have been the novel that Christian readers of *The Fall* might have wished for, surely it would have been Camus' most ambitious work and very probably his most impressive one. Having had his (fictional) say about Algeria, having explored and portrayed the cultural complexities that the French intelligentsia refused to acknowledge, having paid a proper tribute to the dignity and value of his mother's life, would he have returned to the spiritual quest which so dominated *The Fall*? That, alas, we cannot know. But now, at least, we have stronger testimony to Camus' moral integrity, if not to a movement towards Christian faith.

Edward Said has called Camus "the archetypal trimmer," implying that Camus altered his opinions to gain the approval of others. If this were true, then no one could ever have trimmed more ineptly, since Camus' simultaneous insistence upon the validity of Algerian complaints *and* upon the innocence of his family (and others like them) earned him nothing but contempt from both sides. In fact, Said's statement is a monstrous calumny. Camus was a sinner, like all of us, and can be faulted for many things. But in two ways he is, I think, an exemplary figure. He had the wisdom to see that political justice is never simple, and cannot be reduced to simplistic binary oppositions between the oppressors and the oppressed; and he had the courage, in the most stressful of circumstances and in the face of the bitterest opposition, to repudiate the cheap virtue that such oppositions always represent. Perhaps this is a naïve idealization, but I think that Camus' face, in those later photographs, reveals something of his character: stubborn, as Sartre said, but upright, and willing to acknowledge just how difficult it is to discern what Truth or Justice is in any given case. After all, when he died he was very near the age at which, as George Orwell said, every man has the face he deserves.

The Witness

After twenty years of exile, Alexander Solzhenitsyn made a triumphal return to his homeland in 1994. In the scant few years since Mikhail Gorbachev had inadvertently started the collapse of the Soviet Union, almost all of the great writer's long-suppressed works had been published — beginning, at his insistence, with the printing of excerpts from *The Gulag Archipelago* in *Novy Mir*, the journal which had once made him famous and then, later, scorned him. He had recently topped the bestseller lists in his homeland; many looked to him as a prophet whose wisdom would guide this fragile new polity toward its proper future; nearly half of the voters who had just been polled in St. Petersburg considered him the best candidate for the Russian presidency (18 percent supported Boris Yeltsin).

A decade later, such enthusiasm seems almost unimaginably distant, and it is clear that Solzhenitsyn has no definable place or role in his native country. His career as a novelist completed, he has continued to articulate his vision for the future of Russia — in books, articles, speeches before the Duma, even an abortive attempt at hosting a televised interview show — but no one seems to be paying much attention. In a vicious moment of irony, many of his compatriots now link him with precisely those figures he made it his life's work to expose, deflate, and condemn: for today's Russians, Lenin, Stalin, Beria, Molotov, and Solzhenitsyn *all* simply belong to a past it is best to forget. The novelist Victor Yerofeyev proclaims

Solzhenitsyn "comic" and "obsolete"; Dmitri Prigov likewise seeks to "deconstruct" the whole historical crew in order to reclaim them as figures of purely pop culture, as though they were labels on so many Andy Warhol soup cans. And the bookstores of Moscow, their walls lined with Russian translations of Stephen King and Harold Robbins, once again fail to stock *The First Circle* or *Cancer Ward,* though this time the law of supply and demand is blamed rather than the dictates of the Party.

D. M. Thomas's biography of Solzhenitsyn has many flaws, but perhaps its greatest virtues derive from its author's conviction that none of this — not the early celebration, not the current neglect — matters a whit. Solzhenitsyn may be a prophet without honor in his own country, or a man dwelling helplessly in an irrecoverable past; he may be an exemplary hero of resistance to tyranny, or a cruel and arrogant manipulator of those closest to him; he may be all these things. But beyond doubt, he is a figure too large to be contained by the whims of popular opinion. David Remnick has rightly claimed that, "in terms of the effect he has had on history, Solzhenitsyn is the dominant writer of this century." The young Russian rock critic who calls Solzhenitsyn "passé" and asks, dismissively, "Why should anyone now care about *The Gulag Archipelago?*" can be so dismissive in considerable part because of the very work at which he sneers. As Remnick says, "If literature has ever changed the world, his books surely have."

In *Alexander Solzhenitsyn: A Century in His Life,* Thomas — an English novelist and occasional translator of Russian poetry — has not produced a work of scholarship, nor does he claim to have done so. He frequently acknowledges his reliance on the monumental labors of Michael Scammell, whose 1984 biography *Solzhenitsyn* and 1995 collection of KGB files relating to the author provide the bulk of the information on which Thomas relies (excepting Solzhenitsyn's own work). So what does Thomas have to offer us here? He tells us right at the beginning: a novelist's imagination and his "fictive experience" (by which, in defiance of English grammar, he clearly means his experience in writing fictions). Indeed, Thomas inserts in his acknowledgments page one of the most disheartening sentences I have ever read at the beginning of a book: "And may the spirits of Stalin's lawyers and judges, those sticklers for the literal truth, forgive me for having occasionally let imagination make an event more vivid — though I hope never against the grain of the known reality." That Stalin's judicial henchmen — than whom no one less concerned with the facts of a case could possibly be imagined — would be invoked as sticklers for *any* kind of truth defies comprehension. Moreover, with this statement Thomas invites his readers to wonder whether any given episode he relates is augmented by the excessively imaginative application of "fictive experience." And all this in a biography of Solzhenitsyn, no less, whose whole reputation rests on his determination to tell the truth at any cost, and whose most famous speech in the West condemned Harvard University for utter neglect of its motto: *Veritas.*

In the event, I am glad to report, Thomas is less imaginative than he promises (or threatens) to be. To be sure, he stumbles: his commitment to Freudian interpretation, for instance, leads him to devote proportionately much more space to Solzhenitsyn's childhood than did Michael Scammell, and since the documentary evidence for that part of the writer's life is scanty, Thomas ends up writing far too many paragraphs that begin with the words "I imagine" and continue with sheer speculation. And his novelistic instincts too lead him to embroider rich borders on some stories. One minor example: Scammell, citing an early autobiographical poem by Solzhenitsyn, relates the story of how Solzhenitsyn's grandfather Zakhar Shcherbak, as an old man grieving deeply the death of his wife, confronted the Communist authorities who had deprived him of his estate by showing up at their offices with "a rough wooden cross round his neck, like a beggar." In Thomas's rendition — which cites Scammell as source — Zakhar becomes "a crazy old man bowed under a heavy wooden cross," as though he were bearing it on his back, a strange distortion Thomas reinforces by speculating that when Zakhar died soon afterward it might have been due to a heart attack incurred by his attempting to bear such a crushing weight.

Thomas also likes to relate some episodes from Solzhenitsyn's life in a style that is pure pastiche of the writer's own — or that of his English translators. Some readers will undoubtedly find this clever, while others will just wonder why they aren't reading Solzhenitsyn instead of this clumsy imitator. And in at least one respect Thomas's imagination manifestly fails him: he dutifully acknowledges that Solzhenitsyn's Western (and indeed many of his Russian) readers are dismayed and puzzled by Solzhenitsyn's manifest religiosity — his insistence that the fundamental problems of the world have spiritual causes and must therefore find spiritual solutions — but it is clear that Thomas doesn't know how to account for such thinking, and he therefore tends to ignore it.

Nevertheless, Thomas provides a serviceable and generally reliable account of the events of Solzhenitsyn's life for those who lack the interest or stamina required for the nobler course: Scammell's exhaustive scholarship and Solzhenitsyn's own voluminous autobiographical writings. His admiration for his subject and his contempt for Western liberals who refuse to acknowledge Solzhenitsyn's greatness (or the character of the empire he fought) are equally and quite properly evident. Moreover, the latter chapters certainly give an interesting update of events in Solzhenitsyn's life in the dozen years since Scammell's biography appeared. Even given Thomas's moments of waywardness, the story he relates compels the reader's attention. Solzhenitsyn's experiences in the war, his abrupt arrest, his years in the Gulag, his tumultuous relationship with his first wife, his amazing recovery from advanced cancer, his unexpected rise to Politburo-endorsed fame, his fall from favor, his exile, his triumphant return — all this is the stuff of, well, a Russian novel. It could scarcely do less than compel.

Thomas devotes surprisingly little time to Solzhenitsyn's experience in the Gulag; perhaps he feels that this is the part of the writer's life that readers of the biography are most likely to know already. Conversely, he describes in great detail the circumstances that led up to the publication of Solzhenitsyn's first camp story, *One Day in the Life of Ivan Denisovich*, because the improbability of it all could not fail to impress a novelist. That a writer only a few years removed from Stalin's Gulag would have a story of that experience endorsed by Stalin's successor, and would become almost overnight one of the most celebrated men in Russia, beggars the most ambitious imagination. (What Thomas fails to note — and this is a point to which we will return — is that it was precisely the unexpectedness of this fame that convinced Solzhenitsyn that he was indeed a chosen instrument of God, an Elijah to the Ahabs of the Central Committee.) Perhaps it goes without saying that Solzhenitsyn's subsequent fall from political grace — arising from his determination to tell the whole story of the camps — is far less surprising.

But by this point in the story the reader realizes that there is one problem that will not let Thomas go, one puzzle that relentlessly demands to be solved, and that is Solzhenitsyn's treatment of his first wife, Natasha. This becomes the dominant theme of the biography. Thomas understands how the two grew distant from one another during the long prison years, and why Solzhenitsyn ultimately, after his release into exile in Kazakhstan, sought to renew their marriage (he insisted that Natasha abandon her life with Vsevolod Somov, the widower who loved her and wished to marry her, and to whose sons she had become a mother). Thomas even understands, up to a point, why, more than a decade later, Solzhenitsyn determined to divorce Natasha and marry one of his young research assistants. Again and again in this book Thomas offers the most sympathetic readings possible of Solzhenitsyn's actions. But the treatment of Natasha defeats him, as it has many other supporters of Solzhenitsyn.

Thomas is right to worry over this issue, because it goes to the heart of a question that arises in the lives of many of the great: what price are we willing to pay — or rather, are we willing to have *others* pay — for that greatness?

When Natasha realized that Solzhenitsyn would not cease to demand that she grant him a divorce, she attempted to kill herself by taking an overdose of sleeping pills. As she lay unconscious, Solzhenitsyn "raged" to his friends: "How could she do this to me? How *dare* she do this to me?" This reaction seems, to Thomas and, I would think, to any morally sensible reader, outrageous. But Thomas shows that this is of a piece with the whole history of their relationship: all along Solzhenitsyn had spoken to Natasha of his expectations for *her*, never of any obligations *he* might have incurred by marrying this woman. "The question, it seemed, was who could love him with the greatest devotion, not whom he could love." Thus, for Thomas, Solzhenitsyn's reaction to Natasha's suicide attempt is but the logical extension of his insistence that she do everything in her power to enable him to spend almost every waking hour on his writing. She was to work (as a chemistry professor) to pay the bills; she was, in addition, to cook his meals, type his manuscripts, and when necessary help him smuggle the microfilmed typescripts out of the country. And he would later, Thomas notes, have the same expectations — though in less dramatic and dangerous circumstances — for his second wife when they moved with their sons in Vermont and the writer worked on his last great project, *The Red Wheel*, for fourteen or more hours of almost every day, year after year.

In Thomas's view, however deplorable such selfishness might have been in the moral world of ordinary people, it was necessary for Solzhenitsyn if he were to produce his great masterworks. To adapt an old phrase, *ars longa, amor brevis*: art persists, love does not, and the latter must therefore become the handmaiden of the former. Thomas applies the same criterion in discussing the many friends whom, over the years, Solzhenitsyn has condemned or abandoned: "had he been gentle, friendly, 'nice,' he could never have written [*The Gulag Archipelago*]. Had he lolled congenially in bars with . . . the *Novy Mir* editors he could never have written it." Had Solzhenitsyn treated other people with charity and compassion the world of *art* would have suffered the neglect and contempt. Thomas deeply regrets the suffering of those close to Solzhenitsyn, but for him this world of art means almost everything: it is almost surprising that he doesn't quote Faulkner's line about why the truly dedicated writer should be willing to sacrifice his grandmother to his art: "the 'Ode on a Grecian Urn' is worth any number of old ladies." Thomas eagerly looks forward to the day when Solzhenitsyn will be seen clearly as "a writer rather than a fighter for rights." "In the next century of Alexander Solzhenitsyn the embattled politics of his work will fall away and become . . . no more than a backdrop for an exploration of human anguish, fear, courage, cowardice, desire. Already . . . what is most moving about *The First Circle* is its brilliant depiction of experiences that seem timeless." So politics, like love and friendship, is transitory in comparison to the eternal realm of the aesthetic object.

It is hard to imagine Solzhenitsyn disagreeing with Thomas's claim that others had to make terrible sacrifices in order that he, Solzhenitsyn, would be able to fulfill his life's calling as a writer; it is equally hard to imagine him agreeing with Thomas's view of art. Solzhenitsyn is not nor has he ever been a priest of art like James Joyce or Balzac: it was not for the aesthetic object that he and others paid such a price. Here we must consider Thomas's relative inattention to Solzhenitsyn's time in the Gulag, where he came to believe in God and in Russia and in himself. For it was that horrific experience that determined all (both good and bad) that Solzhenitsyn would eventually become.

The quest for understanding here is aided by the most profound, and therefore the most terrifying, body of writing that emerged from the Holocaust, that of Primo Levi. In his devastating last book, *The Drowned and the Saved* — completed just before his death in 1987 — Levi raises once more the question of all survivors of such experiences: Why me? Why am I alive and not another? Again and again Levi was told one of two things: either that survival was random, accidental, or that he had been chosen by God to tell his story and that of his fellow sufferers. But he could not believe in the God invoked by the latter explanation; and the former one seemed to him to contradict utterly his experience in Auschwitz. For Levi saw, or thought he saw, that it was the brave and the selfless who died first, while the cowardly and the selfish lived. Therefore, Levi's survival became to him a badge of shame: had he been better, he would not have lived. And how could he, the living one, tell the story of those who knew the character of the camps to the fullest, since those were the ones whom the ovens destroyed? No wonder, then, that when, in April of 1987, Levi's broken body was found at the bottom of his apartment building's stairs, it was almost universally assumed that he had thrown himself down and willingly joined those to whom he had felt himself always and necessarily unworthy.

It is in the harsh light of Levi's experience that we must consider Solzhenitsyn's. He too wondered about his survival, about what appeared to be his luck. The pattern was too strong not to note. For instance, soon after his arrest for making derogatory comments in personal letters about Stalin, in the latter months of the war, the artillery battery he had commanded was wiped out by the German army. Then, in the camps, he repeatedly found himself in relatively privileged positions, in the "first circle" of Stalin's Inferno. So troubled was he by this that he followed the example of his braver friend Dmitri Panin and found a way to get himself sent to a tougher camp, but even so, he always knew that he had never seen the worst of the Gulag. After his release, there was the cancer which, he was told at one point, left him no more than a few weeks to live; and yet he survived that too. Perhaps one, or even two, of these escapes could have been coincidental, but surely not all of them. The monster — a giant "improbable salamander," as he once called it — that had swallowed so many others spat him out, and he found himself stronger and more purposeful for the experience.

And this had not happened because he was good: indeed, he would write that "in the intoxication of youthful successes" he had believed himself "infallible"; it was the Gulag that taught him that he was "a murderer, and an oppressor." It was the Gulag that taught him that every one has the capacity to become a Stalin, and that therefore "the line separating good and evil passes not through states, nor between classes, nor between political parties either — but right through every human heart." His "bent back . . . nearly broke beneath the load" of this knowledge, but just because it was so heavy and yet so hard to acquire, he had to bring it to others who had not shared the experience. Repeatedly in his three-volume documentation of that improbable salamander he cries out, *"Bless you, prison! . . . Bless you, prison,* for having been in my life!" But — and this above all is what marks Solzhenitsyn as truly great — without retracting that cry of gratitude at all, he adds these quiet words: "(And from beyond the grave come replies: It is very well for you to say that — when you came out of it alive!)"

It is those voices from beyond the grave to whom Solzhenitsyn came to believe himself accountable — those, and the living voices who unaccountably survived the worst the Gulag could offer. In the presence of one such as Varlam Shalamov, author of *Kolyma Tales* (Kolyma in the far northeast being the most horrific of all the archipelago's "islands"), Thomas reports, even the impossibly arrogant Solzhenitsyn was made meek: he had been neither so afflicted nor so brave. It was for the *inarticulate* Shalamovs, for those unable — because of death or shock or mere illiteracy — to tell their own story that he had to speak. This was his calling, and only by meeting this enormous obligation could he justify the repeated miracles by which he was made to survive. He would become for those inside the Archipelago what Anna Akhmatova was to those on the outside, in the greater prison of the Soviet Union. One day, as dozens of women stood in line outside a Leningrad prison, hoping to visit their loved ones, a devastated woman approached Akhmatova and asked, "Can you describe this?" And Akhmatova, whose son suffered somewhere within those walls, replied, "Yes, I can." It was the only reply she, or Solzhenitsyn, could make.

Thus, when Krushchev gave approval for the publication of *One Day in the Life of Ivan Denisovich* in 1962, Solzhenitsyn wrote a prayer to God — a key document in his life, strangely uncited by Thomas — which concludes with these words:

> As I ascend the hill of earthly glory,
> I turn back and gaze, astonished, at the road
> That led me here beyond despair,
> Where I too may reflect Your radiance upon mankind.
> All that I may reflect, you shall accord me,
> And appoint others where I shall fail.

He could not tell everyone's story, or anyone's in full, but what he could tell, he would. And their voices, to borrow a phrase from Akhmatova, would speak through his mouth. To this task he committed all his energies.

Such a commitment does not justify Solzhenitsyn's miserable treatment of Natasha, in part because Thomas is wrong even to suggest that the fulfillment of this task was incompatible with basic charity: Solzhenitsyn could not have fulfilled his vocation by being a clubbable man, but he could have been decent to his wife, and he need not have abandoned her (as, once or twice, he has acknowledged). But one understands Solzhenitsyn better when one sees that he feared above all else anything that would prevent him from the best advocacy possible for those who had no other advocate on this earth. Better, in his (probably unconscious) view, to maltreat his wife than fail in his obligation to his former inmates: her attempt at suicide was to be deplored primarily because it threatened to derail his work, only secondarily because of her pitiable suffering. Such thinking may be deeply perverse, but it is comprehensible.

It also has nothing to do with art as Thomas conceives it. Only in the context I have just sketched can we properly understand Solzhenitsyn's statement upon receiving the Nobel Prize for literature: "In the struggle against lies art has always won, and always will win." For Solzhenitsyn, that which is not true is not art; and, conversely, to present history "just as it really was" — Solzhenitsyn frequently invokes the historian von Ranke's famous definition of the goal of historiography (to tell the story *wie es eigentlich gewesen*) — is the very height of art. "I really cannot envisage any higher task than to serve reality," he said in a 1976 interview. "And I do not consider imagination to be my task or goal. . . . All that was needed was to recreate everything as it was." To be sure, this requires a kind of creative energy properly called imaginative: the writer does not merely repeat what has happened, "for that would not be art at all," even if it were possible (which it is not). But Solzhenitsyn's art "concentrates" reality rather than inventing or bypassing it: it is an art grounded always and firmly in historical actuality and will never (Thomas's hopes notwithstanding) transcend it. Nor need it do so.

Thomas's failure to grasp this conception of the writer's vocation explains his frustration with Solzhenitsyn's last great literary venture, *The Red Wheel*. Thomas can understand Solzhenitsyn's commitment to documentary fidelity in a work like *The Gulag Archipelago*, but finds his inability to abandon the habits of exhaustive research fatal to this Tolstoyan historical novel. As Solzhenitsyn gathered archival material from Stanford's Hoover Institute, Thomas writes, "an artist died. He became, instead, a kind of obsessional 'hoarder'; nothing was to be left to the reader's imagination." Thomas's attempts to explain this approach are bizarre: he wants Solzhenitsyn to be done with history and to explore instead "the heart's dark forest"; he accuses Solzhenitsyn of lacking the courage "to turn a remorseless light upon himself" — imagine saying this of a man who, for all his failings and blind spots, calls himself "a murderer, and an oppressor"! — ; he seems to want Solzhenitsyn to have reinvented himself as John Updike.

Part of the problem here is a failure of empathetic engagement: Thomas should recall that Solzhenitsyn spent almost his whole life in a world where reliable documentation of almost anything was impossible. For such a man there is great pleasure as well as instruction in the simple acquisition of information. But the greater failure stems from Thomas's wildly inaccurate assumption that in writing *The Red Wheel* Solzhenitsyn was in "exile from his great theme, Stalinism and the Gulag" — in other words, that Solzhenitsyn had discharged his obligations to his former fellow prisoners and was now artistically "free" to do as he pleased. But it is perfectly evident that *The Red Wheel* is more than anything else an attempt to follow the Gulag to its source, or at least to one of its major sources: the collapse of tsarism in the Great War. In *The Red Wheel* no less than in *The Gulag Archipelago*, Solzhenitsyn is bound, and justified, by the obligation to tell the historical story just as it was.

This explanation does not, of course, answer the many and legitimate questions about the overall quality of *The Red Wheel*. I tend to agree with Thomas that it is flawed, though I would stress a point Thomas makes but briefly, that "there is much *unfashionable* wisdom in it." And this is just one of the many questions about Solzhenitsyn that remain to be answered, and that will be debated for the foreseeable future: What is his attitude toward the West? Is he opposed to Western democracy *tout court* or just to its current manifestations? How close is his vision for the future of Russia to that of nationalists like Vladimir Zhirinovsky (whom he has denounced as a "caricature of a patriot")? How fully is he imbued with the spirit and character of Russian Orthodoxy, as opposed to the Romantic exaltation of the artist-as-great-man that certainly forms some portion of his character? For me, it is possible to imagine neither the resolution of these questions nor the fading of interest in them. If there is one contemporary writer who will be a subject of vigorous contention a hundred years from now, that writer is surely Solzhenitsyn.

As an epigraph to his 1984 biography *Solzhenitsyn*, Michael Scammell presents a passage from the Mexican poet Octavio Paz in which Paz struggles to describe what precisely it is that Solzhenitsyn represents, what about the man demands our attention. "His example is not intellectual or political or even, in the current sense of the word, moral. We have to use an even older word, a word that still retains a religious overtone — a hint of death and sacrifice: *witness*. In a century of false testimonies, a writer becomes a witness to man." Paz's incisive comment reveals the hopelessness of Thomas's attempt to distinguish between the political-historical and the artistic Solzhenitsyn. All are bound together in his life and work. He came under an enormous weight of conviction that God called him to bear witness, and that what God called him to bear witness *to* was the experience of the camps — especially the experience of those who never emerged to tell their own story. To answer that call faithfully, and nothing else, could justify his miraculous survivals: of the war, of the camps, of cancer, of the KGB. Those in Russia and elsewhere who now disdain or ignore Solzhenitsyn should remember an old Russian proverb that the old inmate of the Gulag cites at the beginning of his great account of that salamander: Dwell on the past and you'll lose an eye; forget the past and you'll lose both eyes.

The Judgment of Grace

First Movement

What I will have to say is framed by a poem. It's by Linda Gregerson, and it's called "Pass Over." Gregerson's poem causes me to think about the dark and strange intertwinings of judgment and grace.

Here is the first of the poem's four sections:

1. Plague of Darkness
You point a camera at a kid, the kid
    will try
      to smile, he said. No matter part

of his mouth is missing, eyelid
    torn,
      the rest of his face such a mass

of infection and half-healed burns they'll
    never
      make it right again. You know

what the surgeon found in his scalp?
    Pencil lead.
      Six broken points of it, puncture wounds

some of them twelve months old. They figure
   the mother
  made him wear a ski mask for those

thousand-and-some-odd miles on the bus
   or why
  didn't somebody turn her in? The kid

is eight, the camera belongs to forensics, and
   he thinks
  he's supposed to smile. Do the math.

If anyone here were in charge, my vote is scrap us
   and start over.

People often say that poetry is the art of indirection — "Tell all the truth but tell it slant," Emily Dickinson famously wrote — but I sometimes have my doubts about the virtues of slanting. I wonder if we can't be *too* content with indirection, too enamored of our subtleties; scorning directness as "simplistic" but, deep down, fearing the pains inflicted by directness. We've all at some time had to face agonizing truths, about ourselves or the larger world, and we know what it can be like; like having pencils jabbed into our scalps, where the lead breaks off and remains, embedded, to infect. Only, for most of us, not nearly as bad.

No wonder we praise indirection. There are depths of experience in every cliché, but never more so than in the one about laughing to keep from crying. When my wife Teri was still in college, her best friend's mother died, suddenly, of an aneurysm. The day after the funeral Teri and her friend sat around a kitchen table and talked about what it took to kill that lady, who for the previous five decades had emerged strong and apparently unscathed from almost every kind of misery, and they laughed and laughed, wildly, frantically, until they were exhausted, and Teri's friend laid her head on the table and went to sleep. That's why we have the Swifts and Voltaires of the world, writers who habitually cause us to look up from the page, blinking, and wonder whether the tears cooling our cheekbones arise from laughter or weeping.

When I read Linda Gregerson's poem I am reminded of a line by Rebecca West, a great (and greatly neglected) writer who is capable of first-order invective: "If the whole human race lay in one grave, the epitaph on its headstone might well be: 'It seemed like a good idea at the time.'" It's okay to laugh, we're supposed to, but only if we know that on a level deeper than we care to go it's really not funny. Gregerson is more blunt: no "might well be," but simply, "my vote is scrap us and start over." Little indirection there; the poem scarcely leans — instead, it seems to be pushing itself, and us, relentlessly and painfully towards the upright.

But Gregerson has her own subjunctive, her own conditional: "*if* anyone here were in charge, my vote is scrap us and start over." This is a marvelously rich and subtle sentence. She doesn't say that no one is in charge; it's just that if anyone *is*, he or she or it isn't "here." Moreover, the cosmic polity seems to be un-democratic: none of us "here" has a vote that counts for anything. But Gregerson doesn't place her decree in the conditional: not "my vote *would be* scrap us and start over," but "my vote *is*." Whether there's anyone in charge at all, whether anyone is listening and counting, Gregerson wants to go on the record with her verdict. Just in case.

And it's an inevitable verdict, she suggests: "Do the math." But we cannot do that math; it's comprised wholly of irrational and imaginary numbers. Gregerson's image calls to my mind a powerful book, *Tell Freedom*, the autobiography of the "coloured" South African writer Peter Abrahams. Abrahams was raised in Johannesburg in the 1920s and '30s, but as a teenager received a scholarship to attend an Anglican "diocesan training college" called Grace Dieu, near Pietersburg in the Transvaal. And there something strange and powerful happened to him, in the company of his friend Jonathan.

> In the months after his visit to the city, Jonathan and I had again and again brooded over the way the white man treated the black. We had worked it down to Christianity. The white man believed in God. He had brought God to us. God taught: 'Love thy neighbour as thyself.' Christ came that we might have life and have it more abundantly. The Church taught that we were all brothers in Christ, one with another. . . . and the

whites, those who had spat on us and on others, were all Christians. The equation did not work out. Where was the error? In the religion? In the white people? In us? In God or in man? And how were we to work it out?

Here, in this peaceful valley, the equation worked out. The Fathers who taught us lived up to their teaching. They were good men and they poured their lives into good work. Belief was translated into reality. We were the witnesses.

But we would leave this peaceful valley and go out into the big world. And there, among the whites, it did not work out. It did not work when whites came to our church. They sat in the front row. What made it so very difficult for us was the fact that the equation did work out with the Fathers and indeed with the Sisters from across the little bridge. But we had proof that the rest of the white Christians of our land were not like the Fathers and the Sisters. If there were any fault that we could lay at the door of the good Fathers and Sisters, it was that they had taught us too well. They had made Christianity a living reality for us, a way of life, a creed to live by, to measure our relations with others by. And the tragedy lay in the measuring.

The equation did not work out. And in the harshness of our youthful idealism we demanded that it work out as logically as a piece of mathematics. And it did not.

The result of Abrahams's inability to solve this equation is simply stated: "I took leave of my dear friend Jonathan and turned my face from that peaceful valley called the Grace of God."

In that "peaceful valley" he had received loving grace; and that grace became for him a perpetual standard of measurement, by which the rest of South African society was weighed in the balance and found wanting. Grace exposed, once and for all, the ungracious; love exposed the unloving. And from then on, to remain in the peaceful valley of grace seemed to Abrahams an evasion: as long as people who looked like him were being spat on, he had to open himself to the same pain. And soon enough, or so it seems from his narrative, the grace of God became no more to him than the deeply ironic name of a pastoral ideal cut off from the sordid realities of Johannesburg. For Abrahams, judgment eclipsed the very grace that had made judgment possible.

It is hard for me not to feel indicted by this story, or, at least, to feel complicit in it. To read it, and poems like Gregerson's, is to be cast into a surreal courtroom as defendant, as one under judgment, accused — but of what and by whom we don't know. It's to become a character in an unwritten Kafka story, and it was Kafka who said, "Our concept of time makes it possible for us to speak of the Day of Judgment by that name; in reality it is a summary court in perpetual session." So. Welcome to the evening lecture on the Day of Judgment.

Here is the second part of "Pass Over":

2. Plague of Frogs
Indicator species is the phrase, I think.

Which means we pour our poisons in the streams
    and swamps
  and these poor creatures grow an extra

leg or lingual tumors or a cell wall so
    denatured
  that the larvae fail. In my new favorite

movie it begins as rain, a burst
    of guts
  and mucus on the hero's car, the hero

such as he is, poor man, who's lost
    his gun and now
  is lost himself before the windshield's slick

indictment, throat of frog, webbed foot
    of frog, split
  belly sliding down the glass in red

and yellow closeup, thence to join
    the carnage
  on the street, boot deep now, bred

of neither air nor water but of God's disgust
    with humankind.
  Behold them, said the prophet, in

thine ovens and thy kneading troughs. And
    then he said, Take,
  eat. This is the body you have made.

Gregerson's "new favorite movie" is *Magnolia,* P. T. Anderson's film from 1999, about which I will say more later. But first I want to consider the claim that the plagues are a sign of "God's disgust." In the Bible and (I think) in *Magnolia,* they are a judgment which is also a gracious gift. They comprise a terrifying act of love.

Why did God not destroy the Egyptians immediately upon Pharaoh's first refusal to free Moses' people? He could have; their slave-holding cruelty had already earned their destruction. But God stayed his hand, and why? Because he so loved the people of Egypt. It's something we all tend to forget, focused as we are on God's care for his chosen people — it is as though we believe that he loved them because they agreed to his proposed covenant. Or as though we believe that he made a covenant with them, made them his "peculiar treasure," because he loved them *instead* of loving others made equally in his image. Some of the people of Israel themselves have thought in this way: when the rabbis who made the translation into Greek that we call the Septuagint came across Isaiah 19:24 — "In that day Israel will be the third with Egypt and Assyria, a blessing in the midst of the earth, whom the Lord of hosts has blessed, saying, 'Blessed be Egypt my people, and Assyria the work of my hands, and Israel my inheritance'" — a severe attack of cognitive dissonance came upon them. *Egypt my people?* Surely the God of Abraham, Isaac, and Jacob would never say such a thing. So they translated it, "Blessed be my people who are in Egypt and in Assyria, and Israel my inheritance."

It was a mistake the reluctant prophet Jonah would not have made. He understood that God loved even sinners so gross as the mobs of Nineveh, and sought their repentance: "I knew that you are a gracious God and merciful," Jonah said, reproachfully, to his Lord; "slow to anger and abounding in steadfast love, and relenting from disaster." So when called to preach to the hated Ninevites, he fled to Tarshish. Or tried to. But that is another story; today we concern ourselves with Moses and Pharaoh.

(I must acknowledge, though I will not try to explain, God's telling Moses that he will harden Pharaoh's heart; just as I must also acknowledge the claims elsewhere in chapters 7 through 9 of Exodus that Pharaoh hardened his *own* heart. For today, I will simply assume that those statements cancel each other out — we are still "doing the math," please remember, as Linda Gregerson counseled us to do, and, as we learned in school, complicated equations require us to simplify them whenever possible. I will therefore treat the Exodus story as one that belongs to the recognizable human moral world. Because I think it does.)

The first plague — turning the Nile to blood — does not move Pharaoh because he has wizards in his employ who can do the same "by their secret arts." But the frogs are more than he had reckoned with, and he gives in, at least for the moment. He asks Moses and Aaron to intercede with God on his behalf, plead for the plague's removal; but when they do so, and the frogs cease to infest the land, Pharaoh refuses to release the Israelites. This establishes a pattern which is continued with the plagues of flies and hail and locusts and darkness, before the final terrible affliction which the Israelites know as the Passover. But the pattern can be continued only because God gives Pharaoh every possible chance to release the Israelites from their captivity; he is, after all, "slow to anger and abounding in steadfast love, and relenting from disaster." The plagues, then, are signs that God does not wish to destroy Egypt — and indeed, he never does, even when his wrath seems to be fully kindled: he only inflicts upon them such pain as is necessary to free Moses and his people. He would rather see them mend their ways. As, centuries later, he asks Ezekiel, "Have I any pleasure in the death of the wicked . . . and not rather that he should turn from his way and live?"

If this sounds increasingly like a sermon, blame Linda Gregerson. She started it. And she did so by describing the plagues of Egypt as a sign of God's disgust rather than (primarily) his forbearance and grace. Even in *Magnolia*, the frogs raining from the skies and splattering onto car windshields and asphalt, and crashing through skylights, and thumping cacophonously onto roofs and gas station canopies, are portrayed as a way for God — or Someone, Something Up There — to arrest the attention of people who are ruining their own lives and the lives of those around them. It's not his disgust that moves him, it is his horror at our self-disgust; he doesn't destroy us, but tries to stop us from destroying ourselves. Hours before the frogs fall from the sky, it's just rain that's falling — though in torrents — and people sit in their living rooms or lie in their bedrooms or half-recline in their cars and softly sing:

> It's not going to stop
> It's not going to stop
> It's not going to stop
> 'Till you wise up

But they don't wise up, most of them. Even when it's just rain pouring down, it does so hour after hour, in a way quite remarkable for Southern California: and long before the rain began, a young African-American boy had rapped to Jim the cop, "When the sunshine don't work, the Good Lord bring the rain in." Yet no one seems to notice the conditions; they always have their backs to the windows; turned inward, eyes downcast or vacant, they continue to eat away at their own guts, oblivious to the external world, muttering the lyrics to a song they seem not to feel the force of. Only the crashing of frogs onto windshields and roofs and through windows and skylights — and in one case, right onto a man's upturned face — is sufficient to shake them from their self-referential stupors.

The arrival of the frogs does strange things to these people. It throws a mother and daughter into each other's arms; it sends an ambulance carrying a woman — a would-be suicide, nearly dead from an overdose of morphine — weaving out of control, crashing onto its side, and sliding right up to the door of an emergency room, perhaps rather more quickly than the driver could have gotten there on his own. One frog, singled out by the camera as though it had been chosen for its mission, plunges through a skylight, knocking the gun from the hand of a man about to shoot himself in the head. The bullet punctures a television instead, and it would appear that the man (a television performer, host of a game show) lives on, perhaps to be held accountable for his sins against his wife and daughter, which are many and vile. Another man confronts his dying father — a father whose sins are also many and vile — in complete obliviousness to the frogs; the pounding on the roof seems but to focus his mind on the dark task at hand. And those fathers themselves, after years of being trapped in the relentless cycle of their sins, are simultaneously and mysteriously prompted to find some way to confess — confess at least some of their violences against others, against themselves, and (if they but knew it) against God.

And what about "the hero," as Gregerson rightly calls him, Jim the cop? Well, for Jim — who has indeed lost his gun, is (as he says himself) a laughingstock among his peers, and has just now (it seems) lost the young woman he met only that morning but with whom he has already fallen in love — the frogs just present another opportunity to serve, to help, to "do good," as he puts it at the beginning of the film. He rescues the man who has taken a frog to the face, and then (falling from a ladder) a mouth full of asphalt and broken teeth; he helps this man try to undo a crime he has committed. And then, rather than arrest the man, he sends him on his way. And here's what he says as he sits in his car and considers his decision — as he does also near the beginning of the movie, he's half-consciously imagining himself in an episode of the reality show *Cops*:

> I have to take everything and play it as it lays. Sometimes people need a little help. Sometimes people need to be forgiven. And sometimes they need to go to jail. And that's a very tricky thing on my part, making that call. I mean, the law is the law, and heck if I'm going to break it. But you can forgive someone — well, that's the tough part. What can we forgive? Tough part of the job. Tough part of walking down the street.

And, by the way, the last thing that falls from the sky in this movie? Jim's lost gun. Well, what you sow you reap. You sow abuse, you get abused by the rain of frogs; you sow kindness, you forget your own loss and turn your attention to the losses of others, you have what you had lost returned to you. What I'm trying to say is that they're *all* gifts, *all* grace.

But more about Jim, the hero, later.

The frogs seem somehow to break the momentum of the spiraling disintegration that so many of the characters are experiencing, or inflicting on themselves and others; the frogs mark a severe mercy — nothing less severe would make a difference, therefore nothing less severe would be merciful, gracious, loving. Certainly, it is because of our sin that we must be spoken to in such a harsh language; but we *are* being spoken to, not destroyed. After all, did not the Lord promise that he would never again bring a flood to drown the creation? The movie's young prophet is right: "When the sunshine don't work, the Good Lord bring the rain in." And when the rain don't work, he brings the frogs — and the darkness, and the locusts, and the river of blood. And something even worse, for those whose hearts have calcified to sheer stone. But his hand never falls on us as fiercely as it could — as it once did, in the time of Noah. To Linda Gregerson I say, no, it's not disgust that moves him, though it surely is grief and even wrath. *Every* judgment, I tell you, is an act of loving grace. Do the math.

3. Plague of Locusts

Because there's never enough. No, not
     in this bright
       field of surfeit: milk rings on the phone bill, tracked-in

honey where the cats came through, lost
     homework,
       last year's coggins on the tackroom floor.

My neighbor back in Somerville had only the
     narrowest
       path to walk, from table to toilet, toilet

to bed, the rest was floor to ceiling with what normal
     people throw
       away. I see how it comes to this. Never

enough of it battened down. I lose my pills, he said
    to me once,
  they're rolling around on the floor somewhere.

The Parsis bring their dead, as Zoroaster
    is construed
  to have taught them, to Malabar Hill, where

when the world was well the birds
    restored them
  to simplicity in ninety minutes flat.

The birds are purpose-built for this, their scabrous
    faces bear
  a nearly paraphrastic kinship to the fetid

stuff they tunnel in. O who will come who will
    not choke?
  The birds cannot keep up.

Here Gregerson pursues the theme of consumption — consumption as destruction — that she began to explore in the last lines of the previous section: "Behold them, said the prophet, in thine ovens and thy kneading troughs. And then he said, Take, eat. This is the body you have made." The frogs fill the kneading-bowls of the Egyptians; they're lodged in the rising dough, they foul it; they clog the ovens, the bakers choke on the smoke of their burning flesh. The people of Egypt are not given, this day, their daily bread. "This is the body you have made," writes Gregerson, the food we have earned by our cruelty — and, perhaps more to the point, by our addiction to ceaseless production and consumption, to the making and ingesting and excreting of unnecessary things. Or so this third section suggests.

    Let's try to trace the arc of the poem — which taken as a whole is a kind of anatomy of our collective sin — as it is now visible to us. In the first section, Gregerson describes the plague of darkness — the darkness in which a poor abused child (one of a multitude) must live, the black shadow we feel cast over our lives when we read such an account; in the second, the plague of ecological catastrophe as embodied in the frogs. She traces the grievous damage we inflict on everyone and everything that surrounds us. But here, in her third section, she turns our attention towards the damage we inflict on ourselves — perhaps because it enables, even necessitates, that violence towards others. And she considers our self-woundings under the rubric of *production,* a ceaseless profligate manufacture of artifacts and images and signs, followed by an equally ceaseless consumptive hoarding. Gregerson is describing a world in which what we produce overwhelms us, encloses us, leaves us scarcely space to breathe. As Dylan puts it in one of his blackest songs, "There's not room enough to be anywhere." He was thinking of the walls of depression closing in, but for Gregerson the most confining walls we confront are those that arise out of our "bright field of surfeit," where the milk and honey of the Promised Land are largely wasted, spilled, tracked onto our floors. "The birds cannot keep up" with all that we pour forth onto and into the Creation, and that we ravenously consume. We are at once, to borrow William Blake's terms, the Prolifics and the Devourers.

It seems to me that this idea has great and disturbing resonance for the artist, especially the Christian artist, who strives to be faithful in representing God's interventions in the world in their doubled aspect of judgment and grace, and who can do so only by making, producing — by adding *more* to the "bright field of surfeit." How do we justify such continued production, in a world already full, arguably far too full, of books and poems and paintings and songs?

Second Movement

The terms "Prolific" and "Devourer" come from Blake's "Marriage of Heaven and Hell":

> Thus one portion of being is the Prolific, the other the Devouring: to the devourer it seems as if the producer was in his chains, but it is not so, he only takes portions of existence and fancies that the whole.

But the Prolific would cease to be Prolific unless the Devourer, as a sea, received the excess of his delights.

Some will say: 'Is not God alone the Prolific?' I answer: 'God only Acts & Is, in existing beings or Men.'

These two classes of men are always upon earth, & they should be enemies; whoever tries to reconcile them seeks to destroy existence.

Religion is an endeavour to reconcile the two.

Note: Jesus Christ did not wish to unite but to separate them, as in the Parable of sheep and goats! & he says I came not to send Peace but a Sword.

As is usually the case with Blake, no one is certain exactly what all this means; but many people have found the distinction intriguing and even compelling. Carl Jung, for instance, was much taken with Blake's pairing, and used it (in his book *Psychological Types*) to introduce his famous distinction between the extravert and the introvert. He believed that the extravert is prolific, the introvert devouring; but the poet W. H. Auden (a careful reader of both Blake and Jung) rightly believed that Blake identified the Prolific with the artist, and also noted that artists are predominantly an introverted crew — since, after all, so much of what they do has to be done in solitude (even for the performing artist, the actual performing is a small part of the job). For Auden it is the consumer, the Devourer, of the artwork who fits the type of the extravert.

What I want to suggest here is that both Jung and the young Auden get the experience of art wrong; and they get it wrong because they accept Blake's view that there are these "two classes of men" who cannot be reconciled or merged with each other.

I contend that Blake, by separating the prolific artist and the devouring consumer of art into two irreconcilable groups — and by favoring the one group as evidently superior, which we see in his comparison of his distinction to Jesus' distinction between the sheep and the goats — has conceived of the relationship of artist and audience in a way that no Christian should accept. The Christian arts community, I believe, should never think of art in terms of production and consumption, but rather in terms of *exchange*, of the giving and receiving of *gifts*. The artist gives from what has already been given to her, from the talents bestowed by God and cultivated through stewardly discipline; the "audience" receives in such a way that that receiving is also a gift, the gift of time and attention — and maybe even, if the artist is especially blessed, money. As Wendell Berry is fond of reminding us, there are other economies than the economy of money; the giving and receiving of gifts (gifts of art, gifts of attention) belongs to the economy of grace. In this economy a one-to-one exchange is more than enough; we have no need to discover what paintings fetch at auction or how one's books or CDs are doing on the Amazon.com bestseller list. One must simply remember the portion of St. Francis's prayer that reminds us that in giving we receive. I think again of Jim, in *Magnolia*, who gets his gun back when he isn't looking for it; having forgotten his troubles and instead given his attention to people in need, at a moment when he least expects or even thinks about it, he receives again what he had lost. Christian artists ought to be like Jim.

And all this comes back around to my theme for this lecture, judgment and grace. An artist can only pay attention to the dark intertwinings of judgment and grace if she recognizes that she herself is under judgment and grace at once. *Simul justus et peccator*, as Luther liked to say: simultaneously justified and a sinner. At once able to give and needing to receive. If the artist considers herself one of the Prolific, then she becomes simply the dispenser of judgment or grace, not equally a receiver of those gifts. In Dante's *Purgatorio*, the repentant sinners hear words, or see images, that restrain them from sin; these, collectively, are called their bridle. They also hear words, or see images, that encourage them towards righteousness; these, collectively, are called their whip. For the Christian artist an understanding of oneself as a sinner under judgment is the bridle; an understanding of oneself as a child of God under grace is the whip.

Without this twofold understanding, the artist can fall back into the invidious distinction that Blake makes, to see herself as someone intrinsically different than the others who are not Prolific. Few spiritual states are more dangerous, as Auden (after he became a Christian) was especially aware. If, when he was a young poet, he could sometimes be caught up in Romantic dreams of prophetic power, after he became a Christian he swerved in the opposite direction. In his great poem "At the Grave of Henry James," written just after his return to the Christian faith of his childhood, he writes movingly of the distinctive spiritual dangers of the artist:

> All will be judged. Master of nuance and scruple,
> Pray for me and for all writers living or dead;
>   Because there are many whose works
> Are in better taste than their lives; because there is no end
> To the vanity of our calling; make intercession
>   For the treason of all clerks.

But after another decade of maturation in the Christian faith, he came to see that this view (however beautifully expressed) was too dramatic; it wrongly saw the experience of the artist as unique. One of my favorite lines in his poetry comes from his great poetic sequence from the early fifties, the *Horae Canonicae,* and is a deceptively simple one: "Can poets (can men in television) be saved?" Whether poets can be saved is indeed a question; but no different than the question of whether "men in television" can be saved. The poet is singled out neither for damnation nor redemption, but simply must muck along as best he can, like everyone else.

Without this knowledge — without the discipline of reminding oneself of it — the Christian artist is in a bad way. Without a constant awareness of being under the same judgment and the same grace as everyone else, we are left with this: "Take, eat: this is the body you have made." Accepting the judgment that falls hard on us, and then accepting the grace that alone can save us from that judgment, we hear another word: "Take, eat; this is my body given for you."

Here, then, is the final section of Linda Gregerson's poem:

4. Hyssop, Lamb

Explain to me the writing on the door posts
    will you, now
  while the angel gorges on them

and theirs, each that was first to open the
    matrix, first
  still matters in this first world,

that much I have seen and do in part
    acknowledge.
  Archived in the space behind the lintel

and its hasty script, a logic of division
    that has made
  the world articulate, a portal for each

fine discrimination of the covenanting
    mind.
  And heaven has its discards too, there's not

a book I know that tells me otherwise.
    I'm having
  trouble reading in this light though.

Was it something in the water, or before?

Earlier, I wrote of Peter Abrahams' decision to turn his back on the "peaceful valley" of Grace Dieu because he could not bear the contrast between its idyllic world and the misery inflicted on other people of color in South Africa's apartheid regime. Abrahams reminds me of what I would rather not consider: that for all my talk about the unity of our experience — all under judgment, all under grace; art as an equal exchange between maker and receiver — the human world is constituted by difference, distinction. "All will be judged," Auden writes, and of course it's true, but all do not respond equally to judgment. Some bow meekly, some accept the verdict but with resentment, some refuse the authority of the Judge; some pronounce their own angry counter-judgments upon any who might dare to judge them. And for each one who receives grace with thankful wonderment, there is probably another who grows wrathful at the very premise of the gracious offering: that the one to whom grace is extended *needs* it. One of the most memorable theatrical experiences of my life occurred more than a decade ago in England, where I saw a small but very accomplished company perform *Measure for Measure*. In the last scene, when the Duke of Venice has returned from his period in disguise, and his corrupt and murderous deputy Angelo kneels before him awaiting judgment, suddenly Isabella — the woman whom Angelo has most offended — falls to *her* knees next to Angelo and prays that the Duke will spare him. And in this lovely performance, the actor who played Angelo, without rising from his knees or indeed moving his body at all, turned his head ever so slowly towards Isabella, his eyes slightly widening, in speechless astonishment that the one whom he has persecuted would plead for him. I saw those actors perform that play four times, and each time I wept at that moment, so beautiful was its depiction of forgiveness unexpected and unlooked-for.

Conversely, I think of John Mortimer's BBC television drama from some years ago, *Titmuss Regained,* in which an English politician, Leslie Titmuss, hires a private investigator to get dirt on his wife's late first husband, whom Leslie thinks she idealizes. When he reveals that that husband had had an affair with a friend of hers, she is devastated and walks out on him. But later she returns and tells him that she has decided to forgive him; to which Leslie (played by that fine actor David Threlfall) replies, stiffening with bitterness, "I don't want to be forgiven. . . . Not by you . . . Not by anyone." To accept forgiveness is to accept the need for forgiveness, to accept one's sins and errors, to acknowledge the propriety of judgment; and this Leslie cannot do. Years later he remembers that moment as the time "when she turned on him and forgave him. . . . She could never be trusted again."

All will be judged. But how will we respond when our moment comes? We will be divided by our responses: on one side, Angelo; on the other, Leslie Titmuss. The logic of division is the logic of non-reciprocity. Likewise, in Peter Abrahams' South Africa, the white Christians spat on the black ones; while the eight-year-old boy in the first section of Gregerson's poem, the one who smiles into the camera with his ruined face, has suffered what he never inflicted and (we hope) never will inflict. In Gregerson's final section, here, she discerns a primal chasm, one marked by the lamb's blood on the Israelites' doors: some children will die, some will live. All will be judged, but some receive a judgment from which others are spared.

Gregerson flinches from the image of this primal severance. At the moment that she considers the most frightening image of division — "And heaven has its discards too, there's not a book I know that tells me otherwise" — her world starts to darken, the book's print becomes indiscernible: "I'm having trouble reading in this light though." But before the darkness descends, she sees and reports that the "logic of division" embodied in the blood-marked lintels is what "makes the world articulate."

There's a sense in which this is true that I am tempted to call trivial, though it may actually be profound: what we articulate is defined or framed by what we leave unarticulated. I say this and not that; you sing one song and leave another unsung, perhaps unimagined; every time that painter draws a line she leaves forests of lines undrawn, and even a lifetime isn't enough to rescue more than a fraction of them from non-being. As I say, I don't know if this is a trivial point or not. But certainly the "logic of division" takes on more heft and force when we must decide what events, what scenes, what images of our world to make articulate. When we must decide whether to portray an Angelo or a Leslie Titmuss. We must find the colors in which to paint both judgment and grace.

I want to move towards an ending by considering this question in light of a great mystery. St. Paul famously spoke of the "mystery of iniquity," but that's not what I refer to here. I am thinking of the mystery of virtue, of simple goodness. The real question, it seems to me, is not why there is evil — look around you, for crying out loud, at this evidently Darwinian world. Actions that all of us call evil when we see them in the human world happen every second in the rest of creation, as is amply (some would say excessively) illustrated in the biologist Lyall Watson's book *Dark Nature: A Natural*

History of Evil — so much so that when people lived closer to nature's patterns of life and death almost no one spoke of the "problem of evil." That "problem" arises as a major philosophical concern in the eighteenth century, and in the cities, among people who rarely saw wild animals and who almost as rarely saw how the meat they ate for dinner got on their table. This is not to say that people who were aware of the harshness of the natural world did not see it as something requiring explanation — they did, and at least from the Middle Ages on they commonly explained the violence of animals as one of the consequences of the Fall of humanity. But such harshness was not seen as a "problem" that had to be answered lest one be forced to abandon Christian belief. Even the fourteenth-century Black Death — though it prompted many questions — did not prompt the *kind* of questions that, say, the Lisbon earthquake of 1756 did: the "how-could-a-good-God-allow-such-suffering" questions. And though Milton (in 1660) says that his goal in *Paradise Lost* is to "justify the ways of God to man," it is perfectly clear that he is less interested in "justifying the existence of evil" than in "justifying the plan of redemption."

It is my view — though I can't defend it in any detail here — that the rise of the "problem of evil" is the result of alterations in the typical European forms of life. It is a function of, among other things, urbanization. The people who first raise the problem of evil — or, at least, who first make it central to European intellectual life — are people of the cities: Paris above all, but also London, Berlin, Edinburgh. They tend to be — in that curious and resonant term borrowed from the French — deracinated, uprooted from their native soil. They have disconnected themselves from the life-forms of their ancestors, and no longer do the work those ancestors did or worship in the parish churches those ancestors occupied. And, as the eighteenth century yields to the nineteenth and then to the twentieth, they live in increasing health: with better nutrition, fewer diseases. In the latter third of the nineteenth century, the great cities begin to clean themselves up, to dispose more healthily of their wastes, to develop cleaner fuels and thereby improve their air. The patterns of life and death, of expected suffering and unexpected health, that were all Europeans had known receded further and further into the fog of history. In 1702, the famous Bible commentator Matthew Henry wrote: "Since I set out in the world, I never was so long without the death of children or others near and dear to me." How long a period is he referring to? Three years. Yet the "problem of evil" was not an issue for Matthew Henry. It is, strangely and yet (when you think about it) understandably enough, only when European and American life gets noticeably cleaner and safer and healthier that certain intellectuals begin to think that the greatest difficulty for Christianity to deal with is the fact that anything bad happens at all.

Even now, we can see that some of the writers and thinkers most attuned to the unexpectedness of blessing, the extraordinariness of even the small graces of daily life, are the ones whose experiences remain connected with, rooted in, the rhythms and patterns of Creation. I think often of a poem by the great Australian poet Les Murray called "At the Aquatic Carnival." The poem elaborates the overlapping of what we might call the economy of nature and the human world, and centers itself on a repeated sentence: "Nature is not human-hearted." It must be given here *in toto*.

Two racing boats seen from the harmonic railing
of this road bridge quit their wakes,
plane above the mirroring shield-forms
and bash the river, flat out, their hits batts of appliqué
violently spreading, their turnings eiderdown
abolishing translucency before the frieze of people,
and rolled-over water comes out to the footings of the carnival.

Even up drinking coffee-and-froth in the town,
prodigious sound rams through arcades and alleyways
and burrs in our teeth, beneath the slow nacelle
of a midsummer ceiling fan.
No wonder pelicans vanish from their river at these times.
How, we wonder, does that sodden undersized one
who hangs around the Fish Co-op get by?
The pert wrymouth with the twisted upper beak.

It cannot pincer prey, or lid its lower scoop,
and so lives on guts, mucking in with the others

who come and go. For it to leave would be death.
Its trouble looks like a birth defect, not an injury,
and raises questions.
There are poetics would require it to be pecked
to death by fellow pelicans, or kids to smash it with a stick,
preserving a hard cosmos.

In fact it came with fellow pelicans, parents maybe,
and has been around for years. Humans who feed it
are sentimental, perhaps — but what to say
of humans who refused to feed a lame bird?
Nature is not human-hearted. But it is one flesh
or we could not imagine it. And we could not eat.

Nature is not human-hearted. So the animals
come to man, at first in their extremity:
the wild scrub turkeys entering farms in drought-time,
the done fox suddenly underfoot among dog-urgers
(that frantic compliment, that prayer never granted by dogs)
or the shy birds perching on human shoulders and trucks
when the mountains are blotted out in fiery dismemberment.

Why, for our fellow creatures, is there even this inchoate sense that humans may, just possibly, grant the prayer never granted by dogs? What instinct or impulse presses them even to take a chance on the possibility of our mercy? Nature is not human-hearted, indeed — but why are *humans* human-hearted? Why do so few of us adhere to that "poetic" that would require children to beat the deformed pelican to death, so few of us embrace the need to "preserve a hard cosmos"?

Similarly, why is Jim the cop — to return to *Magnolia* — why is Jim kind to people? Almost everyone surrounding him is, as I have noted, both self-absorbed and self-destructive (interesting how those go together); yet he repeatedly forgets his problems and occupies himself with helping others. Now, Jim is clearly a Christian — could that be it? An important question arises here: is Jim good because he is a Christian, or is he a Christian because he is good? The answer makes all the difference in the world; because if it's the latter, if Jim is a Christian because he's inclined to be good anyway, then Christianity becomes just an add-on, an accessory to a goodness that's already there, somehow intrinsic to him. No lessons for the rest of us in that. If Jim is good because he's a Christian, though, it's a very different story: then, perhaps, we should *all* be Christians, so we can all be good, or at least have the chance at it. I wish I could think that that's what P. T. Anderson is suggesting, but it's not likely. For in addition to Jim, we have another warm and loving character, a hospice nurse named Phil Parma (played beautifully by Philip Seymour Hoffman), who evidences no religious commitment, no commitments of any kind. As far as we can see, he's just kind, sympathetic — good. Some people are; what can we offer by way of explanation but a shrug?

I want to suggest that we should do more than shrug; that we (and I mean here especially we Christians) need to explore the mystery of virtue as well as the mystery of iniquity, to press our audiences to see the strangeness of goodness, the extraordinary unexpectedness of love and grace. In the last scene of *Magnolia*, Jim leaves the man he has helped undo a crime — return money he has stolen to a safe — and drives to Claudia's house. Claudia's life is a mess; she is sexually promiscuous, living (it appears) with a history of sexual abuse by her father, heavily addicted to cocaine; and Jim is in love with her. Having just asked himself "What can we forgive?" he comes to her apartment, sits on her bedside, and says: "you listen to me now. You're a good person. You're a good and beautiful person and I won't let you walk out on me. And I won't let you say those things — those things about how stupid you are and this and that. I won't stand for that. You want to be with me . . . then you be with me. You see?" And Claudia, sniffling and blotchy-faced, her eyes red with tears, looks up — looks right at the camera — and smiles. Cut to credits.

How does this kind of thing happen? I demand to know. Why is anyone good to anyone else? That we're cruel to one another doesn't surprise me in the least; I want an answer to the problem of goodness. Even if it takes a lifetime, or more, to figure it out.

I'm aware that it's easy for me to ask this kind of question, to think in such positive terms. I might have a different set of issues if my mother had burned my cheek with cigarettes, torn my lip, plunged pencils into my scalp. (Even when a sufferer like Solzhenitsyn cries out, "Bless you, prison! . . . Bless you, prison, for having been in my life!" he always hears, "from beyond the grave," voices admonishing him, "It is very well for you to say that — when you came out of it alive!") Perhaps for that boy — with Linda Gregerson's description of whom I began this essay — the problem of evil might be just a tad more real. After all, if your own mother is the most destructive and hateful element in your world, it is hard to imagine what in your experience you might use to make your life worth living. And it is true that many people who suffer as that little boy has suffered never find their way in this world, and do not mind leaving it as soon as they can. Nevertheless, let us meditate on this: "You point a camera at a kid, the kid/ will try/to smile, he said." In fact, the kid *will* smile — it's no less a smile because his lip is torn and his face burned. And that, when you think about it, is an astonishing thing. It's remarkable enough that Claudia, at the end of *Magnolia,* carrying all her baggage of pain and sin, can smile at Jim and at us; but it strains credulity to the snapping point that that little boy can smile at the camera. *And yet he does.* After all he has been through — enough, indeed, to make a reasonable person vote to scrap us and start over — he finds, from somewhere inside — some obscure and ever-hidden part known only, perhaps, to God the Crucified One — the trust, the hope, to smile when that human-hearted man from forensics points the camera's lens at his poor ravaged face. What that camera records, of course, is a terrible judgment on all of us who have helped make, or have allowed to be made, a world in which a mother can for so long abuse her son so grossly; and that judgment is so terrible that it can conceal from us (as I think it conceals from Linda Gregerson) its other message: that hope and trust are possible even from the most profoundly wounded among us — that humans can be even that resilient, that forgiving, that willing to give the world another chance. What I love about *Magnolia* is that P. T. Anderson had the courage to portray, perhaps slightly less dramatically, that grace, to put it before us either to shame or to bless us, depending on our response. Those who have ears to hear, let them hear.

The Genesis of Wisdom

Leon Kass's meditation on the wisdom of Genesis (*The Beginning of Wisdom: Reading Genesis*) is expansive, curious, fascinatingly rich and digressive. This I claim without reservation, but my next claim begins with a qualifier: *to me*, it is also quite maddening. I emphasize the qualification because Kass didn't write the book for me, or people like me — that is, though Kass says that the book "is addressed to believers and nonbelievers alike," the latter group is likely to be more comfortable with Kass's discourse. This is not really a book for people who believe that Genesis is a sacred text with an unavoidable claim on their lives. Such people may learn much from the book — as I certainly did — but they are not its ideal audience. If we wish to discover whom this book is really written for, we might consider its title: Kass has written a primer for those who would begin the task of reading for wisdom. I must admire such a book; in the event, I find that I must also contend with it. But Kass's generous encounter with Genesis is so thoroughly undogmatic that I doubt he would mind my contentiousness.

The most surprising thing about this book is that Kass wrote it — or so, at least, he himself thinks. After all, he is by training a physician and a biochemist, and is best known for his incisive contributions to biomedical ethics. But he has long demonstrated a wide range of intellectual interests — witness (to take but one example) the collection of essays and reflections on marriage, *Wing to Wing, Oar to Oar*, that he recently edited with his wife Amy Kass. Still, he himself raises the question, "How does a man of medicine and science, raised in a strictly secular home without contact with Scripture, come to write a book on the Bible?" He answers, "It is a mystery, even to the author"; but he suspects "that it all comes from a late-onset, dominant — and, I fear, lethal — rabbinic gene." This suspicion seems unwarranted, though, because Kass goes about his task in a way quite alien to traditional rabbinical commentary.

Kass's approach to Genesis owes little or nothing to the culture of the synagogue, and almost everything to the culture of the university seminar room — specifically, at the University of Chicago, where Kass has taught for many years, and where his interest in Genesis arose. First he taught it in a core course for undergraduates; then he explored it in informal meetings at his home with his wife, a faculty colleague, and a few interested students; but, though his interest grew and grew, he was reluctant to take the next step and offer a whole class of his own on the text. "Public teachers of the book, I then thought and still think, should be either biblical scholars or knowledgeable and religiously observant keepers of the tradition — preferably both — and I was neither." But eventually Kass came to believe that Genesis deserved to be taught in a way that neither the scholars nor the believers were likely to teach it: as a book that offers "wisdom," a book that has "an 'anthropology,' an account of the human being, embedded in its account of the good life." And if no one else at the University of Chicago was likely to teach Genesis in that spirit, he would have to be the one to do it.

Thus emerged a course, at first (in 1980) offering no college credit and populated by "handpicked students," but later offered openly and for credit, in which Kass and his students read Genesis "philosophically, solely for meaning and understanding, in search of wisdom." Now, in this book that has emerged from many years of discussion and reflection on the text, Kass freely admits that there is "a reason to be suspicious of a philosophical approach to the Bible" — indeed, more than one reason. Many of today's philosophers are likely to find Kass's belief in "reading for wisdom" naïve and superannuated; and even those who sympathize with such a quest may well suspect the philosophical quality of the Biblical narrative. Kass also recognizes that scholars dedicated to the textual history of the Biblical books — their origins, developments, and later editorial transformations — may be congenitally suspicious of the belief that some unified picture of wisdom can emerge from these multiply redacted pages. Then there are those believers (and others) who point out that neither the Bible's "manner nor its manifest purposes are philosophical. Indeed, there is even good reason for saying that they are *antiphilosophical*, and deliberately so." Finally, Kass tips his hat to his fellow scientists, who may well be skeptical not only of Kass's project but also and equally of all the other opponents of it. There is something rather winning about the independence and cheerfulness with which Kass acknowledges these objections — and continues on his quest wholly unperturbed by them. Twenty years of experience tells him that wisdom may indeed be found in Genesis, if one seeks it in a philosophic spirit.

What, then, does a philosophical reading of Genesis look like — at least as Kass defines it? He claims, to start, that it means "reading without presuppositions or intermediaries," but he doesn't mean that. He certainly does have a presupposition, and admits it: that wisdom may be found in this text. He states quite forthrightly that "to read in the spirit of thoughtful engagement" — which for Kass is a synonym for reading philosophically, reading for wisdom — requires "suspending disbelief and seeking reasons to trust." And he takes that position in part because of the "intermediaries" of past generations who have venerated Genesis and found reasons to trust it. In presupposing that Genesis contains value, Kass is practicing what Chesterton called "the democracy of the dead" — he's giving the ancestors their votes. So when he says that he wants to read Genesis "without presuppositions or intermediaries," what he really means is that his presuppositions are revisable and his intermediaries do not possess absolute authority: he does not come to the text with faith commitments that *require* him to find wisdom in the text and to obey its commandments insofar as he understands them. He is a pupil of the text, but not a disciple; he does not recognize it *a priori* as being binding upon him.

As a pupil, Kass seeks guidance from Genesis: his approach "attempts to understand the text in its own terms yet tries to show how such an understanding may address us in our current situation of moral and spiritual neediness." But how can the text be shown to address us, given its temporal, spatial, and cultural distance from us? At the outset of his book, Kass suggests some of the connections: "As were the protagonists in the world of Genesis, so are we today troubled by vexing questions of family life." "Contemporary concerns over unbridled technology are anticipated in the story of Babel." "Biblical Egypt should be of special interest for modern Americans." But given the distances that I mentioned, how can these connections be made to seem viable and unforced, richly appropriate comparisons rather than strained allegories?

To achieve his goal, Kass must discover a vocabulary that mediates between the Biblical world and ours. He needs bridges, translators; and he finds them in the language of human problems and human self-understanding. Let me take but two among dozens of possible examples. Reflecting upon what, in accordance with most modern Biblical criticism, he calls "the two creation stories" (roughly, the first and second chapters of Genesis), Kass sums up the lessons of the stories:

> In short, the first story challenges the dignity of the natural objects of thought and the ground of natural reverence; the second story challenges the human inclination to try to guide human life solely by our own free will and our own human reason, exercised on the natural objects of thought.

By "natural reverence" Kass means the persistent human tendency to worship the things of the natural world: "A main teaching — perhaps *the* main teaching — of Genesis 1 is the nondivinity of the cosmos, and in particular of the sun, the moon, the stars." Genesis 1 is determined to "demote the dignity of the cosmos," and, by extension, to refute the idea of "trying to orient human life on the basis of knowledge of nature." Similarly, the second chapter warns against intellectual and moral autonomy. Kass invites us to consider the problems that we modern humans have gotten ourselves into, collectively and personally, and to see if Genesis provides potential answers to those problems.

In a similar vein, Kass prefaces his account of the complex relationships among Noah and his sons by suggesting that the Genesis narrative wishes "to encourage the ambivalent male reader to participate vicariously in the fatherly education of the Hebrew patriarchs," first by showing him "precisely why such an education is needed" and then by "moving him to care about whether in fact it can be obtained." Kass explores the ways in which Noah acts both wisely and foolishly, and discerns in his sons "three fundamental human types":

> the tyrannical man or, alternatively, the man who is focused on sex and bodily pleasure [Ham]; the decent or noble man, the generous man of refined taste and sensibility [Japheth]; and the pious man, the man who takes his bearings from looking up to the divine [Shem].

And Kass suggests that we should consider these types in light of a similar typology offered by Aristotle in the *Nicomachaean Ethics*: the life of pleasure, the life of honor, the life of contemplation.

If these two passages of commentary — on the creation narratives and on Noah — represent philosophical reading, then we may reasonably infer that philosophical reading strives to locate in the text whatever is universal to human experience, and to find ways of describing the particular experiences of particular people in the most broadly relevant terms possible. This requires abstracting the meaning of events from their narrative embodiment; indeed, one reflecting on Kass's procedure might even conclude that the culturally, historically, and narrationally distinctive is the enemy of philosophy, and must be winnowed like chaff.

And might not one readily defend such an approach, at least for the first eleven chapters of Genesis, which narrate the first stage of human history, and which are populated by the common ancestors of all later human beings? After all, the protagonist of the first story is *'adamah* — "the man" or "the human." That's as generic as a character can get. Moreover, by the time God brings down the tower of Babel we have still not yet entered the story of Israel itself — we have not yet even met the "father of believers," Abraham. Does not universal history warrant a universalizing mode of reading?

Perhaps. But we should never forget that the primal history of Genesis was composed, read, and interpreted by the people of Israel, and understood by them as the story of the covenant that constituted them and gave

87

them communal life. Seen in the context of the whole of Genesis, and even more in the context of the whole Pentateuch, the first eleven chapters of Genesis are simply the prehistory of the Abrahamic covenant. It's not merely paradoxical to say that for the Israelites Adam is important primarily because he is the ancestor of Jacob, and that in this book the particular precedes and governs the universal. That key feature of Genesis 1 that Kass rightly points to — the "demoting of the dignity of the cosmos" — only makes sense when one understands that the Israelites were surrounded by people who worshipped the sun, moon, and stars. Their creation narrative is therefore a kind of indirect polemic against Israel's dangerous neighbors, an affirmation that the pagan gods are no more than big lights in the sky, attempts to placate which get you exactly nothing. (The unique combination of arrogance, gratitude, defensiveness, and fear that this situation produced has been imaginatively realized nowhere better than in Frederick Buechner's beautiful novel *Son of Laughter*.) Now, Kass notes just this difference, but he characterizes it merely as a "rejection of polytheism" — as though what was at stake was the choice among a range of religious options, rather than the life or death of a people; and he is more interested in seeking ways of reading the story that "address our current situation of moral and spiritual neediness."

Kass pursues this task about as intelligently and resourcefully as it is possible to pursue it; but I worry about all the history that such an approach must skip over. I think first of the moment when Jacob, traveling between Beersheba and Haran, lays his tired head upon a stone and dreams of a great ladder with angels ascending and descending upon it. God speaks there to Jacob, and pronounces a promise rather different than the ones he had made to Abraham. To Abraham God had promised many descendents, with wealth and power for them, and had pledged to be their God always. But to Jacob he promises, "in you and your offspring shall all the families of the earth be blessed" (Gen. 28:14, in the fine new English Standard Version). This promise would begin to be realized when Joseph lived in Egypt and brought blessing to that land; as a Christian, I believe its ultimate fulfillment comes in the person and work of Jesus Christ. But it is only once that promise works itself out, as the people of Israel bring the blessings of God's word and God's law into alien cultures, that the universal meaning of their sacred narratives becomes accessible to the rest of us.

From one who belongs to a covenant community, then, the appropriation of the Biblical narrative must be done by *historical* rather than what Kass would call philosophical means. Our task is not to find a conceptual vocabulary that will allow us to build analogical bridges between the Biblical text and our experience; rather, we must understand that we dwell in the same history that the people of Israel relate in the Pentateuch — a history that even the Law itself is but a part of. (As David Damrosch has written, "In its presentation of the Law within this vision of the redemptive potential of exile, Leviticus is the very heart of pentateuchal narrative.") Genesis is not *analogous* to our experience; it *is* our experience, in its historical aspect.

If this argument is right, then Kass's non-historical, analogical reading of Genesis isn't ideal even for the first eleven chapters of Genesis; and therefore we should not be surprised when the patriarchal narratives pose rather a challenge for him. As all commentators do, Kass recognizes that the book of Genesis pivots quite dramatically when, having concluded the Babel story with its fragmentation of human society, it turns to a particular man named Abram. Here is how Kass describes the change:

> The failure of the city and tower of Babel brings to a close Genesis's saga of universal human beginnings. Multiple nations arise as the necessary remedy for the proud and perilous project of humankind united. After and because of Babel, God abandons his plan to work simultaneously with the entire human race. But he in no way abandons his universal aspirations for human beings. On the contrary, He pursues the same ends but by different means. Having dispersed mankind into many nations, He now chooses one nation to carry His way as a light unto all the others, and He takes up a prominent role as that nation's educator and guide.

It is not a description I could wholly endorse; my understanding of God does not encourage me to imagine that the whole Babel crisis caught him by surprise and occasioned some late-night strategic revisions in the heavenly office suite. (Kass would surely reply that his reading is consonant with the text itself; to which I would counter that that could be so only if we ignore the Israelite cultural situation in which the text was produced and to which it was addressed.) But in any event, Kass recognizes the shift in the narrative and must shift his own reading strategies accordingly. One can see this shift most obviously in the headings Kass gives to sections of his commentary. In the pre-Abram sections, those headings would often be generalized and abstract, in keeping with the mediating or translating method of reading that Kass favors: "The Meanings of Sexual Complementarity," "Paternity and Piety: Noah and His Sons," "Rational Animal, Political Animal: Speech and the City." But after Babel, the descriptions mime the particularities of the narrative: "Abraham's Final Trial: The Binding of Isaac," "Pharaoh Gets the Message: Joseph Becomes Prime Minister," and so on. Kass must alter his interpretive strategy because the patriarchal narratives are full of events and decisions that cannot be translated into any sort of hermeneutical standard notation; it's often hard to say just what to make of them, at least in general terms, and certainly the narrative itself rarely gives us any pointers. In many cases in the second of the book's two parts, Kass seems forced to provide a kind of summary exposition interlaced with character sketches — something far less "philosophical" than the conceptual allegories he weaves when dealing with the book's first eleven chapters.

No passage in Genesis more notoriously resists interpretive strategies than the binding of Isaac. Indeed, it was just this story that Erich Auerbach, in his magisterial *Mimesis*, employed to distinguish the openness of Homeric poems from the "reticence" of Hebrew narrative, which by contrast is "fraught with background" — background that is never brought into the reader's field of vision. When Kass reaches Abraham's crisis he prefaces his treatment with a truly extraordinary confession:

> No story in Genesis is as terrible, as powerful, as mysterious, as elusive as this one. It defies easy and confident interpretations, and despite all that I shall have to say about it, it continues to baffle me. Indeed, my approach seems even to me to be too shallow, precisely because I am attempting to be reasonable about this awesome and shocking story.

(I scarcely know what to make of this — a scholar confessing that a story exceeds his powers of interpretive ingenuity? Obviously Kass was not trained in literary or Biblical hermeneutics, or he would know that such humility is strictly proscribed by the guild authorities. But I will forgive him this assault on the core values of my profession and move on.) I find it fascinating that, despite this confession of "shallowness," Kass does indeed continue to strive to "be reasonable." We might contrast this determination with the straightforward claim of Kierkegaard's Johannes de Silentio (the "author" of *Fear and Trembling*), who throws up his hands and declares, "Abraham I do not understand, in a certain sense there is nothing I can learn from him except astonishment." For Kierkegaard the story enacts a repudiation of anything recognizable as morality and therefore anything that could possibly be called "reasonable." If the philosophically-minded must have a term for what this story presents us with, Johannes de Silentio is willing enough to provide one: "the teleological suspension of the ethical." The reasonableness of ethics must be suspended in favor of a greater *telos*: trust in Yahweh and his promises — which is not a reasonable thing to do, and may not even be recognizable to philosophy *as a telos*. Johannes's famous term is actually Kierkegaard's shrewd way of indicating the irreconcilability of philosophy with Biblical narrative.

If indeed Abraham's decision to trust Yahweh and lift the knife is definitively unreasonable, and if Kass knows — indeed, announces — that his approach to the story is "shallow," then how could his reading possibly be justified? To defend Kass here would seem to be difficult at best; and in light of what I have written so far I would scarcely be expected to do the defending. But that is just what I hope to do. For it is this most incomprehensible episode of Genesis that brings out the best in Kass; precisely because he knows that no conceptual algebra will solve this equation, he slows the pace of his analysis and allows the story to have its own mysterious and elusive way.

Throughout his reading, Kass is acutely attentive to the story's layers of knowledge. Isaac knows the least; Abraham knows only what he is commanded to do; we the readers know (as Abraham does not) that he is being "tested"; and God alone knows the precise purpose of the horrible test. A recognition of this epistemological complexity itself is sufficient to compel the thoughtful interpreter to avoid precipitous decisions. Above all, Kass is aware that the story's notorious reticences (especially concerning Abraham's thoughts and expectations) make multiple interpretations possible, and force the reader to reckon with them. Thus he enters here, more fully than elsewhere in his commentary, into the conversation about the story, quoting from a range of interpretations, even considering Michael Fishbane's argument that Abraham's willingness to sacrifice Isaac means that he fails God's test. In this sense Kass is more rabbinical in dealing with the binding of Isaac than he is elsewhere in the book; here he joins whole-heartedly in the endless midrashic debate about "this awesome and shocking story."

Nevertheless, he does not follow the example of Johannes de Silentio and throw up his hands in incomprehension: though aware of the likelihood of "shallowness," he offers a reading — his best attempt at figuring it out, at finding a way of construing the narrative's force and purpose. He tries to see what, through this ordeal, God learns about Abraham and what Abraham learns about God. Whatever I or anyone else might think of the specifics of Kass's reading, in the circumstances his offering of it is a gesture both humble and brave.

One could even say that in Kass's treatment of the binding of Isaac we see the ethos of the university seminar room at its best. Though many professors fail to understand this point, the seminar room is not the place for a complete dismissal of the texts under scrutiny as patriarchal or racist or sexist or complicit in violence, or (for that matter) atheistic or blasphemous or immoral; nor is it a place for Johannes Climacus's position, that the story can be accepted by faith and faith alone. Rather, the seminar room occupies an intellectual demilitarized zone, where the text is confronted, wrestled with, puzzled over; where interpretations are offered, perhaps tentatively or provisionally, then debated, revised, withdrawn, or renewed. In such an environment it is vital that such texts *not* be explored as though understanding them is a matter of life and death; and while people of passionate commitment (to faith or unbelief) may often be frustrated by such a deliberate lowering of the interpretive stakes — certainly I have often experienced that frustration — environments that encourage such detachment are socially beneficial. There need to be discursive spaces in our society (spaces that, when functioning properly, can constitute a healthy and vibrant "public sphere") where matters even of eternal life and death can be considered as though they were not quite *that* important. This is another way of saying that the Enlightenment project is not without value, even if it is deeply flawed and has never been well realized. Kass's struggle with the binding of Isaac is a lovely example of the humane and thoughtful intellectual exercise that that classic Enlightenment institution, the secular university seminar room, can, at its best, produce.

Recognizing this point, I am led back to my earlier claim that Kass's book is not for people like me. It will now be clear, I hope, that by "people like me" I mean people of faith who insist that sacred texts demand to be treated as such. Kass's commentary reminds me that a less insistent approach may bear fruit too. It is true that, as I explore the book, it is not always easy for me to keep its virtues in mind; I shudder when I read (for instance) these words in his Epilogue:

> The book of Genesis is mainly concerned with this question: is it possible to find, institute, and preserve a way of life that accords with man's true standing in the world and that serves to perfect his godlike possibilities?

It seems to me that not a single significant word in this sentence accords with what the book of Genesis is about. Genesis, and the culture from which it emerges, doesn't seem to me to give a damn about our "true standing in the world" and our "godlike possibilities"; rather, as far as I can tell, it is about God and what he has done, and is doing, to repair what his rebellious and arrogant creatures have broken: our relations with ourselves, with one another, with the creation, and with God himself.

But even as I make my protest I realize that, if Kass's language would be unrecognizable to the Biblical authors, so too the language I have just employed would ring hollow and strange in the ears of most university students in America today. When reading an ancient text, especially one that makes the kinds of demands on us that Genesis makes — demands not just on our attention but also on our obedient response, on our whole lives — we have to start somewhere, and in the end I'm not sure that it matters much where. Should we begin with the contexts and assumptions of the ancient world and work our way towards the present situation? Should we begin with present forms of understanding and work our way back towards the ancient text's lifeworld? Though we are accustomed to the idea that readers need to be governed by the right hermeneutic, in fact theory and method mean next to nothing in reading. The real question is not where we begin — not what tools we bring to the task of reading (about which we may not have as much choice as we think we do anyway) — but rather what purposes move us and what fortitude we show in pursuing them. Leon Kass, in this book and in his classes at Chicago, is asking people to *pay attention* to this strange old book, to listen very carefully to hear what it might have to say to them; he is, further, suggesting to them that they need wisdom if they are to live well, and that they might find a deposit of it in these stories. Those of us who believe in the sacred power of the Bible shouldn't worry that that power can be shut off by a faulty hermeneutic. If I suspect many of Kass's categories and methods, I do not doubt the force of that invitation simply to read wisely. Kass himself, as he admits forthrightly at several points in this book, is still very much a wayfarer in the pages of Genesis, striving to take hold of the story and perhaps also of the God who fills its pages with his deeds, his words, his mysteries; and this teacher asks students and readers alike to strive alongside him. May he hold fast to the book until it blesses him.

part 2

EXPLORATIONS

The Only Honest Man

Most of us know, now, that Rousseau was wrong: that man, when you knock his chains off, sets up the death camps. Soon we shall know everything the 18th century didn't know, and nothing it did, and it will be hard to live with us.

RANDALL JARRELL

1.

When the great poet, satirist, and philosopher Voltaire died in 1778, at the age of eighty-four, he was buried on the grounds of the Abbey of Sellières, near Romilly-sur-Seine, France. But this would not be his final resting place. In the fervent early years of the French Revolution, before the sovereignty of Terror, the leading revolutionaries agreed that their "glorious Revolution has been the fruit of his works," and decided to bring his body to Paris, where he could receive the honor so rarely granted him in his lifetime. Some such decision had to be made, for the Abbey (along with much other property of the Church) had been confiscated by a cash-strapped government and was to be auctioned off, and some of the new national leaders quailed at the prospect of the great philosopher's remains becoming private property. The site they chose for the hero's reinterment was the newly designated Panthéon — what had been the unfinished church of St.

97

Genevieve, now finally completed not as a house of God but as a monument to those designated by the revolutionaries as *"les Grands Hommes."*

Only two dignitaries had thus far assumed their places in the Panthéon: its original inhabitant, the seventeenth-century philosopher Descartes — the patron saint of Reason as conceived by the Enlightenment — followed in April 1791 by the revolutionary leader Mirabeau, whose unexpected death had bestowed upon him an immediate sanctification. Now, on July 11 of the same year, Voltaire would make the third in this company: his remains were carried on what Simon Schama calls "a monumental chariot, as high as a two-story house," leading an enormous imitation-Roman triumphal procession through the streets of Paris. Notable among the many participants in this cortège were "a troupe of men dressed in Roman costume [carrying] as trophies of glory editions of all Voltaire's works."

Strange to say, this bizarre ritual would be repeated three years later, in October 1794 — when *la grande Terreur* had run its course, its instigator and sustainer, Robespierre, having been at the end of July one of the guillotine's last victims — but now the exhumed hero was Jean-Jacques Rousseau. Again the procession was organized, this time commencing at Ermeonville, thirty miles from Paris, where Rousseau had died and been buried. (Though eighteen years younger than Voltaire, he had outlived him by only a month.) Again emblems of the great man's life and work were displayed for public approval: musicians played Rousseau's compositions, and at the end of this cortège members of the national legislature held aloft copies of the Gospel *du jour,* Rousseau's famous political treatise, *The Social Contract.*

In one sense, nothing could be more comprehensible than this co-elevation of two of the eighteenth century's most versatile and influential writers. Each man had written in a remarkable variety of genres. Voltaire produced tragedies, an epic, a witty philosophical satire *(Candide)* that is his most-read work today, many comic tales, and innumerable pamphlets on his time's most controversial subjects. Similarly, in one astonishing nine-year period Rousseau produced a romantic epistolary novel about love and duty *(Julie, or the New Heloise),* a didactic philosophical tale about the ideal means of educating young men *(Emile),* an extended polemic on the uses and dangers of theaters in various societies *(Letter to d'Alembert),* and a compressed yet ambitious treatise on political philosophy *(The Social Contract)*; such activity left him no time to compose the music which had earlier brought him to the attention of the French. Both Voltaire and Rousseau contributed to the dominant intellectual project of their time, the great ongoing *Encyclopedia* edited by Denis Diderot and Jean d'Alembert. Both were theoretically hopeful about the human race, but by temperament bitterly pessimistic. Above all, both men understood themselves to be celebrants and defenders of Freedom, and therefore enemies of the hierarchies and institutions of France's *ancien régime*. Surely a revolution which itself promised freedom from royal absolutism and aristocratic privilege was right to enthrone these two great men?

Perhaps. But it must also be said that Voltaire and Rousseau had loathed each other; indeed, believed themselves to speak for irreconcilable philosophies. Their relationship — which was conducted wholly in letters, since they only met once — began cordially enough, as the aspiring artist-intellectual Rousseau sent flattering letters to the man already recognized as France's dominant writer (though Voltaire's polemical nature had generated enough highly placed enmity to drive him from his native country and to the suburbs of Rousseau's home city, Geneva). But in 1754, when Rousseau sent a copy of his second significant work, the *Discourse on the Origins of Inequality,* to Voltaire, things began to change. This *Discourse* was Rousseau's first work fully to articulate a position which would later be almost identified with him: that human beings had once lived in a blissfully anarchic "state of nature," the innocence of which we have since lost through the corruptions of organized society. Nothing could be further from Voltaire's view that the disciplined practice of Reason was, or at least could be, gradually emancipating us from the chains of ancient passions and superstitions, and he replied with predictable irony: "I have received, Monsieur, your new book against the human race, and I thank you. No one has employed so much intelligence to turn us men into beasts. One starts wanting to walk on all fours after reading your book. However, in more than sixty years I have lost the habit."

From this point on the relationship deteriorated. Sarcasm became Voltaire's sole mode of response to Rousseau's books, though he sometimes spoke well of the younger man's character. For his part, Rousseau became more and more convinced that Voltaire was his greatest enemy, a consuming suspicion which boiled over in 1760 in a wrathful letter, equally paranoid and megalomaniacal, which insured that they would never be reconciled:

> I do not like you, Monsieur; you have done me injuries of the most harmful kind; done them to me, your disciple and your enthusiastic admirer. You have ruined Geneva, in return for the asylum you have been given there. You have turned my fellow citizens against me as a reward for the praise which I have secured for you. It is you who have made living in my own city impossible for me; it is you who force me to perish on foreign soil, deprived of all the consolations of the dying, cast unceremoniously like a dog on the wayside, you who, alive or dead, enjoy in my homeland all the honours to which a man could aspire. I despise you.

(Incidentally, far from being a dying, impoverished, and rejected man — and far from striving to return to Geneva — Rousseau at the time was living comfortably on the bounty of his friend and patron, the fantastically wealthy and powerful Maréchal de Luxembourg.) Voltaire never responded to this letter, which perhaps only intensified Rousseau's paranoia and determination to oppose the older man in all things. If Voltaire would praise philosophy, Rousseau — who as an aspiring writer had self-consciously given up music for philosophy — would repudiate it. If Voltaire would elevate Reason, Rousseau would condemn it in favor of the more sure way of the heart: "I have abandoned reason and consulted nature," he wrote to a Genevan friend when his alienation from Voltaire, his old friend Denis Diderot, and the whole world of the *philosophes* had become evident to everyone involved, "that is, the inner feeling."

And they quarreled about God. Voltaire always maintained a belief in the existence of some kind of deity — the argument from design appealed to him — but he wasn't sure exactly what kind, since it was obvious to him that this beautifully made world was also filled with incomprehensible evil. When a great earthquake destroyed much of Lisbon, Portugal, in

November of 1755, Voltaire wrote a bitter poem which mocked the very idea that such a disaster could be attributed to the sovereignty of a benevolent Providence, and asked whether a good deity could even be thought to rule over this world at all. Rousseau responded — this was before their decisive break — with a long letter pointing out, reasonably enough, that many of the people died not from the earthquake as such but because their cheaply constructed and grotesquely crowded houses caved in on them: the disaster was more due to the systemic evils of life in unjust human society than to the acts of God. Rousseau warmly affirmed his belief in Providence and in the immortality of the human soul. (For this affirmation, Diderot came to believe, Rousseau had earned the admiration of "the devout party" — that is, the Christians — and would therefore remain popular with and accepted by them. In this he was wrong.)

Voltaire in turn replied only with an apology for not having time to answer substantively, though he proclaimed affection for Rousseau. And so the conversation appeared to end. But when *Candide* appeared two years later — with a repudiation of the idea of Providence, and those who believe in it, still more fierce than that of the poem — Rousseau understood it to be Voltaire's belated reply to his passionate letter. "I wanted to philosophize with Voltaire; in return he made fun of me." If such was the attitude of the age's greatest apostle of philosophy and reason, then who needed philosophy and reason? And indeed mockery would be from this point on Voltaire's characteristic response to Rousseau: for instance, he amused himself by spreading the rumor that Rousseau had at one time been valet to France's Ambassador in Venice. (In fact, Rousseau had been the Ambassador's secretary and therefore an important member of the diplomatic corps himself; but since at one time he had indeed been a footman in the household of a rich man, the false report had a particular sting.) And to his fellow *philosophes* he spoke of "that fool Rousseau, that bastard of Diogenes's dog."

Were Voltaire and Rousseau right in thinking that they, and their intellectual positions, were irreconcilable? Or had the Revolutionaries correctly discerned some hidden complicity of the two antagonists, some common vision that lay beneath the surface and which Voltaire and Rousseau themselves could therefore never see? Or could both views be true?

There is another way to put these questions: was Romanticism an alternative to the Enlightenment, or its natural heir? For it is Jean-Jacques Rousseau who stands at the confluence of these two great movements in Western intellectual history; his life and work, more than those of any other single figure, show us how the two were related to each other. And if Rousseau's life is full of confusions and contradictions, that is largely because he represented within himself movements which were now harmonious, now dissonant; now moving on parallel tracks, now on a collision course. Rousseau is the modern world.

2.

Maurice Cranston's three-volume biography of the extraordinary Jean-Jacques is as full and scholarly and vivid a portrait as we are likely to have; but alas, it is not all that one might hope for. Chiefly this is because Cranston, a longtime professor of political science at the London School of Economics, died before he could complete the third volume. Sanford Lakoff, who was entrusted with the task of putting the manuscript in order, writes that Cranston had finished seven of that volume's eight chapters when he died, but one can only assume that Cranston was hurrying his work, since these chapters cover momentous events in Rousseau's life at a much quicker pace than the first two volumes had maintained. The reader of those sweeping yet detailed books cannot but be disappointed at the thinness of the third.

Such disappointment testifies both to Cranston's skill as a biographer and the extraordinary richness of Rousseau's eventful life. Even the briefest sketch of Rousseau's experiences is enough to illustrate the need for a multi-volume biography. At the outset of his second volume, Cranston summarizes Rousseau's first forty years:

> Rousseau's early life was that of a wanderer, an adventurer, the life of a
> hero of a picaresque novel. Orphaned by the early death of his mother
> and the defection of his father, he had run away from his native Geneva
> at the age of sixteen to escape the life of a plebeian engraver's appren-

tice, and found refuge as a Catholic convert in Savoy. Making his own way in the world as a footman in Turin, a student at a choir school in Annecy, the steward and the lover of a Swiss baroness in Chambéry, the interpreter to a Levantine mountebank, an itinerant musician, a private tutor in the family of Condillac and Mably in Lyons, secretary to the French Ambassador in Venice and research assistant to the Dupins at Chenonceaux, he set out with his great friend and contemporary Denis Diderot to conquer Paris as a writer, and, much to his own surprise, did so almost overnight at the age of thirty-eight with the publication of his *Discourse on the Sciences and Arts.*

After this came the prodigious decade already mentioned, in which almost all the works that would make Rousseau famous were written. But these increasingly controversial works alienated the more conservative elements in French Society — especially Roman Catholics — and in 1762 two of them *(Emile* and *The Social Contract)* were formally condemned. Rousseau fled France under threat of arrest, and it is with this departure that Cranston ends his second volume. For most of the rest of his life he lived in Switzerland, though his reputation as an infidel made him unpopular, and he had to move from town to town. For a while he lived in England under the protection of the philosopher David Hume, but Rousseau's increasing paranoia ruined that friendship as it had ruined many others, and he returned to the Continent. Eventually, in 1767, he was received back in France, and in the years leading up to his death in 1778 was once again celebrated in the salons of Paris, where in lengthy readings of his work-in-progress, the *Confessions,* he praised himself and cursed his enemies to the applause of society.

Again, until the Swiss exile Cranston is a masterful relater of this history. But it is not just the rushed narrative of Rousseau's later years that creates problems for this biography's readers: also problematic is Cranston's desire to rescue Rousseau from at least some of the bad repute that disfigures his memory. Cranston is consistently sympathetic to Rousseau, and tries whenever possible to reconcile Rousseau's versions of events — especially as those versions appear in Rousseau's pathbreaking and self-exculpating *Confessions* — with the available evidence. Sometimes he has to give up the attempt with an almost audible sigh, but for the most part he manages to make Rousseau's view of the controversies that always surrounded him seem comprehensible and even plausible. But Cranston achieves this, at least in some cases, by a kind of withholding of evidence. Rousseau's letters are full of passages that show him in a very bad light indeed, and often Cranston simply doesn't quote such passages; or if he does quote them, and cannot explain them away, he leaves them without comment. To some degree he is reacting against earlier biographers and critics who have calumniated Rousseau, but given a work of such scope it is difficult to condone a reluctance to confront the whole truth about the subject.

One may approach this problem, and simultaneously approach what is of crucial importance about Rousseau, by returning to the quarrel with Voltaire. In 1759 Rousseau wrote a letter to an old Genevan friend whom he was coming to distrust because he knew the man to be one of Voltaire's regular visitors. He was particularly concerned to respond to a semi-rhetorical question his friend had asked him: "How is it that the friend of humanity is hardly any longer the friend of men?" The question had angered Rousseau, and in defending himself he insisted, "I am the friend of the human race." When Voltaire saw this comment he seized upon it: "Extreme insolence is extreme stupidity, and nothing is more stupid than a Jean-Jacques talking about 'the human race and I.'" (All of this Cranston relates.)

One might think that Voltaire was unfairly mocking a passing figure of speech, but Rousseau's distinction was by this time in his life fundamental to his character — fundamental in a way that Cranston is reluctant to acknowledge. Three years after the exchange I have just described, Rousseau wrote, "Oh why did Providence have me born among men, and make me of a different species?" And one does not have to read far in Rousseau's letters, or indeed his published works, to figure out what species he thought he belonged to: he was the world's only *honnete homme*, that is, the only truthful and wholly honorable man.

Almost from the beginning of his time in Paris, Rousseau took pains to emphasize his difference from others. He early on learned to make capital of his peculiarities — he had more than a few — and to convince people that what would be rudeness or thoughtlessness in others was virtue in him. He called himself a "bear" and liked it when others did the same; he commented frequently on his inability to make polite conversation or to dissemble his feelings in any way. When friends suggested that he owed some gratitude to Madame d'Épinay, who had befriended him, he replied bluntly: "As for kindnesses, I do not like them, I do not want them, and I do not feel grateful to those who force me to accept them." (He does not explain how exactly she "forced" him to take her gifts, which included a house in which he lived; later he would complain similarly of being "forced" to receive presents from an admiring Prince de Conti.) When the Maréchal de Luxembourg installed Rousseau in his "petit chateau," Rousseau wrote a letter to Madame de Luxembourg insisting, "I shall not praise you. I shall not thank you. But I inhabit your house. Everyone has his own language, and I have said all in mine." This had the exquisitely subtle effect of flattering his aristocratic patrons while simultaneously maintaining the manner of a "bear" who simply cannot behave as other men do.

Rousseau found every possible means of insisting upon his difference from other men. Thus his habit once he was established in Paris of referring to himself, and having others refer to him, as "citoyen de Geneve," when in fact he had repudiated his Genevan citizenship as a young Catholic convert: he found it useful to represent himself as the outlander, the plainspoken burgher from the wild Alpine lakes. In his Swiss exile he even wore a flamboyant Armenian costume on his daily walks (and then wrote letters complaining that the locals mocked him). His virtues could only be made evident by contrast with the vices of everyone else. In a reproachful letter to a woman who had failed to return his affection, he roundly declared that "there cannot be any peace between J.-J. Rousseau and the wicked" — and who wasn't wicked? "What distinguishes me from all the other men I know, is that with all my faults, I have always reproached myself for them, and that my faults have never made me despise my duty or trample on virtue; and, moreover, that I have struggled for virtue and conquered at times when everyone else has forgotten it." It is this conviction above all that underlies the most definitive statement of his uniqueness, on the first page of his *Confessions*: "I am made unlike anyone I have ever met; I will even venture to say that I am like no one in the whole world."

Rousseau consistently maintained belief in his uniqueness, and almost as consistently belief in his superiority to human beings — but at times the latter stance grew difficult. Especially when word got out that his mistress had borne him five children and he had promptly sent each of them to Paris's Foundling Hospital, he had some explaining to do, and knew it. He writes to several friends, at various times in his life, about that decision, and wavers between staunchly defending himself — on the grounds that he had lacked the resources to raise his children properly and that in the orphanage they would have been educated into an honest trade, which was more than he would have been able to do for them — and expressing remorse. But his general tone of each letter is more or less the same: that he had shown his nobility of character in performing the "rational" act of abandoning his children, and that he continues to show the nobility of his character by experiencing deep remorse even over such a fully justifiable decision. Whether in acting or in lamenting his actions, then, he lived up to his self-description as *l'honnete homme*.

In this case and in many others, Rousseau presents himself as a man whose behavior would be vicious if practiced by others, but on his part is sheer virtue. In a lengthy and extraordinary letter to Madame d'Épinay (one to which Cranston does not refer), Rousseau refuses her attempts to reconcile him to his former friend, the *philosophe* Diderot. He describes for her at some length his expectations in friendship — expectations unmet by Diderot — and concludes the description by saying: "I require from a friend even a great deal more than all I have just told you; even more than he must require from me, and than I should require from him, if he were in my place, and I were in his."

But what does Rousseau mean when he speaks of his "place"? This is important, since the distinction between his place and that of Diderot seems to justify the grossest inequalities in friendship. He immediately goes on to explain, "As a recluse, I am more sensitive than another man" — and it is Rousseau's status as a "recluse" to which he almost obsessively returns in his letters and memoirs. In Rousseau's philosophy, only the recluse can be virtuous, because only the recluse evades the corrupting influences of society and thereby retains a pure natural honesty. Rousseau the recluse, then, becomes the living embodiment of his own "noble savage," and Cranston is right to title his second volume with that phrase.

In his *Confessions*, therefore, Rousseau writes that he "first began to live" on April 9, 1756, for on that day he retired from society into a "Hermitage," utterly isolating himself from his Parisian acquaintance. Well, perhaps not "utterly." No self-respecting hermit could have found Rousseau's residence satisfactory, since it was a former hunting lodge on Madame d'Épinay's estate, and he could visit with her whenever he chose. Moreover, in Cranston's words, this was no "Gothic cottage but a dignified and symmetrical house, with good-sized rooms, an elegant door and windows, with both ornamental and kitchen gardens and an orchard, surrounded by fields and the forest." And to top it off, this supposedly remote and isolated habitation was less than a dozen miles from Paris; Rousseau would sometimes chastise his friends for not walking out to visit him.

Later, when living still more elegantly in the Maréchal de Luxembourg's "petit chateau," he would often visit the Duke's house in Paris. This was awkward for Rousseau, not only because of his status as "recluse" — when first invited there he replied, "Why do you disturb the peace of a hermit who has renounced the pleasures of life in order to be spared its fatigues?" — but also because he had vowed never to set foot on the streets of Paris again. But then he realized that the Duke's carriage would take him directly into the garden of the great town house: thus "I could say with the most exact truth that I never set foot on the streets of Paris."

3.

Nevertheless, these various "cottages" and "hermitages" were sufficiently removed from the day-to-day distractions that bedeviled Rousseau in his Parisian years that during the nine years that he lived in them he wrote almost every word that would later make him famous. For all his posturing, Rousseau was never reluctant to work, and he was intellectually ambitious as well as prolific — even though he made almost no money from his books and tried to support himself by copying music.

But if one looks at those works from the great decade in isolation from what we know about Rousseau, they are not often impressive. Jules Lemaitre may have exaggerated when he said that the enormous popularity of Rousseau's first book, the *Discourse on the Sciences and Arts,* constituted "one of the strongest proofs ever provided of human stupidity"; in that book, and in each of Rousseau's books, there are certainly striking and provocative ideas. But the works lack coherence of development, and indeed some of them are wildly self-contradictory, as Rousseau himself saw: in the case of his novel *Julie,* he noted some of the contradictions when the book was being prepared for press, but decided not to remedy them. (Perhaps he didn't know how; or perhaps his attitude anticipated that of Walt Whitman a hundred years later: "I contradict myself? Very well, I contradict myself. I am large; I contain multitudes.") Even the book by which Rousseau is best known today, *The Social Contract,* was not widely read in his lifetime — in part because it was frequently censored — and first became influential when the Revolution initiated its cult of Rousseau.

What is particularly important about this first celebration of Rousseau is that, like those that would come afterwards, it was dictated by Rousseau's self-presentation in the *Confessions.* Indeed, the *Confessions* was Rousseau's only book to have precisely the effect he intended it to have: while the others were thoroughly misread or not read at all, this one hit the mark. In the depths of a profound paranoia, convinced that his former friends were conspiring at least to destroy his reputation and perhaps to have him murdered, Rousseau wrote this book to convince the world that he was in fact a new kind of saint: the saint as reclusive hermit, as noble savage — as *honnete homme.* "I publicly and fearlessly declare," he says at the end of the *Confessions,* "that anyone, even if he has not read my writings, who will examine my nature, my character, my morals, my likings, my pleasures, and my habits with his own eyes and can still believe me a dishonorable man, is a man who deserves to be stifled." It was largely because this rhetorical strategy convinced his revolutionary readers that he was installed in the Panthéon — not because of the influence of the *Social Contract,* which few among the revolutionaries had read, and which was appealed to not because of its argument but because of a couple of striking phrases. There was the famous first sentence of the book — "Man is born free, but everywhere he is in chains" — a resonant utterance in the mouths of self-proclaimed liberators; and then there was the notion of the "general will" of the people, the collective desire or purpose of a culture, a will for which the rebels were quick to claim that they spoke, though they cared little what Rousseau meant by that phrase.

No, it was the Jean-Jacques of the *Confessions* who was the real popular hero, because he stood against the complexities and hierarchies and dissimulations of the *ancien régime* by standing for an unaffected "natural" sincerity. On the first page of that book, he stakes out his territory in memorable terms as he imagines going before the Judgment Seat of God, not bowing or kneeling, not weeping penitent tears, not in awe or fear, but boldly, with a copy of the *Confessions* in his hand. Indeed, Rousseau imagines the whole company of Heaven suspending their customary adoration of the Lord to listen, as raptly as the attendants of a fashionable Parisian salon, to the honest man read his story:

> I have displayed myself as I was, as vile and despicable when my behavior was such, as good, generous, and noble when I was so. I have bared my secret soul as Thou thyself has seen it, Eternal Being! So let the numberless legion of my fellow men gather round me, and hear my confessions. Let them groan at my depravities, and blush for my misdeeds. But let each one of them reveal his heart at the foot of Thy throne with equal sincerity, and may any man who dares, say "I was a better man than he."

This astonishing declaration needs to be read in conjunction with Rousseau's desire to "stifle" anyone who does not hear his tale with full approval. In other words, the honesty with which he proclaims his every action transmutes those actions, however base they may seem, into the pure gold of virtue. Rousseau claims justification neither by faith nor by works, but by sincerity: sincerity alone enables him not only to transcend his fellow human beings but also to throw his *Confessions* in the face of God, daring even him to judge Jean-Jacques.

4.

What is so noteworthy, here and elsewhere in Rousseau's writings, is the fierceness with which he demands the recognition and approval of others, even while simultaneously claiming to despise their company and to owe them nothing (not even gratitude for *un petit chateau*). So even when he descends to the public's level and provides just the sort of sensationalistic writing they want to read, he sophistically contends that they are merely getting what they deserve and are able to comprehend. He blames the age rather than himself for the bad taste of his *Julie, or the New Heloise*, as he explains in the Preface to his novel (referring obliquely to his own condemnations of theaters and novels in his *Letter to d'Alembert*): "There must be theatres in large cities and novels for corrupt peoples. I have observed the morals of my time, and I have published these letters. Would that I had lived in a century when my duty would have been to throw them in the fire!" In other words, just as his aristocratic patrons were "forcing" him against his will to accept their lavish gifts, so French culture as a whole was "forcing" him to write corrupt, and corrupting, novels.

This kind of argument had for Rousseau a twofold beneficial effect. On the one hand, it relieved him from the responsibility for any of his actions that might be considered shameful. On the other hand, by condemning so bluntly the very people to whom he addressed his works, he maintained in their eyes his reputation for being bearish, blunt, unaccommodating — in short, honest. One cannot but admire the rhetorical panache with which Rousseau carries this off: to become famous and celebrated by relentlessly praising oneself and belittling everyone else is no easy feat and must be managed with great care.

Here again the contrast with Voltaire is instructive. Voltaire was happy to participate in what he liked to call the "Republic of Letters" and its "Reign of Critique," and enjoyed not only the honors showered upon him by his fellow intellectuals (such as membership in the Académie Française) but also, when they came, those bestowed by the monarchy. Rousseau by contrast looked upon, or tried very hard to look upon, or pretended that he looked upon, all honors as invitations to corruption: for instance, he claimed to have *refused* membership in the Académie. Likewise, his insistence on earning his bread by copying music — while all the time his patrons were slipping money to his mistress — served to increase the esteem of those already inclined to admire him.

As Paul Cohen shows in his admirable book *Freedom's Moment*, the key to understanding this phenomenon is provided by the sociologist Pierre Bourdieu, who coined the term "consecrated heretic" to describe a recurrent character in French society — a character, Cohen says, created virtually from whole cloth by Rousseau. Again and again since Rousseau, famous French intellectuals have made, or enhanced, their public reputations by the ostentatious refusal of public honors. (Thus the anthropologist Claude Levi-Strauss, in his own narrative of encounters with "noble savages," *Tristes Tropiques,* speaks for the entire French intelligentsia when he celebrates Rousseau as "our master and our brother. . . . Every page of this book could have been dedicated to him, had it not been unworthy of his great memory.") In repudiating every form of recognition by the society at large — and even by the counter-cultural intellectual elite — these thinkers demonstrate their intellectual autonomy and integrity. As Cohen points out, the greatest of all such masters of refusal was Jean-Paul Sartre, who in the aftermath of World War II publicly and vocally declined election to the French Legion of Honor, then, encouraged by the admiration this decision elicited, went on to refuse (like Rousseau) the Académie Française, then the Collège de France, and finally, in the grandest gesture of all, the Nobel Prize for literature.

The point of such repudiations, especially in the context of the sixties, is clear: Sartre was determined to avoid being "co-opted" by the Establishment, that is, lulled into complacency and acceptance of the status quo by the soporific drug Honor. But this determination only made him more heroic in the eyes of the intelligentsia: thus for his very heresy he was consecrated. At times, Sartre seems to have suspected that his inability to get himself persecuted by his society compromised his claim to heretical status. After all, would a truly subversive thinker be so lionized? It must have been particularly galling for Sartre when, in 1960, President de Gaulle shrewdly declined to have Sartre imprisoned for subversive activities, saying "one does not arrest Voltaire" — a neat twist of the knife, that phrase, given Voltaire's enthusiastic acceptance of public recognition!

In this respect Sartre could only have envied Rousseau. As long as he was celebrated and coddled by Madame d'Épinay and the Maréchal de Luxembourg, Rousseau's pride remained more or less in check: his complaints about being forced to accept gifts and his insistence that he is a reclusive hermit betray doubt about the moral validity of his position. But when he came under genuine persecution and his books were banned and he was driven into real solitude and exile, his self-regard escalated into megalomania: every new misfortune, every word of criticism, confirmed his superiority to the human beings among whom he was doomed to live. Rousseau became the ultimate heretic, consecrated not by society — whose praise would have been gall and wormwood to him — but by the only authority whose right to consecrate he could accept: his own heart.

5.

Scholars in many disciplines have identified Rousseau as a decisive figure in the development of modernity. Political theorists have discerned in *The Social Contract*, especially its notion of the "general will," adumbrations of later totalitarian regimes; historians of education have pointed to *Emile* as the originating document of the "liberating" tradition of pedagogy that Americans associate primarily with John Dewey; his "primitivism" and his love of wild mountain scenery (scenery "sublime" rather than merely beautiful) have been acknowledged as sources of the Romantic movement in literature, painting, and music. One could go on. But Rousseau's true gift was for self-creation, and it is this art which he has bequeathed to the whole modern world. He could well have said what Oscar Wilde would later say, that only his talent went into his work: it was his life that exhibited genius.

Peter Gay has defined Rousseau's life as "that melodramatic vagabondage punctuated by angry letters." A brilliant and incisive phrase, but not fully adequate. Those letters — including *The Confessions*, which may fairly be called the longest and most rhetorically crafted among them — are not always angry: often they rail, to be sure, but equally often they plead, and, as occasion warrants, lament, sneer, enthuse, celebrate, scold. But each of these moods or tones is put in the service of one comprehensive and never-forgotten goal: to justify the ways of Jean-Jacques to the world. The image Rousseau offers us on the first page of the *Confessions*, of his striding up to the Throne with his book in his hand, is the only one we really need if we wish to understand this remarkable man.

Remarkable, but not — oh, how Jean-Jacques would protest here — not unique. For in many ways his audacious confrontation of all the host of Heaven is but the logical culmination of the key doctrine he shares with Voltaire and all the *philosophes*: the doctrine of innate human innocence. Voltaire and Rousseau, for all their differences, alike inherited what may well be the decisive event in the last thousand years of intellectual history: the widespread rejection of the Christian doctrine of original sin. Voltaire, Rousseau, and all the *philosophes* never waver in their conviction that innocence is our birthright, just waiting for us to claim it.

But why, then, has the Rousseauean picture of humanity become so much more potent and lasting than the *philosophes'* picture? Why are we the heirs of Jean-Jacques rather than Diderot or Condillac or even Voltaire? It is an easy question to answer. Note what each party says:

Philosophe: 1) People behave badly. 2) They do so because they follow the dictates of passion and superstition rather than those of reason. 3) Therefore an education which systematically disciplines the passions and places them under the sovereignty of reason will remedy most human ills.

Rousseau: 1) People behave badly. 2) They do so because they live in societies which have miseducated them, led them astray, and made them deaf to the call of their own pure hearts. 3) Therefore an education which isolates them from the corrupting influences of society and liberates them to hear and heed the innocent and natural promptings of their inmost being will remedy most human ills.

Which of these would *you* be more likely to receive as good news? The *philosophe* tells you that your sins and crimes result from a combination of acts (for instance, feeding your passions) and failures to act (for instance, not training those same passions), for both of which — the acts and the failures — you are responsible. The good news that you are naturally virtuous is scarcely sufficient to compensate for this tough lesson in accountability and the need for hard moral work.

Rousseau, on the other hand, gives you not only the good news of innate virtue, but also the still better news that your habitual failure to realize such innate virtue is always someone else's fault. So omnipotent is this belief in our time that I once quoted, in a classroom full of young Christians, Sartre's famous dictum — the summation of Rousseau's thought, in four words — that "Hell is other people," only to have several students nod approvingly and one mutter, "That's so true." So pernicious is this belief in our time that, despite Rousseau's defense of the goodness of God and whatever approval from "the devout party" he received therefrom, a retreat from Rousseau's principles to those of the *philosophes* would be a salutary move for our society. It is true, of course, that anyone attempting to follow the *philosophes'* program for moral improvement would be hindered and ultimately defeated by the recalcitrance of the fallen human will. But this defeat could be instructive and even redemptive. Rousseau's brand of self-regard, by contrast, eliminates *a priori* the learning of such lessons.

Which leads us back to the French Revolution. As that movement progressed, it came increasingly to be dominated by its more radical parties, until the most radical of all rose to power: the Jacobins. And foremost among the Jacobins came to be Maximilien Robespierre. As Paul Cohen explains, Robespierre's "idol" was none other than Rousseau: from Rousseau he derived his whole rhetorical-ethical apparatus, especially its relentless division of the sheep from the goats. "There are only two parties in France," he declared, "the people and its enemies": the party of "corrupt men and that of virtuous men." But as Robespierre's Reign of Terror progressed, it began to frighten or dismay even those who had been enthusiastic at its inception; and as he saw his colleagues deviate from the true path — "there are not two ways of being free," he insisted — the party of the goats grew ever larger, while that of the sheep inexorably shrank. More and more Jacobins found themselves peremptorily arrested, tried, and guillotined, in a terror which claimed to be the instrument of virtue: for, as Robespierre famously said, it may be that without virtue "terror is harmful," but without terror "virtue is impotent."

But how did Robespierre know that his way was the way of virtue? He knew because, like his idol and model Rousseau, he had attended to the testimony of his heart — indeed, this was how he discerned the few good citizens among the many bad: "I believe patriotism not to be a matter of party but of the heart." One can see where this, inevitably, is headed: toward the paranoia of Rousseau, who came in the end to trust no one but himself, no heart but his own. Thus a caricature that appeared in 1795, showing a formally dressed man releasing the guillotine's blade onto the neck of a solitary victim, with this caption beneath: "Robespierre guillotining the executioner, having guillotined all of France." It is the tragic culmination of Rousseau's logic: since other people impede my achievement of virtue, in the very name of virtue they must be destroyed. In July 1794 the Jacobins who remained had little choice but to turn on Robespierre and execute him; he would have gotten each of them eventually. And Rousseau had said it all before him: "I publicly and fearlessly declare that anyone, even if he has not read my writings, who will examine my nature, my character, my morals, my likings, my pleasures, and my habits with his own eyes and can still believe me a dishonorable man, is a man who deserves to be stifled." The child of pride is Terror.

Iris Murdoch's Added Vowel

Some years ago an academic conference at the University of Chicago convened to celebrate the theological importance of the writings, especially the novels, of Iris Murdoch. It was striking to me at the time that the attitude many of the theologians involved have taken was one of nearly abject gratitude to Murdoch for taking religion seriously — not many noted artists do so, after all, nor, come to think of it, do all of the theologians themselves. Confronted with the spectacle of these highly trained men and women genuflecting in the direction of a novelist, however brilliant, I struggled to recall that theology was once named Queen of the Sciences.

Yet if any contemporary writer, in the English-speaking world anyway, deserves this kind of attention it is Iris Murdoch. For many years she taught philosophy at St. Anne's College, Oxford, and her five philosophical books would by themselves indicate a pretty substantial career. But her reputation chiefly rests upon her twenty-five novels, which collectively constitute one of the more impressive bodies of fiction produced in English in this century. Interestingly, her most ambitious — and, I would argue, most successful — work in both fields was produced well after her sixtieth birthday. Throughout the 1970s and 1980s and even into the 1990s — until she began to feel strongly the effects of Alzheimer's disease — she turned out complex, challenging, and lengthy novels at the rate of about one every other year, pausing only long enough to publish, in 1992, a substantial expansion and revision of her 1982 Gifford Lectures under the title *Metaphysics as a Guide to Morals*. But when *The Green Knight* (and at 472 pages her briefest novel in more than a decade) appeared in Great Britain in 1993 it became clear that the completion of *Metaphysics* had scarcely exhausted her energy. She would publish only one more book, the disastrously bad *Jackson's Dilemma* (1996), whose lack of energy and coherence clearly showed that something was terribly wrong with her, even before news of her Alzheimer's became public. I was so shocked by its failure that I had to throw my copy away as soon as I had finished reading it.

Metaphysics as a Guide to Morals and *The Green Knight*, then, mark the real culmination of Murdoch's work, and in them we can clearly discern a clarification and focus of her key themes. She seems there to have expressed her philosophy more directly and forcefully than ever, connecting it with the whole range of her interests. And, though it may seem inappropriate to say so about so expansive a writer, I believe that focus is directed chiefly upon a single question, one might even say a single letter: the letter "o." The presence or absence of that letter can determine the ground of our moral lives.

What I mean can be discovered in a single sentence near the end of *Metaphysics as a Guide to Morals*: "Good represents the reality of which God is the dream." Or: "We can lose God, but not Good." Murdoch is a Platonist, to a degree and with a purity almost unknown in modern thought: it is The Good that she seeks, the Idea or Form of the Good. (Platonist thought requires the frequent use of capital letters.) All else, including God, is an image or a substitute for this utter Good, and may be useful to us as we move towards that perfection; but because our human tendency is to substitute the image for the reality, the guidepost for the destination, even the worship of God may distract us from our proper pursuit.

Nevertheless, Murdoch is convinced that each of us pursues the Good according to our understanding of it; evil, in her thinking, is little more than the natural consequence of misinformation about or a misconception of the Good. As such it gets little attention in her writings: a consideration of the view that people are evil and human life miserable takes up but one part of the shortest chapter in *Metaphysics*, and most of the characters in her novels are basically decent people who are rather puzzled when they come upon what appears to be evil. Even a murderer in *The Green Knight* seems more confused than malicious, though malicious he is to a degree. (He is a scholar whose remarkable intellectual integrity suggests that he has simply failed to extend the morality he exhibits in one activity to the rest of his life.) A typical Murdoch character, it seems to me, is young Edward Baltram in *The Good Apprentice* (1986). Edward surreptitiously, jokingly, gives a friend a dose of LSD, and when the friend in mid-trip leaps or falls from a high window to his death, Edward, overwhelmed by guilt, begins to seek some understanding of his experience, some moral or spiritual categories within which it can be comprehended, perhaps even some kind of redemption. On the last page he and his stepbrother (whose quest for a moral life gives the book its title) and stepfather drink to "the good things in the world," though they admit not being sure what those things are. They drink, one might say, to an unknown Good.

Perhaps this one sample from Murdoch's work is sufficient to indicate that she takes the moral life more seriously than almost any other well-known contemporary novelist; and moreover that the virtues and vices of her work are tightly interwoven. Her insistence that a good life is possible, and that many people actively pursue it, including those who don't know that they are doing so, marks a fresh and exciting alternative to the more common themes of today's "serious" fiction: detailed descriptions of adultery in the suburbs, or of the mental worlds of serial killers, or of the contents of a kitchen cabinet in a trailer home in rural Missouri. But in order to make the pursuit of goodness seem both attractive and possible, Murdoch tends to avoid raising hard questions about those who quite evidently aren't interested in goodness, or those who fight with little success against their evil impulses. As a Christian I would say that the great lack in Murdoch's moral philosophy is an adequate concept of the *will*. Augustine's *Confessions* turns up from time to time in *Metaphysics*, and I kept hoping that at some point she would consider the philosophy of will elaborated there; but I was disappointed. Her only reference to it merely notes that Augustine "pictures will as a blend of intellect and feeling."

Nevertheless — I always find myself going back and forth in this way when I think about Murdoch — she does understand as well as any modern novelist just how complicated our moral lives can be, which is perhaps why she tends to write big novels, since their open and expansive form can make room for complexity and for a certain quite realistic lack of coherence. In one particularly stimulating chapter of *Metaphysics* she questions the pre-eminent position of tragedy among literary genres: "If it must be a play, is it not necessarily too short and simple?" Moreover, doesn't the association of tragedy with death enforce a certain too-neat closure? Murdoch suggests that *King Lear* would be a still more powerful — indeed, perhaps unbearable — play if Lear did not die at the end, but was forced to go on living with his crushing burden of knowledge and guilt. (Though she does not note it, this is of course what does happen to Oedipus at the end of Sophocles's first play about him.) Murdoch suspects the Aristotelian doctrine of catharsis because a play which obeys it settles too many issues and closes too many emotional doors. More generally, referring to philosophy as well as art, she says that "the achievement of coherence is itself ambiguous. Coherence is not necessarily good, and one must question its cost. Better sometimes to remain confused." (Thus she praises the novel because "in the traditional novel the people, the story, the innumerable kinds of value judgments both illuminate and celebrate life, and are judged and placed by life, in a reciprocal process. We read great novels with all our knowledge of life engaged, the experience is cognitive and moral in the highest degree." Such experience is also too diversified to be fully coherent.)

I am not wholly comfortable with Murdoch's suspicion of coherence; it links up too readily with her resistance to stopping the pursuit of the Good with Jesus or Yahweh or Allah. The traditional believer is not confused about the object of his or her worship, which is for Murdoch often too bad. But that (important) point noted, Murdoch's willingness to tolerate confusion is valuable in its recognition that the moral life cannot be reduced to rule-governed behavior. Not that she is against moral rules: they are, she argues convincingly, an "indispensable," if insufficient, part of the moral life. Especially interesting in this regard is her rehabilitation of the Kantian notion of duty, so scorned by many modern moral philosophers for "imposing" a supposedly external or, to use Paul Tillich's word, "heteronomous" standard upon the moral agent. "A realistic view of morality cannot dispense with the idea," she argues; "duty is for most people the most obvious form of moral experience." It is where moral neophytes — a category which includes but is not confined to children — find their starting point. As one grows morally and spiritually, one moves toward a more natural selflessness; but "meanwhile requirements and claims . . . demand to be met." And it is good for all concerned that we acknowledge and meet those demands.

This position, admirable in itself, is put to some troubling uses by Murdoch. Rules, structures, and duties, along with symbols, rites, even gods and all other objects of worship — in short, all given forms of the religious life — are in her view useful primarily as training wheels, to be replaced or removed when the rider no longer needs them. Thus she often portrays characters who begin their moral quests by seeking a place within the structures of more-or-less traditional religious belief. Bellamy James in *The Green Knight*, for instance, finds a cloistered priest to serve as his spiritual advisor, and seeks to live a monastic life in the world, hoping that ascetic discipline will give him a clearer vision of Christ. But such characters are not allowed to find lasting satisfaction within those structures: internal and external circumstances tend to force them into more individualistic and amorphous modes of religious experience. Bellamy's spiritual advisor seems to embody the thinking of his creator when he leaves the Church and tells Bellamy to "remember Eckhart's advice (for which he was deemed a heretic): do not seek for God outside your own soul." He also says, "You should stay with Christ, that presence need not fade, it can be an icon" — but of course this is a significant demotion, from Savior to mere sign or token of an impersonal and unrepresentable Good. In one of the two dialogues in her book *Acastos*, Murdoch has Socrates tell a young man that if he prays to whatever God he knows, he will be answered. But it is clear that she also believes that, if one is not spiritually stagnant, any God will eventually cease to answer, at which point one must move on to higher and better things. The French statesman Georges Clemenceau famously remarked that he would disown his son if the young man were not a Communist at age twenty, and would do the same if he were still a Communist at age thirty. Murdoch seems to have the same attitude toward adherence to traditional forms of religion: admirable and necessary in a moral beginner, unforgivable in a morally mature person. It is this conviction that lies behind her claim that she is a Christian Buddhist, or Buddhist Christian: she envisions a Christianity in which Jesus plays the same role that Buddha does in the more sophisticated forms of Buddhism, that of (at most) an avatar of a transcendent Good that he cannot exhaust or even adequately represent. This belief should not be confused with what has often been called "ethical Christianity." Murdoch repeatedly insists that morality, as commonly conceived, is not self-supporting. She rejects the liberal humanistic tradition which believes that morality itself can be the ground of a good life; to the contrary, she argues, morality itself must be grounded in religious commitment. Religion, as Murdoch defines it, demands more of us than any mere morality can; it requires our unswerving allegiance, its claims upon us are absolute. In this sense, while the desire to be good or to be a better person may be a merely moral project, the pursuit of the Good is genuinely religious. The true encounter with Christ (or the Buddha, or whoever) will be a mystical vision of the Good that shines through him, not a simple acknowledgment of his ethical superiority and the value of following his example.

But the religion Murdoch envisions — as many of her characters come to believe, as Socrates preaches in *Acastos,* and as Murdoch herself repeatedly argues in *Metaphysics* — is necessarily, for reasons that by now should be obvious, a religion without gods. Not only *can* we lose God, but if we are to retain Good, at some point we *must* lose God. "The 'demythologisation' of religion is something absolutely necessary in this age." Moreover, the abandonment of the "old dogmatic literalistic myths" may well, she thinks, be going on right now in churches around the world without anybody noticing. This process can happen silently because "a Christian who loses belief in God and resurrection and immortality, while remaining religious [in the sense of the word just noted], is not necessarily making a radical change in his value world." Murdoch is aware that some people will doubt that the transformation she recommends is so simple:

> Can one simply decree this sort of status for the risen Christ and still keep a Christian structure and observance as before, as if it did not matter all that much? The transformation of Christianity into a religion *like*

Buddhism, with no God and no literally divine Christ, but with a mystical Christ, may be, if possible at all, a long task. . . . Or could an individual perhaps one day decide to 'look at it in this way'? Do not people so decide? And suppose a good many of them do? Is one being too rigid and solemn about it all? Do not a large number of those who go to church already think in a new non-literal way without bothering about theology and metaphysics?

This, it seems to me, is wishful thinking. Even the most superficial investigation of the demographic data reveals that, while most Christians would agree that they care little for theology or metaphysics, those who actually go to church on a regular basis (and this is as true in Great Britain as it is in North America) tend to believe pretty literally in the creeds they recite each Sunday. Those who do not so believe tend eventually to stop going to church altogether, finding the Sunday *New York Times* — that "parish magazine of affluent and self-congratulatory liberal enlightenment," as Alasdair MacIntyre has so vividly called it — a less demanding way to meet their spiritual needs. One may deplore or applaud this tendency, but one cannot simply ignore its existence, or assert its opposite. Murdoch is quite unusual in her assumption that the structures of religion are of greater importance than the beliefs which have historically generated and then undergirded those structures. It may seem obvious to her that, in British Christianity, the abandonment of a belief in a personal God would be of little significance, while the loss of the Authorized Version of the Bible and Cranmer's Prayer Book marks a religious disaster of the first magnitude; or that if "our minds are . . . full of readily available religious imagery . . . there is no need to expel [it] simply because . . . we do not believe in God." But it is difficult to imagine that others will find such notions equally obvious, or perhaps even comprehensible. And at times Murdoch acknowledges that those who believe that untrue ideas should simply be dispensed with have an argument worthy of consideration.

Religious forms and structures are important to Murdoch for pragmatic reasons: they are pegs on which to hang spiritual experiences that might otherwise be too amorphous and indefinable to be made sense of, or, as I said earlier, training wheels without which one cannot learn to ride the spiritual bicycle. But the Good itself, well, that is another matter — isn't it? Surely Murdoch, as a self-proclaimed Platonist, believes in something like a "literal way" in the existence of the Good — doesn't she? One might so conclude, if one had read only the first five hundred or so pages of *Metaphysics as a Guide to Morals*. But right at the end she gives away the game.

There is a story which Murdoch tells in this book, a Tibetan story, she says:

> A mother asks her son, a merchant setting off for the city, to bring her back a religious relic. He forgets her request until he is nearly home again. He picks up a dog's tooth by the roadside and tells the old lady it is a relic of a saint. She places it in her chapel where it is venerated. It begins miraculously to glow with light.

At its first telling this little tale illustrates a point about the role of stories in religion. It does not seem very important. But Murdoch returns to it several times, and finally, near the end of the book, it suddenly appears to be something like the key to her whole philosophy:

> Keats says that 'what the imagination seizes as beauty must be truth, whether it existed before or not.' It *must* be *truth*. Simone Weil quotes Valéry: 'The proper, unique and perpetual object of thought is that which does not exist.' Here we may make sense of the idea of loving good. 'At its highest point, love is a determination to create the being which it has taken for its object.' Here indeed we come back to the Ontological Proof in its simpler version, a proof by perfection, by a certainty derived from love. The good artist, the true lover, the dedicated thinker, the unselfish moral agent solving his problem: they can create the object of love. The dog's tooth, when sincerely venerated, glows with light.

Murdoch neatly escapes a recurrent dilemma of Platonism, which is to explain the mode of existence of the Good and of all the Forms, by denying that they have an existence at all independent of those who believe in them. The Good is not worshipped because it exists, but exists insofar as it is worshipped. It may be indispensable — unlike God — but this indispensability is purely pragmatic and heuristic. We cannot live in the way we most want to live, or at least the way some of us want to live, without it. Murdoch's Good is what the poet Wallace Stevens called a "supreme fiction": a story, a metanarrative, by which we can direct our lives, and the origin of which is our own creative imagination. If, as Jean-François Lyotard has claimed, postmodernism may be defined in a phrase as "incredulity toward metanarratives," then Iris Murdoch (like Stevens) is a modernist; that is to say, one whose incredulity is limited to metanarratives written by others.

Many of the more curious features of Murdoch's novels become more comprehensible once one understands this belief that the Good is an imaginative creation: for instance, the seemingly minor yet recurrent instances of paranormal phenomena. In *The Philosopher's Pupil* (1983) a man's life is changed by his vision of a flying saucer; a key episode in *The Good Apprentice* turns on what appears to be the effects of a love potion; a young girl in *The Green Knight* exerts an involuntary telekinesis over the stones that she has collected in her room; in the same novel the goodness of a man named Peter Mir (Mir meaning, in Russian, both "world" and "peace," as several characters note) seems to be contagious, bringing sweet dreams and love to those with whom he comes in contact. But more questions, I think, are raised than are answered, of which I will note but three.

First, why do the various spiritual seekers of her novels tend to move in the same direction, that is, to conceive of or imagine goodness in roughly the same way? I can imagine several plausible answers to that question, but as far as I know Murdoch doesn't give any. Second — a point noted earlier — how are we to explain those people who do not seem to give a damn for the Good or for moral action in any form? Do they simply have deficient imaginations? Moreover, how should we respond to them? What kinds of arguments, if any, could we formulate that would call them to account for their behavior, and even to see the error of their ways? In *The Green Knight*, the good Peter Mir confronts the murderer mentioned earlier, and seems to have no resources with which to bring about moral conviction in the man; their several conversations end in frustration and no closure is reached. At one point in *Metaphysics* Murdoch quotes, approvingly so far as I can tell, Wittgenstein's claim that certain moral questions cannot be profitably discussed: "There are, indeed, things which cannot be put into words. They *make themselves manifest.* They are what is mystical." But of course, there are many people to whom such "things" are obviously not manifest. What then?

The third question is, in my view, the most important. Earlier I quoted Murdoch's claim that "the 'demythologisation' of religion is something absolutely necessary in this age." Throughout the book she takes it for granted that the "old dogmatic literalistic myths" must go, indeed have gone; the only question is what "we" will replace them with. The recurrent use of the plural pronoun and her constant reference to traditional religions in the past tense — "Should we let [the word 'God'] dwindle and go, together with the *person* whom it used to designate?" — are equally telling. That Murdoch feels qualified to speak for a "we" which presumably includes all of her readers is indicated by the fact that she offers neither a defense nor even an explanation for her determination to demythologize. To Murdoch it goes without saying that historic Christianity is not an option. Yet it does not seem to me likely that her audience is as uniform as all that; and even those readers who do not share my commitment to traditional religion may still wonder whether, if we are going to create our own object of worship, the exchange of a personal, loving God for an impersonal, unresponsive Good is an appealing trade. Why — this is my third question — should anyone agree to such an exchange? Insofar as Murdoch does answer this question, the answer is only implicit, and appears to be pragmatic. It is a matter of what "we" can bring ourselves to believe in. From time to time she notes that "we can no longer believe" in traditional Judaism or Christianity — that is, in the notion of a personal God, or a Savior who rose from the dead, or personal immortality in the familiar sense. It is a common sort of statement, and yet it begs many, many questions. Many people do believe in these things; many people in the past did not. Many contemporary skeptics would find it easier to believe in a personal God than in "a Christ who . . . is to be found as a living force [only] within each human soul." If indeed Murdoch thinks her philosophy is for the modern person more "believable" than the historic religions, I need to be convinced and not just told.

This is an important issue because Murdoch implicitly acknowledges from time to time that her Good is in many ways less appealing, less satisfying than a personal God. Her nostalgia for the ancient Jewish and especially the Christian faith is palpable throughout *Metaphysics,* and in a less direct way in many of her novels. "The charm, attraction, and in many ways deep effectiveness, of faith in a personal God must constantly strike the critical or envious outsider." Of the Gospels she writes, contrasting them with the forceful rhetoric of Paul's letters, that they "are in a sense easy to read, can seem so (even I would think for a complete stranger to them), because they are the kind of great art where we feel: It is so." And that this is not a merely aesthetic reaction may be indicated by these curiously ambivalent words, from the same page: "What happened immediately after Christ's death, how it all went on, how the Gospel writers and Paul became persuaded He had risen: this is one of the great mysteries of history. It is difficult to imagine any explanation in purely historical terms, though the unbeliever must assume there is one." The narratives of Christ's redemptive acts touch Murdoch because they reveal a God who, in the Apostle Paul's formulation, came to save us while we were yet sinners, before we had loved him. The Platonic Good can be, like the Jewish and Christian God, lovable; "however, God sees us and seeks us, Good does not."

That Murdoch cannot find a way to accept this God who sees and seeks (who redeems), but instead embraces an impersonal and probably fictional Good, makes it ironic — perhaps contradictory would not be too strong a word — that she would conclude her book with these words from Psalm 139 (in the Authorized Version of course):

> Whither shall I go from thy spirit, whither shall I fly from thy presence? If I ascend into heaven thou art there, if I make my bed in hell, behold thou art there. If I take the wings of the morning and dwell in the uttermost parts of the sea, even there shall thy hand lead me, and thy right hand shall hold me.

Ironic and contradictory because each property here attributed by the psalmist to the Lord is that of a person, one whose love is active and (in the old word) prevenient. Murdoch concludes her long, confusing, and stimulating book by appealing to an image of the Ultimate which she has, overtly and firmly, if regretfully, abandoned.

The Gospel — and not just the Gospel, but the fundamental Jewish and Christian belief in a loving personal God — is, according to the apostle, "foolishness to the Greeks." We believers are fools. But Murdoch's rejection of God in favor of her supreme fiction, the Good, is worse than foolish, it is empty. Her interpolated "o" adds nothing; in the end it proves to be a zero. Another Fool may have understood, though his words seem harsh: he told his master Lear, "now thou art an O without a figure. I am better than thou art now; I am a Fool, thou art nothing."

Wole Soyinka's Outrage

1.

Like many teachers of literature, I am sometimes asked to name the Greatest Living Writer. (I can hear the capital letters in the voices of those who ask.) Invariably I name two candidates: the Polish-Lithuanian poet Czeslaw Milosz and the Nigerian playwright Wole Soyinka. These names are usually greeted by puzzlement, for, though both have won the Nobel Prize for literature — Milosz in 1980 and Soyinka in 1986 — and both have been on the *MacNeil-Lehrer News Hour,* neither has entered the American public consciousness in a potent way. Milosz is more likely to be familiar, though, and apparently my interlocutors think him a more plausible choice; my claim for Soyinka almost always earns skeptical looks. I imagine that this skepticism derives from the still-common picture of Africa as the dark continent, full of illiterates if not of savages (a picture that the Western media do little to dispel); and also from the suspicion that any African Nobel laureate must be the beneficiary of multicultural affirmative action. But if anything, Soyinka is a more comprehensive genius even than Milosz. Here is a writer of spectacular literary gifts: he is an acclaimed lyric and satirical poet, a brilliant novelist of ideas, a memoirist both nostalgic and harrowing, and almost certainly the greatest religious dramatist of the twentieth century. The assumption that he has come to our attention only because of academic politics is profoundly unjust — though perhaps understandable, given the number of mediocre talents who have assumed recent prominence for just such reasons.

That assumption also carries a heavy load of irony, because of the distance between the triviality of American academic politics — what Henry Louis Gates, Jr., has aptly called our "marionette theater of the political" — and the *real* political crises which have continually afflicted Soyinka and his work. Soyinka's book on the political collapse of his native Nigeria, *The Open Sore of a Continent,* teaches us how absurdly misbegotten our whole literary-political conversation tends to be. Through this book, and through the shape his career has assumed, Soyinka brings compelling messages to our warring parties. To the traditionalists who deplore "the politicization of literary discourse," Soyinka serves as a living reminder that writers in some parts of the world don't get to *choose* whether their work will be political; that is a privilege enjoyed by those who happen to be born into stable and relatively peaceable societies. Others have politics thrust upon them. But Soyinka also tells our Young Turks that their cardinal principle — Everything is Political — is true only in an utterly trivial sense. To adapt a famous phrase from George Orwell, if everything is political, some things are a hell of a lot more political than others.

Whichever side of this dispute one tends to be on, or even if one isn't on either side, Soyinka's story is worth paying attention to, because his career has been virtually derailed by the collapse of his native country into political tyranny and social chaos. Soyinka has not eagerly thrown his energies into protest and polemic in the way that, for instance, Aleksandr Solzhenitsyn did in the days of the Soviet empire; unlike Solzhenitsyn, he is no *natural* polemicist. However, Soyinka has also been unable to follow the route of Solzhenitsyn's older contemporary Boris Pasternak, which was to combat political tyranny by ignoring it, by cultivating a realm of personal feeling impervious to the corrosive solvent of Politics. (As Czeslaw Milosz writes of Pasternak, "confronted by argument, he replied with his sacred dance.") Soyinka has felt called upon to respond to the collapse of Nigeria, and as a result his career has taken a very different direction than it once promised to do. It is hard to question his choice; it is equally hard to celebrate it, for it has led a fecund and celebratory poetic mind into an abyss of outrage.

2.

Soyinka's homeland has suffered from the same consequences of colonialism that have afflicted almost every modern African state. The area now called Nigeria is occupied by many peoples, the most prominent among them being the Hausa, the Yoruba, and the Ibo. The boundaries of the country do not reflect the distribution of these ethnic populations: there are Ibo people in Cameroon, Yoruba in Benin, Hausa in Niger. The physical shape of Nigeria is an administrative fiction deriving from the way the colonial powers parceled out the "dark continent" in the nineteenth century. (Somalia alone among African countries is ethnically homogeneous.) So when the British granted independence to Nigeria in 1960, this most populous of African nations had some considerable work to do to make itself *into* a real nation, as opposed to a collection of adversarial ethnicities. These problems have been exacerbated by almost continually increasing tensions between Christians and Muslims in the country. No wonder, then, that civil rule has been the exception rather than the norm in Nigeria's history, and that civilian governments have served only at the behest of the military, who have been quick to take over and impose martial law whenever they have sensed the coming of chaos, or genuine democracy — for them the two amount to more or less the same thing. And with martial law has always come strict censorship of all the media, which makes it difficult for even the most apolitical writer to avoid politics. Besides, respect for intellectuals is so great in most African cultures that writers can scarcely resist the pleas of their people for help.

Wole Soyinka's people, in the ethnic sense, are the Yoruba, and there is no culture in the world more fascinating. The Yoruba are traditionally among the greatest sculptors in Africa, and their labyrinthine mythology is so coherent and compelling that even the selling of many Yoruba people into slavery could not eradicate it: especially in places where great numbers of Yoruba were transported (most notably Brazil and Haiti) it survived by adapting itself, syncretistically, to certain Catholic traditions. The chief Yoruba gods (the *orisha*) became conflated with the popular saints; the results can be seen even today in religions (or cults) like Santaria. The notorious Haitian practice of voodoo is largely a corruption of Yoruba

medicine, which typically seeks to confuse the evil spirits who cause ill-
ness and draw them from the ill person into a doll or effigy, which is then
beaten or destroyed. This form of medical treatment is crucial to one of
Soyinka's earliest, and most accessibly powerful, plays, *The Strong Breed*
(1959).

Perhaps not surprisingly, the Yoruba have long practiced the arts of
drama, and Soyinka is an heir of that tradition. It is really inaccurate to
say that Yoruba drama is religious, because even to make such a statement one must employ a vocabulary which distinguishes between religion and other forms of culture in a way alien to much of Africa. For the
Yoruba, every aspect of culture is religious through and through — it
simply *is* worship or celebration or healing or teaching — and religion is
thoroughly cultural. In Africa, the notion of "the aesthetic" as a distinct
category of experience is unthinkable. No Yoruba arts can be identified
as part of the human realm as distinct from that of the gods and spirits. In
part this is because of the animism of Yoruba culture, but such a complete integration of religion and culture does not require animism. It
seems to have characterized ancient Israel, for instance: the poetry of the
Israelites is inseparable from their covenantal relationship with Yahweh.
Similarly, Westerners seem to have difficulty understanding why Muslims insist upon the universal application of *sharia,* or Islamic law, and
tend to think that Muslims don't know how to respect the appropriate
cultural boundaries. Yoruba drama arises from what one might call such
a "total culture."

Soyinka, though, was raised in a Christian home. His mother's brand
and intensity of piety may be guessed at from this: in his memoirs he refers to her as "Wild Christian." But it seems that his chief interest in the
doctrines and practices of Christianity derives from their similarities to
Yoruba traditions. Biblical themes always echo in his work, especially
early in his career: the story of the prodigal son in *The Swamp Dwellers*
(about 1958), the Passion (with staggering force) in *The Strong Breed*. But, as
in his fascinating adaptation of Euripides' *The Bacchae* (1973), so do the
themes of classical tragedy. It is clear that Soyinka has been interested in
the primordial mythic truths that lie behind the doctrines and practices of
particular religions: he shares the Jungian view that all religions are

concretized and particularized versions of universal experiences. More-over, he seems to espouse the Feuerbachian projection theory of religion: as he says in his critical book *Myth, Literature, and the African World* (1976), "myths arise from man's attempt to externalise and communicate his in-ner intuitions," and more recently he has written, in oracular tones, "THE WILL of man is placed beyond surrender.... ORISA reveals Destiny as — SELF-DESTINATION." These universalistic and syncretistic tendencies are more easily reconcilable with Yoruba than with Christian beliefs: for the Yoruba, as for most African peoples, it is understood that different cultures will have different gods and practices, but very similar needs and concerns. Soyinka's imagination is thus secondarily and derivatively Christian at best, despite his upbringing and his long-term fascination with Christian doctrine. And in recent years, as we shall see, that fascina-tion itself has been repudiated in rather frightening ways.

When, as a young man, he came to study in England at the University of Leeds, it is not at all surprising that he fell under the influence of the controversial Shakespearean scholar G. Wilson Knight. For Knight's ca-reer was devoted chiefly to the contention that Shakespeare's plays, how-ever "secular" they might appear, were really Christian (in a mythic or ar-chetypal sort of way) through and through. It must have seemed perfectly natural to Soyinka, coming from his Yoruba world, that such would be the case; indeed it must have been hard for him to think of drama in any other terms. No wonder he ultimately decided to adapt *The Bacchae*: the Euripidean original, so obviously shaped by and angrily responsive to the Athenian worship of Dionysos, was a clear picture of what he had always understood drama to be. Soyinka's version, a turbulent tragic fantasy half-Greek and half-African, is one of the most striking and provocative plays of our time, and in its exploration of irreconcilable worldviews often seems a veiled commentary on the troubles of modern Africa.

3.

Soyinka's plays are often said to be about the modern "clash of cultures" in Africa between Western and African traditional ways, but this is a phrase for which Soyinka has a singular contempt. In an "Author's Note" to what may well be his greatest play, the tragedy *Death and the King's Horseman* (1975), which is based on a historical event, he complains that "the bane of themes of this genre is that they are no sooner employed creatively than they acquire the facile tag of 'clash of cultures,' a prejudicial label which, quite apart from its frequent misapplication, presupposes a potential equality in every given situation of the alien culture and the indigenous, on the actual soil of the latter." One might think that Soyinka is here reminding us that the British came to Africa with technologies and forces that traditional African cultures could not hope to resist; in other words, that he is reminding us of his people's status as victims. That would be a misreading. The British did indeed bring superior physical force to Nigeria; but Soyinka is more concerned to point out that the spiritual and cultural forces upon which the Yoruba relied were far more impressive. Now, Soyinka is never shy about offering potent critiques of his culture, and not just in its modern manifestations; from those early plays already mentioned, *The Swamp Dwellers* and *The Strong Breed*, we can see a fierce indictment of how power corrupts even at the level of the village, where leaders pervert their people's traditions and manipulate them for their own gain. But those traditions themselves, Soyinka is always eager to say, have enormous power, and when rightly used and respectfully employed can overcome the humiliations inflicted upon the Yoruba by British imperialism. This is indeed the central theme of *Death and the King's Horseman*, where tradition finds a way to rescue the dignity of a people even when the colonial power seems to have things well under control.

In Nigeria during the Second World War, a king has died. Oba Elesin, the king's horseman and a lesser king himself ("Oba" means "king" or "chief"), is expected, at the end of a month of ceremonies marking the king's passing, to follow his master into the spirit world of the ancestors. In other words, he is to commit ritual suicide. It is his greatest wish to do so, and in the village marketplace, surrounded by people who love and respect him, he awaits the appointed time.

All is prepared. Listen! [*A steady drum-beat from the distance.*] Yes. It is nearly time. The King's dog has been killed. The King's favourite horse is about to follow his master. My brother chiefs know their task and perform it well. . . . My faithful drummers, do me your last service. This is where I have chosen to do my leave-taking, in this heart of life, this hive which contains the swarm of the world in its small compass. . . . Just then I felt my spirit's eagerness. . . . But wait a while my spirit. Wait. Wait for the coming of the courier of the King.

But Simon Pilkings, the district officer in this British colonial outpost, intervenes to prevent the suicide, which he considers to be a barbaric custom and which in any case violates British law. His intervention succeeds in part because at the crucial moment Elesin hesitates, and thereby cooperates with Pilkings in bringing shame upon himself, his people, and his king (who is by Elesin's cowardice "condemned to wander in the void of evil with beings who are the enemies of life"). Elesin's son Olunde — who had been in England studying medicine, and returned when he heard of the death of the king — explains this to Simon Pilkings's wife Jane before he knows that the interference has succeeded. When she suggests that Elesin "is entitled to whatever protection is available to him" — that is, available from her husband as instrument of the colonial law — Olunde quickly replies,

> How can I make you understand? He *has* protection. No one can undertake what he does tonight without the deepest protection the mind can conceive. What can you offer him in place of his peace of mind, in place of the honour and veneration of his own people?

And it is Olunde — the one who Elesin feared would in England forget or repudiate the old tribal ways — who finds a way to rescue his people and his king from the shame brought by Elesin.

In his preface to the play Soyinka insists that the colonial situation of the play be seen as but a catalyst for an exploration of what is permanent in Yoruba society: the play is about "transition," the transition from this world to the world of the spirits and the ancestors, and as such cannot be reduced to a single historical moment. The colonial era simply troubles the waters, it cannot dam the river of Yoruba tradition. "The confrontation in the play is largely metaphysical, contained in the human vehicle which is Elesin and the universe of the Yoruba mind — the world of the living, the dead, and the unborn." Simon Pilkings thinks he holds the power in this situation, that he participates in a story which his people are writing and of which they are the protagonists; but Soyinka reveals him as merely a plot device, a means by which "the universe of the Yoruba mind" is explored.

4.

This potent tragedy marks a return to Soyinka's early themes and concerns, and arrests a drift towards political satire which had begun some years before. One sees this tendency in his two wickedly funny plays about the shyster preacher and self-proclaimed prophet Brother Jereboam (*The Trials of Brother Jero* [1960] and *Jero's Metamorphosis* [1968]), who ultimately becomes the "general" of a Nigerian version of the Salvation Army, sending his "troops" out into a dangerous world while he remains secure in his office. Lingering just below the surface of these plays is a commentary on the ambitions and absurdities of Nigeria's hyperactive military. The Jero plays were followed by Soyinka's darkest, bitterest play, *Madmen and Specialists* (1970), which reveals Soyinka's disgust at the crisis of Biafra in 1969. Biafra was the new country proclaimed by leaders of the Ibo people of eastern Nigeria; but their attempt to secede from Nigeria ended when they were beaten and starved into submission. (Soyinka's sympathy for the Biafran rebels led to his arrest and lengthy detainment, an experience chronicled in his searing memoir *The Man Died* [1972].) Soyinka's play emphasizes the ways that the lust for power, and not just power itself, corrupts gifted men and turns them into tyrants who cannot abide dissent or even questioning.

One can easily see why after writing this play and *The Man Died*, Soyinka would produce *Death and the King's Horseman*, with its passionate commitment to the maintenance of a great spiritual tradition which cannot be extinguished or even derailed by the traumas of political history. But as passionately as Soyinka expresses that commitment, what speaks still louder than the brilliance of the play is the fact that in the two decades since it appeared Soyinka has severely curtailed his theatrical writing. (And most of the plays he has written are topical political satires, like the bizarre comedy *The Beatification of Area Boy*, originally written in 1994 but not performed until some years later.) It is hard to imagine a greater loss for modern drama.

This is not to say that Soyinka has fallen silent. But it may be significant that since the mid-'70s he has mostly avoided the communal and necessarily collaborative work of the theater. Instead he has become a political commentator, a memoirist and celebrator of his family, and for a time early in the 1990s a government official. Perhaps the most remarkable product of this period is not the properly celebrated memoir *Aké: The Years of Childhood* (1981), but rather its successor, *Isarà: A Voyage around "Essay"* (1989). "Essay" is Soyinka's father, the schoolteacher S. A. Soyinka, and this novelistic attempt to imagine and describe Essay's youth and young manhood is a moving act of filial devotion, a tribute to a wry, dignified man and his colorful circle of friends. Interestingly, the plot of the book revolves around the successful attempt by Essay and his friends to influence a matter of *local* politics, the selection of the Odemo (or chief) of the town of Isarà. The frustrations of trying to shape a nation must have made such local concerns seem less painful and more rewarding. But in any case, we see in all the works of this period Soyinka's continued determination to follow E. M. Forster's famous advice: "Only connect!" Connection is Soyinka's constant goal, his natural tendency as a writer; but it is immensely sad to see him cut at least some of his ties to the theater in order to participate in a political realm from which he seems to find little real hope of connection.

5.

Soyinka's experience as a minister in the Nigerian government ended badly, as he probably knew it would. He had been in trouble with governments too many times before to retain many illusions, and if Nigeria's leaders thought that by giving him high place they would muzzle him, they were mistaken. The national police forced him out of the country, claiming that they could not protect him from others who wanted to kill him; and eventually he was charged in absentia by a Nigerian court with treason against the state. In 1997 General Sani Abacha, the country's military dictator, issued a sentence of death against him, though when Abacha died in 1998 Soyinka returned to Nigeria. He has lived alternately in exile and in his homeland for the past two decades, depending on the political situation *du jour*, and often launches his rhetorical missiles from Massachusetts or London. His book *The Open Sore of a Continent*, for instance, is not less a book than a collection of some of his more heavily loaded projectiles. It provides much information about what was at the time of its publication the most recent political crisis in Nigeria, the 1993 annulment by yet another military government of democratic elections. But one needs already to know a good bit about Nigerian history in order to make sense of the story Soyinka tells. Only rarely do Soyinka's literary gifts shine through, but some of a great dramatist's flair for characterization is evident in this comparison of Abacha with his predecessor, General Ibrahim Babangida:

> Babangida's love of power was visualized in actual terms: power over Nigeria, over the nation's impressive size, its potential, over the nation's powerful status within the community of nations. The potency of Nigeria, in short, was an augmentation of his own sense of personal power. It corrupted him thoroughly, and all the more disastrously because he had come to identify that Nigeria and her resources with his own person and personal wealth.
>
> Not so Abacha. Abacha is prepared to reduce Nigeria to rubble as long as he survives to preside over a name — and Abacha is a survivor.... Totally lacking in vision, in perspectives, he is a mole trapped in a warren of tunnels. At every potential exit he is blinded by the headlights of an oncoming vehicle and freezes. When the light has veered off, he charges to destroy every animate or inanimate object within the path of the vanished beam. Abacha is incapable of the faculty of defining that intrusive light, [or] even to consider if the light path could actually lead him out of the mindless maze.

But prose so vivid is rare in this book. Mostly, it is the wrathful detailing of the indignities Abacha and his henchmen inflicted on Nigeria, a detailing interrupted only by the repeated mastication of what have become for Soyinka the fundamental questions: in Africa, is the concept of "nation" viable? Does "Nigeria" exist? Has it existed? Can it exist? In moments like these, Soyinka is not quite ready to abandon the project of nationhood, but he is not far from it.

The lover of literature, and of Soyinka's work in particular, will find few rewards from this kind of writing; and its tone is sadly ubiquitous in Soyinka's last few books, including *The Burden of Memory, the Muse of Forgiveness*, which begins with the assertion that in 1992 the United States "stood a reasonable chance" of electing the white supremacist David Duke as president. It is hard to imagine that Soyinka finds many rewards in writing this kind of thing; and the shrillness of his political writings infects also his recent writings about art and literature. In 1994 Soyinka published a collection of essays titled *Art, Dialogue, and Outrage*, and there, as in *The Open Sore of a Continent*, outrage is certainly the chief note sounded. One is tempted to ask what, exactly, Soyinka *wants*, since everything seems to make him so angry. What, for instance, is a plausible alternative to the almost-bankrupt project of the Nigerian nation-state? What artistic practices does he find healthy and proper? I think the answer to these questions is pretty clear: Soyinka today is concerned, as was T. S. Eliot, with the "dissociation of sensibility," with the fragmenting of a culture and thus of the minds that inhabit it. He wants unity and wholeness. And this can only be achieved within the context of a particular ethnic tradition, that is, for him, within the Yoruba tradition. Furthermore — and here we are moving into territory quite alien to the syncretistic Soyinka of the 1970s — the Yoruba tradition can only flourish again if its competitors are, forcibly if necessary, extracted from the cultural space of Nigeria. Olunde's victory over Simon Pilkings was local and temporary; greater victories will require more drastic measures.

In a scathing 1975 essay titled "Neo-Tarzanism: The Poetics of Pseudo-Tradition," Soyinka responds to critics who have thought him insufficiently African in his allegiances by gleefully trumping their best cards. He makes a proposition: "That the very existence and practice [in Africa] of non-traditional religions be declared retrogressive and colonialist. So let us . . . ban these religions from our continent altogether. This is a serious proposition as [my critics] will discover when they find the energy and determination to launch a movement for the eradication of islam and christianity from the black continent. I cannot alas find the will to place myself at the forefront of such a movement but I shall readily play John the Baptist to their anti-christ." (This is followed immediately by an ironic reflection on how even an "anti-christian" statement finds itself drawing on "the metaphors of christian religious history": such is the "endemic effect of great religions.") It is hard to be sure if Soyinka really believes wholeheartedly in this "proposition," or rather has been driven to it by his critics' accusations; but the fact that he chose not only to write the essay but place it as the concluding piece in *Art, Dialogue, and Outrage* seems telling.

If this radical excision of the alien faiths, and a consequent restoration of Yoruba cultural purity, are the only ways in which Soyinka's anger can be soothed, then outrage will continue to be his portion. And that is not only because Christianity and Islam are now too deeply implicated in Nigeria for their removal, but also because all such dreams of cultural purity, of "unified sensibility," are illusory and deceitful. No human culture ever has been or ever could be whole and pure and undefiled by external "contamination." And such laboratory purity, if achieved, would be lifeless: as Mikhail Bakhtin repeatedly insisted, it is at the boundaries of culture, languages, and faiths that the real excitement happens; the most dynamic cultures are those called to respond to the strange, the other, the different in their midst. Soyinka's plays amply testify to this: it is Olunde's *response* to Pilkings's colonial paternalism that energizes *Death and the King's Horseman;* it is the *competing* understandings of sacrifice in the Yoruba and the Christian traditions that give *The Strong Breed* its peculiar power. Soyinka's desire to eliminate cultural and religious otherness from Nigeria is not only regrettable as an example of what some people call "the new tribalism"; it would mean death to the very Yoruba tradition he wants to save.

6.

Whenever modern cultures reach a certain stage of political development they seem to turn towards their artists and intellectuals for guidance and leadership: one thinks also of Vaclav Havel in the Czech Republic, and Mario Vargas Llosa in Peru. (Earlier examples from Africa include the first president of Kenya, Jomo Kenyatta, who was an anthropologist, and the first president of Senegal, Leopold Sedar Senghor, who was a poet.) None of these men seems fully comfortable with his political role. But this is work that they know they must do, a call they cannot refuse. Soyinka continues to proclaim the continuity of Yoruba tradition and its ability to survive the traumas of history; but he plays the role of the political protestor too. This twofold commitment finds expression in *The Open Sore* when he says that he accepts the definition of man as a "political animal," but "for purely strategic reasons," as a warning to dictators that their subjects are not sheep; he goes on to insist that "man is first a cultural being. Before politics, there was clearly culture." Now, however, is not the time to celebrate the Yoruba way of life. Now is the time to bear witness to suffering and injustice. And in the long run this may not be a less "religious" thing to do than the composition of ritual dramas; perhaps if Soyinka were today to write more plays like *The Strong Breed* and *Death and the King's Horseman* he would be failing not just in his political but in his religio-cultural obligations.

But if Soyinka is, in books like *The Open Sore*, meeting those obligations, he does so by appealing to a notion of shared humanity which he condemns Sani Abacha and his henchmen for disregarding. And how can this contempt for the inhumane be reconciled with Soyinka's equally fierce contempt for Christians and Muslims? After all, the only way for Christianity and Islam to be banished from Africa is for Christians and Muslims to be so banished. It is hard not to think that Soyinka, for all the brilliance and moral sensitivity demonstrated repeatedly in his plays, novels, poems, and memoirs, has descended into a bitterness which is not always clearly distinguishable from the cynicism of the dictators he rightly deplores. In his most recent play, *King Baabu* (2001), the mockery of dictatorship — in this case clearly that of Sani Abacha — seems constantly to turn laughter into a kind of screaming. One wonders if Soyinka any longer has a sense of what legitimate government would be; and one wonders if he remembers that Sani Abacha is dead. In *King Baabu* Soyinka dances, endlessly, on the grave of his enemy.

This descent is not pleasant to watch; would that it were arrested and the direction of Soyinka's thought reversed. But there is something inevitable about such bitterness, I think, for ethically earnest intellectuals living in the various post-Christian worlds. The moralistic humanism which is Soyinka's chief weapon against the dictators arose in Western culture in the eighteenth and nineteenth centuries as a substitute for a Christianity which was then thought to be dying. But, it turns out, belief in a common humanity seems to require the support of Christian doctrine and cannot be sustained without an appeal to the *imago dei* and Christ's universal offer of salvation. (The spirit of humanism is fundamentally alien, I believe, to Islam.) And when humanism collapses, as it must, what is left but Sani Abacha's will to power or Soyinka's retreat into tribalism? Indeed, the two choices may be one: I cited earlier Soyinka's own prophetic claim that "THE WILL of man is placed beyond surrender." The Yoruba tradition is rich and potent; while often cruel, it is in many ways beautiful; but it lacks the resources necessary to wage the political battle Soyinka now finds himself called upon to wage. Thus the last movement of a brilliant literary career may necessarily echo with rage and wrath.

The Republic of Heaven

In the world of literature for adolescents, or "young adults" as the book covers call it, fantasy stories have a particular power to inspire loyalty. Even the casual reader can reel off a lengthy list: J. R. R. Tolkien's sagas of Middle Earth, Ursula K. LeGuin's Earthsea books, Lloyd Alexander's Chronicles of Prydain, Madeleine L'Engle's Time quartet, and so on. These writers' ability to construct what Tolkien called "secondary worlds" — complex, fascinating environments sufficiently like our own to be recognizable but sufficiently different to generate excitement and wonder — is the chief means by which they secure their readers' devoted allegiance. One feels that something consequential is at stake when judging books of this kind: they offer a world to respond to, not just a story.

With *The Amber Spyglass*, the English writer Philip Pullman concludes the trilogy that began in 1995 with *Northern Lights* (or *The Golden Compass*, as its U.S. edition is inappropriately titled) and continued in 1997 with *The Subtle Knife*. The collective title of the series is *His Dark Materials*, and it clearly marks Pullman as a masterful maker of secondary worlds. Looking at Pullman's distinguished career as a writer of children's books, one would not have expected an achievement like this. His series of mysteries set in Victorian London (the Sally Lockhart books) and his comic fantasy-adventure tales for younger children (*I Was a Rat!, Count Karlstein*) are much and rightly admired, but none of these even approaches the scope and ambition of *His Dark Materials*. Indeed, almost the only themes that would connect these powerful novels with Pullman's earlier work are a predilection for female protagonists and a sentimental genuflection before the mystery of adolescent sexual awakening. In other respects *His Dark Materials* seems to come out of nowhere — but readers and critics alike have recognized the scale of Pullman's new exploit. The previous books in the series have reaped almost every award available to them, including England's Carnegie Medal and places on the "best of year" lists offered by *Publishers Weekly*, *Booklist*, and the American Library Association. Further, the readers' reports on amazon.com — always a vivid source of information about real readers — run into the hundreds and are almost uniformly adulatory. Clearly these books are on their way to commanding the kind of praise and devotion reserved for classics of the genre.

Like many fantasies, Pullman's trilogy is theologically freighted, but his project is a distinctively and explicitly *anti*-theological one. The phrase "his dark materials" comes from Milton's *Paradise Lost*, and early in *The Golden Compass* the reader can already see that Pullman is retelling that great epic and, by extension, the Biblical narrative on which Milton's work is based. In these dazzling novels Pullman is making a Creation story in which the familiar roles are reversed. If, as William Blake famously said, "Milton was of the Devil's Party without knowing it," Pullman knows perfectly well whose side *he's* on.

Whatever party the reader supports in this ancient contest, it is deeply disappointing to see how often, in *The Amber Spyglass*, the tale's momentum is interrupted by politico-theological polemic. Pullman's anti-theistic scolding consorts poorly with his prodigious skills as a storyteller. For in imaginative potency and narrative drive he has few peers among current novelists. *His Dark Materials* is an extraordinarily powerful story, filled with scenes that I will remember for years; some moments indeed I am likely never to forget. For such gifts to be thrust so forcibly into the service of a reductive and contemptuous ideology is very nearly a tragedy.

2.

His Dark Materials is a story of multiple worlds. The first volume takes place wholly in a universe similar to, but in crucial ways very different from, our own. The plot is driven, at first, by its heroine Lyra Belacqua's attempt to discover who is kidnapping poor and neglected children in England, including her own dear friend Roger; but as Lyra's quest continues ever-deeper levels of meaning are revealed, until we learn the titanic role that this girl, an orphan herself, will play: she has, one character says, "a great destiny that can only be fulfilled elsewhere — not in this world, but far beyond. Without this child, we shall all die." In the second book, set partly in our own world, we are introduced to a determined and resourceful, but troubled, boy named Will, whose ability to wield the "subtle knife" makes him the apt partner for Lyra, whose story he joins. In *The Amber Spyglass* the strands of the plot converge: the fates of many worlds depend upon the outcome of a prodigious battle, a War in Heaven, a universal Armageddon.

Pullman's brilliance makes itself known from the first sentence of *The Golden Compass*: "Lyra and her daemon moved through the darkening hall, taking care to keep to one side, out of sight of the kitchen." In Lyra's world each person is accompanied by a lifelong companion in the form of an animal; this daemon is a kind of material projection of one's character, and since a child's character is not fully formed, children's daemons are capable of changing shape. Puberty, then, involves not only hormonal change but also the "settling" of one's daemon into its permanent form. The daemons play a vital role in the story, and Pullman brilliantly exploits the strange appropriateness of his invention. He has found a potent way to embody a human dilemma which adolescents feel particularly strongly: we fear being alone, but dread still more the uncomprehending or disapproving gaze of others. In these novels, the perfectly companionable daemons are always a comfort, never a burden.

But Pullman's resourcefulness scarcely ends there. There are the *panserbjørne*, the sentient, inscrutable Arctic bears with their magnificent self-forged armor (their king, Iorek Byrnison, is one of the most memorable characters in the book); the lovingly rendered culture of the "gyptians," or gypsies as we would have it; Lyra's alethiometer, the marvelously intricate "symbol reader" which she uses to acquire almost any knowledge she seeks; and the "subtle knife" used by Will, whose infinitely sharp blade can cut anything — literally *anything* — and whose blunter edge opens windows into an infinity of worlds. It is hard to think of another fantasist whose invention is so prodigious: classic writers like Tolkien, and the currently celebrated Joanne Rowling, work with more conventional iconographies; Pullman is another kind of writer altogether.

Yet he too draws constantly on literary traditions. In addition to the Genesis narrative, his story often echoes classic texts: for instance, Lyra and Will's truly harrowing descent into Hell, which largely fulfills their joint quest and constitutes the key episode of the entire trilogy, pays due homage to previous treatments of the theme, from Homer to Virgil to Dante — with a fascinating variation based on another terrifying (but non-infernal) masterpiece, Aeschylus' *The Eumenides.*

One of the most interesting things about this episode, which occupies several chapters of *The Amber Spyglass,* is its occasional echoes of C. S. Lewis's *The Great Divorce* — interesting because Pullman utterly loathes Lewis. He has called the Chronicles of Narnia "one of the most ugly and poisonous things I've ever read," with "no shortage of . . . nauseating drivel," and has identified himself with those "who detest the supernaturalism, the reactionary sneering, the misogyny, the racism, and the sheer dishonesty of [Lewis's] narrative method." So the echoes of Lewis are revisionary gestures, given Pullman's hatred not only of Lewis but also of the Christianity which Lewis represents. This hatred becomes central (all too central) to the development of Pullman's story.

3.

In the early pages of *The Amber Spyglass,* two angels named Baruch and Balthamos explain to Will certain decisive events from the origin of the cosmos:

> The Authority, God, the Creator, the Lord, Yahweh, El, Adonai, the King, the Father, the Almighty — those were all names he gave himself.

He was never the creator. He was an angel like ourselves — the first angel, true, the most powerful, but he was formed of Dust as we are, and Dust is only a name for what happens when matter begins to understand itself. . . . The first angels condensed out of Dust, and the Authority was the first of all. He told those who came after him that he had created them, but it was a lie. One of those who came later was wiser than he was, and she found out the truth, so he banished her. We serve her still. And the Authority still reigns in the Kingdom. . . .

("The question of Dust," as it is sometimes called here, is too complicated to explain in this context. Suffice it to say that Dust is the embodiment in particulate form of *either* Original Sin *or* the creative energy of humanity.) This is religious polemic disguised as explanation, but the polemic appears undisguised often enough: in *The Subtle Knife* we hear a witch — and the witches in these books are almost unimaginably virtuous — proclaim that "every church is the same: control, destroy, obliterate every good feeling." In *The Amber Spyglass* Xaphania, the angel whom Baruch and Balthamos serve, tells a woman named Mary that "she and the rebel angels, the followers of wisdom, have always tried to open minds; and Authority and his churches have always tried to keep them closed." Mary, a former Christian, seems generous by contrast when she offers a merely condescending verdict: "The Christian religion is a very powerful and convincing mistake, that's all."

To understand further the nature of Pullman's assault on Christianity, we need to recognize that the rebel angels' Creation story is not Pullman's invention: it closely resembles the one that Milton's Satan tells, in response to the seraph Abdiel's invocation of God's creative power, in Book V of *Paradise Lost*:

We know no time when we were not as now;
Know none before us, self-begot, self-raised
By our own quickening power, when fatal course
Had circled his full orb, the birth mature
Of this our native heaven, ethereal sons.
Our puissance is our own, our own right hand

Shall teach us highest deeds, by proof to try
Who is our equal: then thou shalt behold
Whether by supplication we intend
Address, and to begirt the almighty throne
Beseeching or besieging. This report,
These tidings carry to the anointed king.

In other words, Satan believes that Creation was determined by some impersonal principle of destiny ("fatal course") — just as Pullman's rebel angels contend that Dust inexplicably "condensed" into the personal beings of angels. God holds his throne, Satan says elsewhere in Milton's poem, only by the "thunder" which has made him greater than those who are by birth and rank his peers. There is no question, then, of eternal Right of sovereignty, so Satan's debate is a purely strategic one: whether to "beseech" or "besiege" the Authority in his Kingdom. Eventually, of course, he chooses war and loses, after which, unwilling to submit, he finds a third course, to be pursued on Earth rather than in Heaven: deception, "guile" rather than "force." From this new strategy results the temptation in Eden, and the subsequent history of pain and brokenness with which we are all too familiar.

It is widely thought that the book of Revelation envisions a final battle yet to come between the old antagonists, perhaps on the plain of Megiddo, or Armageddon, and Pullman tells a version of that story too, thus extending his narrative from Creation to Apocalypse. The aforementioned Lord Asriel chooses to besiege: he initiates another War in Heaven, marshaling a vast army of mortal and immortal troops to assault the forces of the Authority and his Regent, the rather dubiously named Metatron. I have called Asriel a Satanic hero, and he proves his fitness for the role by repeatedly announcing his determination to "break free" of the Authority's tyranny, for the good of himself and all humanity. He exploits the whole rhetorical apparatus of the self-proclaimed Liberator, and it is not clear that Pullman realizes how much Asriel sounds like all the other Liberators, from Robespierre to Stalin.

The first step in Asriel's war is the building of a bridge between the worlds, which was also the first task of Milton's Satan. (The scene from

Paradise Lost in which *his* bridge-building is described gives Pullman the title and epigraph to his trilogy.) Ultimately Asriel re-enacts Satan's voyage, but not to become the familiar serpent: Pullman divides the Satanic role and gives the task of temptation — or, as he would have it, intellectual and moral liberation — to the pleasant and innocuous Mary. She is a former postulant in a convent and now a scientist, converted from Christianity to a vague neo-paganism by the attractions of a single all-too-pleasant evening on the Mediterranean, and is clearly supposed to receive our full sympathy. Meanwhile Asriel engages in dubious battle with the Almighty's army.

This great War is one of the least successful parts of the trilogy. For some reason, Pullman's narrative energy flags markedly here: at a crucial moment in the battle, it's not even very clear what's happening; only later was I sure who had died and how. And what I can only call the ultimate anti-theological moment towards which the whole narrative has seemed to be heading is passed over in a few lines, after which the characters involved turn to other things that more greatly interest them. I suspect that Pullman does this deliberately, in order to make the *truly* anti-theological point that whether God lives or dies is not in the long run a very significant matter: at one point Mrs. Coulter suggests that we could best prove our love for a decrepit God by "seek[ing] him out and giv[ing] him the gift of death." But even if this is intentional it's still a problem: a writer who draws for a thousand pages on the narrative energy generated by the promise of Armageddon, only to toss the theme aside at the last moment, has not exercised good judgment. This reader feels cheated.

By this point in the story Pullman the storyteller has also been cheated — by Pullman the village atheist. Powerful alternative versions of the Biblical narrative can only be told by people who are themselves passionately theological: Pullman invokes Milton and Blake as his models, but he could scarcely be less like either. Pullman's oft-professed materialism and anti-supernaturalism clash not only with Milton but still more with the great London magus of the following century who, when he looked at the sun, saw not "a round disk about the size of a guinea" but rather "a multitude of the heavenly host crying Holy, Holy, Holy is the Lord God Almighty." In his attempts to diminish God Pullman diminishes his own story: when the Regent of the Almighty, "a being whose profound intellect had had thousands of years to deepen and strengthen itself, and whose knowledge extended over a million universes," is instantly ruined because he can't resist a seductive babe, or when Asriel attacks the Deity with some sort of hovercraft straight out of *Star Wars*, one contemplates absurdity, but not that of Christian doctrine.

Again and again Pullman's mocking of religious belief gets him into aesthetic and moral trouble. There is a bitter irony in Pullman calling Lewis's narrative method "dishonest," because dishonesty is perhaps the signal moral trait of Pullman's trilogy. For instance: one sees a number of unequivocally evil people in these books, and one sees a number of Christians. These are always — *always* — the same people. Everyone associated with the Church is cruel, remorseless, and only rarely less than murderous. Conversely, everyone outside the Church's scope is blindingly righteous, Lord Asriel being the only partial exception. (And his most indefensible deed proves to be the cause, however inadvertent, of — in the narrative's terms — an immeasurably great thing.) And these decent, compassionate folk regularly utter their denunciations of religion and God, while the monsters who run the Church utter scarcely a word in their own defense — just to make sure that no reader comes to a conclusion Pullman doesn't want.

These pronouncements of anathema are almost comically overt, but Pullman also employs a more insidious method, one which becomes available to him through the multiple-worlds device. In *The Amber Spyglass*, Mrs. Coulter says of the Church, "Killing is not difficult for them; Calvin himself ordered the deaths of children" — upon reading which I said to myself, No he didn't! But then I remembered that Mrs. Coulter and her audience are from Lyra's world, and in Lyra's world the Reformation took a different course, as can be inferred from a reference in the first book to "Pope John Calvin" and his decision to move the papal seat to Geneva. I don't know whether Pullman believes that John Calvin ordered the deaths of children, but if I were to challenge him on that point he could merely reply that Calvin did just that in Lyra's world. This is a nice trick: other universes thus become places where Pullman's enemies can be made to do any imaginable evil, so that he can better justify his hatred of them. Meanwhile, who knows how many readers go away from this book believing that John Calvin massacred innocents with the calloused enthusiasm of King Herod?

Omission serves Pullman's purposes as well. In the whole trilogy he refers just once, I believe, to Jesus Christ: after all, his teachings, character, and influence do not fit very well with the picture of Christianity Pullman wants his readers to have. And how many people, especially young people, know enough about Christian doctrine or the Biblical narrative to realize just how deceptive Pullman's treatment is? How many will know, for instance, that the sin of Adam and Eve had nothing to do with their love for each other, or even with sexuality, despite Pullman's contentions in *The Amber Spyglass* that the Authority wants a world of ice-cold celibates and that erotic love is a form of rebellious creativity?

But Pullman soldiers doggedly on in his dismal campaign. His Deity doesn't even reward his servants, but rather condemns all the souls who have ever lived to a horrifically vacuous underworld (very like the one that Odysseus visits in Homer's *Odyssey*). Pullman, unlike this Authority, proposes to save these souls — whose agony he powerfully describes — by annihilating them. Some readers may protest that annihilation is a poor sort of salvation, but Pullman, anticipating this criticism, portrays his characters' obliteration as a kind of joyous merging with the Cosmos: he even says of one character that the "atoms of his beloved" were waiting for him when he disintegrated.

Now this is the very height of narrative fraudulence. If I am vaporized to atoms, there is no longer an "I" to be rejoined with any equally nonexistent beloved. Atoms are just atoms, and if that's how we end, let's not prettify it with misty-eyed descriptions of children expiring in a "vivid little burst of happiness [like] the bubbles in a glass of champagne." In the end Pullman shies from the implications of his premises; he gilds the dark truth which he prides himself on being brave enough to face. Such gilding fits with Pullman's general disregard for truthfulness: his heroine Lyra, though virtually everyone she meets calls her "innocent," almost always saves the day with lies, and if in this final installment of the story her lies finally get her into trouble, the lesson is certainly not that lying doesn't pay but rather that lying doesn't *always* pay: there *may* be times when truthfulness is prudent, and discernment consists in identifying those (apparently rare) occasions when straightforwardness serves your purposes better than deception. Pullman shouldn't accuse anyone else of dishonesty.

4.

If Christianity, and religion more generally, are what Pullman is against, what does he stand *for*? Well, he's in favor of open minds and against closed ones; he thinks that when people have to choose between God and love — as, he thinks, we all must — they should choose love. Certain events near the end of the story suggest that positive energy in the world (Dust) is produced not just by our loving one another but by specifically erotic love. Mary, that admirable tempter, asserts that "all we can say is that this is a good deed, because it helps someone, or that's an evil one, because it hurts them." One could illustrate the positive component of Pullman's moral vision merely by quoting from Beatles songs.

But then there is the bright, shining, explicitly *political* vision that emerges near the end of this trilogy. Cue the violins for King Ogunwe's speech:

> Mrs. Coulter, I am a king, but it's my proudest task to join Lord Asriel in setting up a world where there are no kingdoms at all. No kings, no bishops, no priests. The Kingdom of Heaven has been known by that name since the Authority first set himself above the rest of the angels. And we want no part of it. This world is different. We intend to be free citizens of the Republic of Heaven.

I suppose as an American I should resonate with this — to help me, Pullman prefaces this novel with an apocalyptic epigraph from Blake's "America: A Prophecy," and of course there is sympathy for anyone facing the prospect of Prince Charles as monarch — but I don't. Politics and morals would be simple if the genuine and manifold abuses of authority could be rectified by the elimination of authority. But of course that's not what a republic is: republics have authorities too, and the rule of law. Without at least *that* governance we have, as Hobbes in his cruel clear-sightedness foresaw, something very different than a triumphant War in Heaven: the endless "war of every man against every man." Pullman certainly would not desire such a thing, and would be genuinely shocked if his vision, once realized, bore such bitter fruit. But in the light of the last two centuries — in *our* world, that is, whose history is not to be neglected in the creation of alternate universes for one's enemies to be cruel in — he has no excuse for being shocked.

Ultimately the flaw that cripples Pullman's ambitious tale is just this unwillingness to reckon with European history since the Age of Revolution. He renews the splendid anti-authoritarian rhetoric of that era without acknowledging the complexities of a world in which neither all Authorities nor all Revolutionaries are the same, and in which even the best-intentioned rebels can see their lovely plans turn foul. For Pullman, Blake is the *terminus ad quem* of history: he positions himself and his readers in that wonderful moment of imminent hope, before anyone could see, in the cold light of the morning after, the tangled consequences of even the most principled revolutions.

It is this refusal of historical understanding that leads to the simplistic Manicheanism of Pullman's moral world: closed versus open minds, tyrants versus liberators, the vicious Church versus its righteous opponents. It is hard not to be reminded of Robespierre's famous dictum: "There are only two parties in France, that of corrupt men and that of virtuous men." (Late in Pullman's story Mary says that "people are too complicated to have simple labels." Apparently Christians are simply not "people.") And such crudity cannot be excused by the purported audience of these books: novels for young people, even more than others, should avoid such ostentatious haranguing of their readers. Moreover, adolescents already spend too much time separating the sheep from the goats — the cool from the uncool, the socially approved from the socially ostracized; they certainly need no encouragement to practice binary division. A writer who tells young people that good folks are so readily distinguished from evil ones, and on the single criterion of religious belief, is not doing them any favors.

In the end, it's impossible to say whether the luminously gifted Philip Pullman tells this kind of story because he wants to provide his young readers a pragmatic template for evaluating the people they meet, or because he really believes it. In either case, a work so imaginatively potent will surely inspire the kind of loyalty we have seen given to the secondary worlds of Tolkien and the other great fantasists. But I hope the Pullman devotees will not overlook the deception that, in one form or another, lurks at the heart of his beautiful yet ultimately misbegotten endeavor: "the rhetorician would deceive his neighbours," as Yeats said, "the sentimentalist himself."

The Re-Invention of Love

Anne Carson's translation of the poetry of Sappho (under the title *If Not, Winter*) seems an act of veneration. Sappho is the most archaic and mysterious, and probably the most celebrated, of ancient lyric poets; later Greeks would call her the "tenth Muse." She lived in the seventh and sixth centuries B.C. on the island of Lesbos, off the coast of Asia Minor, not far south of Troy. Most of her poems, which were always set to music, describe erotic passion and its consequences; many of those poems concern desire for other women. There is a legend that Sappho, desperately in (unrequited) love with the "most beautiful of men," a dashing sailor named Phaon, threw herself from the cliff of Leukas, on which stood a temple to Apollo, though the great Byzantine scholar Photios claims that this happened to "another Lesbian woman" named Sappho, not the poet. Various sources supply her with various family members, including a husband and children; one of those sources says she was short, dark, and "most ill-favored."

These are tiny shards of data, and no one will ever know whether they offer us knowledge. Similar doubts haunt Sappho's very language: in one of the poems, for instance, Sappho uses a puzzling word that, Carson tells us, is elucidated by a lexicographer named Pollux: "a word *beudos* found in Sappho is the same as the word *kimberikon* which means a short transparent dress." Undoubtedly any translator or editor is thankful for Pollux's help, sufficiently so, perhaps, to refrain from wondering how trustworthy this claim is, given that the scholar worked some eight hundred years after Sappho and hundreds of miles from Lesbos, in Egypt. And the music Sappho wrote, and to which she set her verses, has been wholly and irretrievably lost.

The poems themselves, moreover, survive chiefly in fragments, and strangely enough — or so I contend — their shreds and patches contribute to their fascination, and to the reverence which I have identified as a feature of Carson's edition. If this is true of a single word like *beudos* — "Who would not like to know more about this garment?" asks Carson — it is still more true of a "poem" that looks like this:

]bitter
]
]and know this

]whatever you
]I shall love
]

]for
]of weapons
]

Carson uses brackets to indicate tears or defacements of the papyrus on which some words have survived. She does not do this systematically, since "this would render the page a blizzard of marks and inhibit reading"; rather, the brackets couple with the words to create a kind of frame for speculation. To "read" a fragment like the above is, inevitably, to fill the gaps, to complete the weave, to make rather than receive a narrative — in the same way that your brain fills in that portion of the visual field left empty by your blind spots. ("Brackets are exciting," writes Carson. "Even though you are approaching Sappho in translation, that is no reason you should miss the drama of trying to read a papyrus torn in half or riddled with holes or smaller than a postage stamp — brackets imply a free space of imaginal adventure.") Carson shows her artfulness nowhere more than in her delicate deployment of these brackets, which lead us so quietly from the abiding love to the weapons. There's a kind of Zen to it.

The other sort of Sapphonian fragment — the line or two cited by later writers — does not offer Carson, or us, the same "free space of imaginal adventure." In these cases we cannot know what sort of poem the line appeared in, how long the poem was, anything:

having come from heaven wrapped in a purple cloak

goes one such line;

do I still yearn for my virginity

goes another one, and no one will ever tell us who descended in that cloak, or whom we overhear meditating on her lost virginity. So, lacking context, even the limited context provided by the papyrus scraps, Carson offers what she can: white space. Each of those lines is given its own page, and this alone contributes to the sense of veneration I have noted — as though these brief phrases carry as much freighted meaning as an ordinary page stuffed full of words. Such lines appear on the book's right-hand pages; on the left is the original Greek, printed in a beautiful blood-red ink. (The same red is used in the book's apparatus for section headings, notes, title pages, and so on.) Given the spareness of the text, it is good to note that the paper itself is good stock, faintly beige in color, thick and rough-cut. The book comprises 397 pages, but easily could have been fewer than a hundred; without the Greek, fewer than fifty.

Reverence indeed. How to account for it? Perhaps by looking more closely at the work of Anne Carson, who, the book's jacket tells us simply and flatly, as though discouraging further inquiry, "lives in Canada." It is possible to learn more: for instance, that Carson taught classics at McGill University in Montreal until her recent move to the University of Michigan, and that she has published several books of verse and prose, the first of which was called *Eros the Bittersweet* (1986) and began with a discussion of Sappho's compound coinage *glukupikron*, literally "sweetbitter." ("Eros the melter of limbs [now again] stirs me — /sweetbitter unmanageable

creature who steals in"; so Carson renders the fragment in *If Not, Winter*.)
One does not have to browse for long in Carson's books before discovering that eros is her great preoccupation, and that she repeatedly takes fragments of ancient erotic poetry and filters them through a contemporary sensibility. In *Plainwater* she takes pieces of Sappho's contemporary Mimnermos and sculpts them into something that can seem very like a translation until it invokes a memory of a hotel in Chicago. Likewise, in *Autobiography of Red*, a retelling and expansion of the fragmentary *Geryoneis* of Stesichoros, she seems to begin with straightforward translation of some of the pieces, only to lead us to this:

> If you persist in wearing your mask at the supper table
> Well Goodnight Then they said and drove him up
> Those hemorrhaging stairs to the hot dry Arms
> To the ticking red taxi of the incubus
> Don't want to go want to stay Downstairs and read

All of which presages Carson's transformation of the red, winged monster Geryon — slain by Herakles in the midst of his famous Labors — into a fairly normal, if homosexual, North American teenager. Who remains, nonetheless, red and winged. "The fragments of the *Geryoneis* read as if Stesichoros had composed a substantial narrative then ripped it to pieces," writes Carson; clearly, she finds great pleasure in reassembling the pieces, and at least some of that pleasure comes from not knowing whether her edifice bears much resemblance to what Stesichoros had composed. Carson's reputation as a scholar seems quite high, but in passages like these (and many others) she seems to be winking at scholarship, or at what we normally take to be scholarship. And the wink has a certain piquancy when offered by someone who has undergone the disciplinary rigors of training in the classics; English professors and literary theorists, by contrast, froze their faces into such a wink so long ago that the expression is no longer recognizable. People just think we're scowling.

Carson obviously cares less for the strictures of scholarly knowledge than for the power of scholarship to liberate ancient texts for our uses and purposes today. But what *are* "our uses and purposes today"? Carson, it seems to me, is one of the most gifted and articulate writers to participate in a curious project, a project that might be called (with apologies to Tom Stoppard) the re-invention of love: an attempt to reject a model of erotic experience that is generally called "romantic love." and is often thought to have some connection with Christianity. That Western literature and culture, from at least the twelfth century on, engaged in a more-or-less purposeful conflation of *eros* and *agape* — romantic or sexual love and holy love — has always been recognized, but it was in the 1930s that this conflation became the subject of widespread scholarly notice and even a kind of consensus. (I cannot explain this convergence of attention.) Anders Nygren's *Agape and Eros* (1930), C. S. Lewis's *The Allegory of Love* (1936), and Denis de Rougemont's *Love in the Western World* (1938) each explored the entanglements of divine and sexual love; each, to some degree at least, though not for uniform reasons, deplored the entanglements; each seemed to see the entanglements as permanent features of, well, love in the Western world. Lovers have learned to pay tribute to the beloved — elevation, adoration, worship — that properly belongs only to God. They have come to see the encounter with the beloved as a fertile field where meaning and value, even ultimate meaning and value, can be cultivated. How can such lessons be unlearned, such knots untangled?

Carson and many others have devoted much scrutiny to the possibility of un-knotting. The romantic picture of love seems to them too metaphysical, too drenched in the "spiritual," and for that very reason inattentive to the *physiology* of desire, its residence in the body. Casting about for an alternative to the romantic synthesis, they follow the example of Nietzsche and seek in archaic (especially pre-Socratic) Greek thought and art a thoroughly physical — and therefore a thoroughly demystified, disenchanted — account of erotic experience. Nietzsche himself, I should add, never really extended his "revaluation of all values" into the sexual sphere; he was, for reasons both personal and philosophical, too prudish or ascetic for that; but in the twentieth century he found adventurous disciples. They are not necessarily the people one would expect: many of the century's most famous apostles of sexuality, from Freud to D. H. Lawrence, retain many of the core beliefs of the old romantic synthesis. Indeed, it would be late in the century before the project of re-inventing love got seriously under way.* I discern two exemplary figures in this endeavor — two rarely linked with each other: Michel Foucault and Iris Murdoch.

We typically think of Foucault as a master of suspicion, a subverter of all trust, a reducer of all relations to power relations; Murdoch, by contrast, in large part because she wrote large, technically conventional novels instead of tortured academic treatises, seems to belong to a wholly different culture. And in some respects this is true. But on the matter of eros Foucault and Murdoch are kindred spirits. For both of them eros is a powerful force with which we must find some way to negotiate; it is always threatening to engulf us, and this is naturally frightening, yet there is something strangely desirable about being engulfed. Thus, in Murdoch's last major novel, *The Green Knight*, a young woman muses:

> . . . he will never forgive me, he will despise me and cast me out, he warned me against the ambiguous Eros, the deceiver, the magician, the sophist, the maker of drugs and potions. Of course I am in love, yes, this *is* love, and I am *sick* with it — but what follows? Do I really believe that I shall give over my life, the whole of my life, which is only just now *really beginning* to another person? . . . What has happened to my soldierly completeness with which I was so content, my satisfaction and my pride? At the first trial I am broken.

Murdoch seems never to tire of depicting the person who is thus swept away; and she is equally tireless in delineating the opposite number, the magician, who deploys the potions of eros to control the object of his desire.

It is just this kind of situation that Foucault has in mind when he says — in a formulation both literal and metaphorical — that "sexual relations are not reciprocal: in sexual relations, you can penetrate or you are penetrated." And when eros is so described, pleasure inevitably recedes from consciousness, to be replaced by a ceaseless meditation on power. Thus,

---

*Stoppard's wonderful play *The Invention of Love* tells a different version of this story, featuring the late-Victorian poet A. E. Housman and, instead of Greek sources, Latin love elegists like Catullus and Horace. I consider my story a complement rather than an alternative to his.

in 1983, when he was in the midst of writing his multi-volume *History of Sexuality* — but, as he knew, also dying and therefore unlikely to finish the work — Foucault announced to an interviewer that "sex is boring." The real point of interest, he had discovered, lay in "techniques of the self," because these techniques enable one to manage the traffic patterns of erotic power: when and how to penetrate, when and how to be penetrated. Even the refusal of sex — in the Christian tradition a practice linked with the pursuit of righteousness — is reconstituted here as nonmoral "technique," an ascetic enterprise in the service of one's own personal therapeutic aims: chastity for control freaks. And in this exploration of technique Foucault attended chiefly to the example of ancient Athens — as did Murdoch for her purposes. She even wrote a lengthy dialogue in the Platonic mode, featuring Socrates, Plato, and others as characters; she called it "Art and Eros."

It is this (new) tradition in which Carson works; thus her veneration of Sappho. Consider three quotations from *Eros the Bittersweet:*

Eros seemed to Sappho at once an experience of pleasure and of pain.

Eros moves or creeps upon its victim from somewhere outside her: *orpeton.* No battle avails to fight off that advance: *amachanon.* Desire, then, is neither inhabitant nor ally of the desirer. Foreign to her will, it forces itself irresistibly upon her from without. Eros is an enemy. Its bitterness must be the taste of enmity. That would be hate. . . . love and hate construct between them the machinery of human contact. Does it make sense to locate both poles of this affect within the single emotional event of eros? Presumably, yes, if friend and enemy converge in the being who is its occasion.*

[In describing this experience] Sappho and her successors in general prefer physiology to concepts.

---

*The Greek words here are from the fragment quoted earlier about "Eros the melter of limbs" (number 130): eros "steals in" *(orpeton)* from somewhere outside and is "unmanageable" *(amachanon).*

In these few words the post-Nietzschean, or neopagan, erotic is neatly encapsulated. First, and perhaps most centrally, eros is an "experience": that is, it occurs *within* me. I discern its character by attending to the testimony of my senses, my body: here I find pleasure, there I find pain. (Thus, physiology rather than concepts.) Moreover, it is this experience itself that must be reckoned with; assessed; treated as friend or enemy, or as both in alternation.

When confronted with this picture, one schooled in what I have termed the romantic synthesis will have a pointed question: Where is the beloved? And the answer can only be that the beloved matters little to this neopagan sensibility: "the beloved" is merely the incidental provocation of desire — not even truly the "occasion" of the "single emotional event," eros itself (says Carson) being that occasion. What the romantic would call the beloved remains wholly outside me; it is eros that "steals in" and occupies my body, eros that I must respond to and deal with — and therefore eros itself that is truly the beloved; when it is not the enemy.

"No simple map of the emotions is available here," writes Carson in *Eros the Bittersweet*. "Desire is not simple." Perhaps; yet desire is simpler than romantic love, and the model offered by Carson (and Foucault, and Murdoch) limits complexity — as demystification and disenchantment always do. (The rigid and universal formula of disenchantment: x is *only* y.) In the neopagan model, love is bound to a limited repertoire of experiences: pleasure and pain, desire and fear, possessing and being possessed, frustration and satisfaction. Perhaps these interior incidents are sufficiently numerous to make any "simple map of the emotions" impossible, but a skilled cartographer could get it all on one page. The complexity of the romantic synthesis, by contrast, would fill a library, just because of the presence in its calculations of another person, with his or her own pleasures and pains, desires and fears. (There is a moment in the interview with Foucault I cited earlier that would be funny if it were not so sad. Near the end of his life, obsessed with his project of self-technique, he pauses to ask this question: "Is the pleasure of the other something which can be integrated in our pleasure?" The merest possibility of reciprocity, of something other than penetrating and being penetrated, finally occurs to this brilliant man, but only when he is too near death to think further. He can but leave it as another avenue of research unpursued.) If one has true regard for one's beloved, and wishes above all — even above the satisfaction of one's desires — the beloved's well-being, complexity increases geometrically, not arithmetically. Every possibility must be considered, even renunciation, and renunciation not for one's own ascetic good: rather, what must be considered is the voluntary abandonment of hopes for marriage, for life together — if that would be best for the beloved. It has been done. As many tales relate.

Carson seems, not only in her translation and her scholarship but even in her poetry, to decline such complications. In her poem "The Glass Essay" (and all of Carson's poems are essays) she writes of a mother's reaction to her daughter's new lover:

Well he's a taker and you're a giver I hope it works out,
was all she said after she met him.
Give and take were just words to me

at the time. I had not been in love before.
It was like a wheel rolling downhill.

The experience detaches from the person who (one might think) prompted it and rolls away, taking the speaker's volition with it. Well, many of us have been there; but I doubt the *sufficiency* of the image to the experience of love. More disturbing is Carson's account of the failure of a marriage in her book *The Beauty of the Husband:*

Loyal to nothing
my husband. So why did I love him from early girlhood to late middle age
and the divorce decree came in the mail?
Beauty. No great secret. Not ashamed to say I loved him for his beauty.
As I would again
if he came near. Beauty convinces. You know beauty makes sex possible.
Beauty makes sex sex.

Again a detachment: this time not of experience from persons, but rather of a trait — a strictly *physical* trait — from the one to whom, in ordinary language, we would say it belongs. Not "the beautiful husband" but "the beauty of the husband": the beauty is not intrinsic to him; rather, he carries it about like an amulet or charm. And it's this amulet that convinces, that makes sex possible, that makes sex sex. The bearer of the amulet has nothing to do with it; the husband stands to one side, bemused or indifferent or whatever he is, and observes the wife's desperate wrestle with eros, her friend, her enemy. Eventually he rolls away, like a wheel down a hill.

For Carson, Sappho is the *fons et origo* of this model of love, love as eros only. Is that fair to Sappho? I don't know. Certainly the fragments delineate the moods and motions of desire; certainly Sappho is deeply attentive to eros as experience. Yet there are passages which seem also attentive to the desired one — seem, I say, because I have only fragments to draw on, and my knowledge of Greek scarcely exceeds the ability to recite that language's alphabet. In the end I cannot contest Carson's uses of Sappho; I can but suggest that the fragmentary character of the poems renders them open to many uses; and then I can turn to another model from the ancient world.

Regard for the beloved was not invented by the troubadours of twelfth-century Provence, nor by the forgotten makers of the story of Tristan and Isolde. It may be found in a poem probably older than any of Sappho's: the Song of Songs, which is Solomon's. This poem matches any of Sappho's in its evocation of the power of desire: "Eat, friends, drink, and be drunk with love" (5:1 NRSV). But there is something more:

Set me as a seal upon your heart,
    as a seal upon your arm;
for love is strong as death,
    passion fierce as the grave.
Its flashes are flashes of fire,
    a raging flame.
Many waters cannot quench love,
    neither can floods drown it.

If one offered for love
    all the wealth of one's house
    it would be utterly scorned.

What is "more" is the affirmation of permanence, of the deathlessness of true love. Eros, by contrast, is famously flighty; the desire that overmasters you one day can evaporate the next. Sappho's one surviving complete poem asks Aphrodite to change the inclination of some desired one, to turn her heart towards Sappho, and Aphrodite agrees:

For if she flees, soon she will pursue.
If she refuses gifts, rather will she give them.
If she does not love, soon she will love
    even unwilling.

But this answer reveals that if the desired one changes, so too will Sappho: her desire will be gone; she will flee from the one who has fled from her. It's the way of the world, surely, and accepted as such by Sappho and Aphrodite alike; but in Solomon's Song we are repeatedly warned against the reckless invocation of a power greater than that of mere desire:

I adjure you, O daughters of Jerusalem,
    do not stir up or awaken love
    until it is ready! (8:4 etc.)

And why should the daughters of Jerusalem be so circumspect? Because if it is the true Love that is awakened, it will not again sleep; and no floods can wash it away. And — continuing the catechism — why is that? Why will this love not sleep, nor be washed away?

    Because it is grounded not in desire, not in eros, not in any "experience," but in the beloved (a word I have used in this essay with Solomon's song always in mind): in the bride herself, or the bridegroom himself. Love is the proper and adequate response to the excellence of the beloved. "We will exult and rejoice in you," say the daughters of Jerusalem to the bride: "rightly do they love you" (1:4) — *rightly.* When she tells them to find her beloved and tell him that she is "faint with love," they reply with a question:

> What is your beloved more than another beloved,
>   O fairest among women?
> What is your beloved more than another beloved,
>   that you thus adjure us? (5:9)

And the bride can answer, with more than the simile of a wheel rolling downhill, and with more than a claim for his beauty — though beauty there is, beauty there certainly is: he is "distinguished among ten thousand" (v. 10); "he is altogether desirable" (v. 16a). But above all, "This is my beloved and this is my *friend*, O daughters of Jerusalem." Friendship implies a kind of reciprocity — even Foucault acknowledges this idea — alien to the understanding of Eros that Carson derives from Sappho: as we have seen, the great plea to Aphrodite simply *assumes* that desire will be unequal and asymmetrical. But it is reciprocity in which the bride places her trust; her limitless regard for the bridegroom is matched by his limitless regard for her; and so she can tell the daughters of Jerusalem with perfect assurance, "I am my beloved's and my beloved is mine" (6:3).

In this poem, then — which rises from a culture as alien to ours as Sappho's, and which is perhaps still freer from metaphysics than any of her poems (I share Dietrich Bonhoeffer's belief that the interpretation of it as an "ordinary love song" is the most "Christological exposition") — we find a richer, more complex model for erotic relationship than anything contemplated by Carson or Foucault or Murdoch or, as far as I can tell, Sappho. Long before the romantic synthesis was dreamed of, we find in Solomon's song a more fully *human* picture of the love between man and woman, a more stately yet more joyous picture, than anything made available by the trifling arithmetic of desire. No wonder Foucault came to believe that "sex is boring." It certainly becomes so, when there are so few counters to play with. "I will do anything to avoid boredom. It is the task of a lifetime," Anne Carson once wrote, but I wonder if, in taking hold of the neopagan model of eros, she has not courted the very boredom from which she would flee.

Sappho too wrote about marriage, about the joy of marriage:

blest bridegroom, your marriage just as you prayed
has been accomplished
        and you have the bride for whom you prayed

It seems sad to me that she wrote such lines for others, while for herself lines of longing and loss. But then, I do not understand Sappho; in the end, all I have to guide me are these poor fragments. If I held the unredacted papyri in my palm, I could pour them on the table in a snow of archaic confetti. It seems so little from which to sculpt a way of love, a way of life.

part 3

EXPERIMENT

Computer Control (the Virtues of Resistance)

FIRST STAGE

1.

In 1986 a musician, composer, and computer programmer named Laurie Spiegel used her Macintosh to produce the first version of an application she called Music Mouse. Music Mouse is not easy to describe, but, in Spiegel's own account, it works like this: "It lets you use the computer itself as a musical instrument, played by moving the mouse with one hand while you control dozens of available musical parameters from the Mac's 'qwerty'. It's a great musical idea generator, ear trainer, compositional tool, and improvising instrument. The software does a lot of harmony handling for you (you control the variables it uses for this), so it's useful — as are all 'real instruments' at any level of musical training, experience, or skill, from beginning through professional." The effects produced by Music Mouse are more striking than any description of the application, as many laudatory reviewers of Music Mouse have noted. If you have a Macintosh — or, buried somewhere in your basement, a by-now ancient Atari or Amiga computer — you can discover Music Mouse for yourself (a free demo of the most recent Mac version can be downloaded at http://retiary.org/ls/programs.html); but for the great majority who dwell in GatesWorld, alas, Music Mouse has never been ported to Windows.*

Music Mouse is interesting and fun to play with; but perhaps, in light of recent developments in computer-assisted and computer-generated music, it doesn't seem earth-shattering. But in its early years it certainly knocked a lot of socks off; including the rather distinguished socks of Richard Lanham, a professor of rhetoric at UCLA, who wrote approvingly of Music Mouse in a 1989 essay called "Literary Study and the Digital Revolution." That essay was reprinted in Lanham's pathbreaking book *The Electronic Word: Democracy, Technology, and the Arts* (1993), and the book's subtitle alerts us to one of the reasons for Lanham's enthusiasm. For Lanham, the work of people like Spiegel uses technology to democratize the arts: it enables ordinary people, even people who have not had access to formal musical training, not only to *listen* to music but to *make* it. Spiegel understands Music Mouse in similar terms, and sees it as emancipating "musicality" from "sheer physical coordination" and "the ability to deal with and manipulate symbolic notation"; these, in her view, are "irrelevant" and "have nothing to do with musical ability."

Much as I enjoy Music Mouse, I am dubious about some of the claims made by both Lanham and Spiegel — in part because it is my habit, whenever I hear someone proclaim that they have achieved my liberation from anything, to make sure my wallet is still in my back pocket. Precisely what *sort* of liberation is this? Instead of struggling with the limits of my physical coordination, limits that have for so long interfered with my desire to play the guitar like the Edge or Chet Atkins, I *could* simply play Music Mouse; but this does not often strike me as a desirable alternative. For one thing, I'm not sure that one gets *better* at playing Music Mouse, or at least not markedly better, and it is generally rewarding to improve one's skills; for another, the many "variables" in harmonization, tempo, and voicing

---

*However, music-making software similar to — but funkier and funnier than — Music Mouse *is* available for Windows as well as Mac: C. Todd Robbins's Sound Toys (formerly just Sound Toy — it has grown in recent years). It can be seen, and bought, at http://voyager.learntech.com/cdrom/catalogpage.cgi?soundtoys. Sound Toys, whose sound palette is primarily blues-based, with some world-music and electronica inflections, goes beyond Music Mouse in that it allows you to record and save your "compositions."

that the program offers me don't seem to approximate the range of musical sounds I can make even with my rudimentary guitar-playing skills. But more centrally, the claim that Music Mouse can liberate my "musicality" from the defects or limits of my physical skill makes me wonder if one couldn't say the same for an EA Sports computer simulation of professional football or baseball: those tacklers I could never escape in the real world, those curve balls I always swung ten inches over, pose little challenge to my skills with a mouse or joystick. The only problem is that when I'm sitting at the computer I'm *not playing a sport;* I'm playing a computer game that offers a shrunken and two-dimensional visual representation of a sport. And similarly, when I use Music Mouse I am *not making music* — or at least that's how it feels to me: rather, I'm offering the computer some extremely simple prompts which allow *it* to make music, and only the kind of music it knows how to make. The computer sports game actually demands much more skill from me than does Music Mouse, which for Laurie Spiegel is the beauty of her program; but that's not the only way to think about the matter.

In his essay, Lanham acknowledges this point in passing: imagining a series of further developments of computerized musical technology, he exclaims, "All these permutations are available to performers without formal musical training. (The computer training required is something else.)" The point deserves far more than parenthetical notation. What Lanham is referring to is the skill in using certain fairly complex computer applications which the making of electronic music can require; but that's not always the case (Music Mouse is about as simple to use as a program can be), and in any event, there's a deeper significance hidden in Lanham's comment. What about the computer training — and musical training! — required to *write* a program like Music Mouse? I am able to use the application so readily because so much of Laurie Spiegel's expertise in both fields has been employed so thoroughly in its making. One could argue that the *amount* of skill necessary to make instrumental music is a constant; what varies is merely its *distribution.* I could not build a guitar; perhaps the person who designed the guitar likewise lacked the skills of guitar construction; but then, the people who built my guitar may not have been able to play it, and may have had no sense of design. The responsibility for such music as I can make with my guitar seems to be divided fairly equally among these three parties. But in the case of Music Mouse, Laurie Spiegel has done almost all the work; all that's left for me is to twiddle the mouse. Am I "emancipated" by this situation? Or am I merely reduced to the level of a *very* junior partner in the music-making enterprise?

Computer technology seems to have this curious effect on many people: it makes at least some of us feel that *we* are doing things that, in point of fact, the computer itself is doing, and doing according to the instructions of people who have certain highly developed skills that most of us do not have. When this happens to me — or, more precisely, when I *realize* that it has happened to me — I feel as though I had temporarily convinced myself that I am the Wizard of Oz; I've forgotten that I'm just a little man hiding behind an enormous shield of technology that, in this case, I didn't even make myself.

Lanham's book is actually a brilliant one, and his exploration of how electronic text changes our orientation to writing and reading is compelling and provocative. The same is true of another humanist's foray into the world of computer-based critical literacy, George P. Landow's *Hypertext 2.0*. If Lanham's emphasis falls on the infinite revisability of electronic text, Landow is greatly fascinated (as are most theorists of hypertext) by the concept of the *link*. He describes in some detail the way that links perceptually work, how they break the linear flow that we are accustomed to from our long acquaintance with the discourses generated by print technology. For Landow, these traits of hyperlinks are liberating and empowering because "the linear habits of thought associated with print technology often force us to think in particular ways that require narrowness, decontextualization, and intellectual attenuation, if not downright impoverishment."

Everything about this sentence strikes me as highly arguable, but let's not argue now. Instead, let's think for a moment in a far more mundane way about how links are available to us in the typical web browser — because thinking in this way will, I believe, lead us to a deep problem with Lanham and Landow's celebratory rhetoric. So. Here we are, on-line, reading a page. A link offers itself (by its color or by its underlining); we click on the link. The page we are reading now disappears and another replaces it; or, in certain situations, a new window displaying a new page appears superimposed on the page we had been reading, which now lurks in the background, mostly or wholly hidden from view. The new page also presents links which will take us still elsewhere — eventually, perhaps, back to the page where we began. Pages of electronic text seem to circulate without a clear directional force; they seem to form an infinite *web*, with interstices at which we can turn in any direction.

But web browsers need *not* have been configured in just this way. What if, when we clicked that link, the new window appeared beneath, or beside, the one we had been looking at, so that both are equally visible, though in smaller portions? What if that process of subdividing the screen were to continue up to a limit set by the user — say, four pages displayed at a time, perhaps numbered sequentially, with earlier pages relegated to the History menu (as *all* previously viewed pages now are)? There are, of course, very good reasons why browsers are not configured in this way, most of them involving the size of the typical monitor; but my point is that they *could* have been configured in this way, and if browsers had evolved along those lines, people like Landow would talk about links in a different way than they now do. This "tiling" of a screen's open windows was in fact the method used by the very first version of Microsoft's Windows, released way back in 1983, when all the windows contained was plain text — and, very likely, was one of the chief reasons Windows 1.0 flopped. But if that model had caught on — which could have happened if the technology of monitors had enabled larger and more precisely rendered images than they did at the time — today the *experience* of linking would be different because the software architecture would produce a different experiential environment.

Similarly, the computer scientist David Gelernter has argued for some years now that computer users have become unnecessarily fixed on the metaphor of the "desktop," as though that were the only way to conceive of our relationship to the information stored on our computers. In his book *Machine Beauty* and elsewhere, he points out that the desktop metaphor had a particular historical origin — in research done by some scientists working for Xerox, later appropriated by Apple for the Macintosh and then by Microsoft — and contends that the role that computers currently play in many of our lives calls for a different metaphor, one based on the organization of *time* rather than the organization of *space*. Thus he and his colleagues have created a software environment called Lifestreams that provides an alternative interface with our computers, and with what we store in them. As a writer for *Wired* put it, Lifestreams is "a diary rather than a desktop." (The project, still in its early stages, can be investigated at www.scopeware.com.) If the Lifestreams model of presenting information to us in the form of time-stamped "cards," with our most recently viewed documents occupying the foreground of our screen, had been developed twenty years ago — and there was no technological barrier to this having happened — then writers like Lanham and Landow might be equally enthusiastic about the effects of computers on writing and learning, but the effects about which they enthused would be quite different ones. I am somewhat troubled by what appears to be a matching of ends to the available means: we become excited about doing whatever our technology is able to do; if its architecture enabled other actions, would the pursuit of those actions automatically become our new goal?

It is because I worry about this that Gelernter, who is a deeply humane thinker and anything but a naive enthusiast about computer technology, nevertheless makes me somewhat uncomfortable when he writes (in *Machine Beauty*) about the goals of software engineering: "Complexity makes programs hard to build and potentially hard to use"; therefore what we need is a "defense against complexity." For Gelernter, "software's ultimate goal [is] to break free of the computer, to break free conceptually. . . . The gravity that holds the imagination back as we cope with these strange new items is the computer itself, the old-fashioned physical machine. Software's goal is to escape this gravity field, and every key step in software history has been a step away from the computer, toward forgetting about the machine and its physical structure and limitations." In one sense this is exactly what I want — what all of us want who have been frustrated by our inability to get the computer to perform a task, either because of a bug in the software or because our machine doesn't have enough memory or a fast enough processor. But were it ever to happen that such frustrations were eliminated, that the computer became "transparent" (as Gelernter sometimes puts it) to my wishes and desires, would that be because the computer had matched itself to my character and interests? Or, rather, because I had gradually and unconsciously re-shaped my character and interests in order to match the capabilities of the technology?

Whatever emancipation or other benefit we receive from computer technology (from any technology) depends on decisions made by people who know how to design computers, other people who know how to build computer components, and still other people who know how to write code. Given the increasingly central role that computers play in our lives, how comfortable are we — and by "we" I mean average computer users — with knowing so little about how these machines came to be what they are, and to do what they do? How content are we simply to roll a mouse across a pad and let someone else's music tickle our ears?

2.

I didn't think much about these matters until about two years ago, when I was reading Neal Stephenson's roller-coaster ride of a novel, *Cryptonomicon*, and noticed that the book had its own website: www.cryptonomicon.com. The novel is full of arcane and fascinating information about cryptography and cryptanalysis, the first digital computers, the possible alternatives offered by analog computing, gold mining, undersea data cables, data havens, secret societies, the ethics of computer hacking, and so on; and I thought the website might offer further information about at least some of these topics. Alas, it did not; but it did contain a curious essay-cum-manifesto (downloadable as a plain-text file, and since published as a short book) by Stephenson, called *In the Beginning Was the Command Line*. It's an absolutely brilliant piece of polemic, and I'll have more to say about it later, but this is the passage that first caught my attention:

> Contemporary culture is a two-tiered system, like the Morlocks and the Eloi in H. G. Wells's *The Time Machine*, except that it's been turned upside down. In *The Time Machine* the Eloi were an effete upper class, supported by lots of subterranean Morlocks who kept the technological wheels

turning. But in our world it's the other way round. The Morlocks are in the minority, and they are running the show, because they understand how everything works. The much more numerous Eloi learn everything they know from being steeped from birth in electronic media directed and controlled by book-reading Morlocks. So many ignorant people could be dangerous if they got pointed in the wrong direction, and so we've evolved a popular culture that is (a) almost unbelievably infectious and (b) neuters every person who gets infected by it, by rendering them unwilling to make judgments and incapable of taking stands.

Morlocks, who have the energy and intelligence to comprehend details, go out and master complex subjects . . . so that Eloi can get the gist without having to strain their minds or endure boredom.

What I realized as I was reading this passage is that, in relation to computers particularly, I am an Eloi. I may be as much or more of a "book-reader" as the most adept Morlock, I may hold a PhD and have a subject to profess, but in relation to the technologies and interfaces that make an obvious and daily difference in how our lives are structured I am as ignorant as can be. After all, I don't read the books *they* read — standing in line at Borders, I clutch *Mansfield Park* or *The Divine Conspiracy*, while they lug *Programming in C++* or *Unix Administration in a Nutshell*. Stephenson is just being kind to people like me when he identifies the Morlocks who control our society simply with book-readers: his point about the enormous influence of the very few adept becomes more forceful when we realize that it is the *technologically* adept who are really in charge. The book-reading George Lucas may dream up the scenarios, but it's the cyberwizards at Industrial Light and Magic who *really* make the movies.

Now, you may think that my ignorance should not have been news to me, but it was, and the reasons may be significant. Spending most of my time around "humanities types" as I do, I do not regularly confront people with a great deal of expertise in using computers. Indeed, some of my colleagues and students have even made the mistake of crediting me with significant computer literacy, largely because I can use some applications that daunt the more helpless Eloi and because I know the meanings of a number of computerese acronyms. (The fact that some of the applications I know how to use — web-design program Dreamweaver, for instance — are considered by Morlocks to be crushingly simplistic and inflexible, little more than the web-design equivalent of Music Mouse, has only recently become fully evident to me, and that of course is part of the story I have to tell. And knowing that CSS, in web-design lingo, stands for Cascading Style Sheets does not enable one to explain very clearly what Cascading Style Sheets *are* or why they're always cascading.) In short, living among the Eloi of Eloi — that is, people who are accustomed to relying every day on computers, applications, and operating systems whose organization and structure they have literally no understanding of whatsoever — I have gotten used to thinking of myself as a kind of minor-league Morlock.

But I'm not. I really don't know anything. And I'm wondering if it might not be time for me to learn a thing or two. But how does one become a Morlock, even a minor-league one? The more I thought about this question, the more my attention came to focus on one issue: the computer's operating system (OS), the set of routines and instructions that govern the basic functions of the computer, and on top of which other applications (word processing programs, web browsers, graphics programs, whatever) run.* Plus, Stephenson's *In the Beginning Was the Command Line*, which prompted so many of my reflections, is primarily a meditation on the way that operating systems, more than anything else, determine the character and quality of our experience on our computers.

But as I read more about these matters, I discovered that when you learn something — even learn a lot — about how an OS works, how one OS differs from another, you've managed to grab only a few small pieces of the puzzle. That is, while such knowledge gets you considerably closer

---

*The OS is usually thought of as a single program, or super-program, but in fact it is an assemblage of the most common and valuable actions (or, in the jargon, subroutines) that a computer is called upon to perform. For instance, the OS allows you to open all files in the same way, and to enter text via the keyboard in the same way; it would be quite cumbersome for every application program to have to provide its own subroutines for such universal actions, and confusing for users, so instead the writers of such programs rely on the OS's way of doing things.

to how the computer "really works" than one gets by clicking a mouse button to open a file or application, you're still several removes from the elemental instructions which allow the different parts of the computer — the memory, the processor — to be aware of one another's existence and to negotiate some kind of ongoing relationship. Even if I were to become a masterful manipulator of an existing operating system I would remain only a user. But by some miracle were I able to learn a few programming skills, even manage to write some code that would a tiny subroutine in an OS, I *still* wouldn't have any idea what was going on at that deeper level. I still wouldn't have the complete knowledge of the computer's workings that the true Morlock should have. Or so I tend to feel.

However, it may be that no such true Morlock exists. As W. Daniel Hillis explains in his admirably lucid book *The Pattern on the Stone* — the book to which I owe whatever limited knowledge I have of the basic workings of computers — today's machines are so complex that *no one* completely understands how one works:

> Often when a large software system malfunctions, the programmers responsible for each of the parts can convincingly argue that each of their respective subroutines is doing the right thing. Often they are all correct, in the sense that each subroutine is correctly implementing its own specified function. The flaw lies in the specifications of what the parts are supposed to do and how they are supposed to interact. Such specifications are difficult to write correctly without anticipating all possible interactions. Large complex systems, like computer operating systems or telephone networks, often exhibit puzzling and unanticipated behaviors even when every part is functioning as designed. . . .
>
> It is amazing to me that the engineering process works as well as it does. Designing something as complicated as a computer or an operating system can require thousands of people. If the system is sufficiently complicated, no one person can have a complete view of the system.

Now, this does not sound like good news to me. If we are making machines that none of us understands, are we not, perforce, making machines that none of us can control? Images of Frankenstein and Arthur C.

Clarke's Hal 9000 come instantly to mind; and what does this state of affairs do to my hopes for Morlockian knowledge?

3.

Curiously, though, for many people who know a lot more about computers than I do, our ability to make machines that transcend our abilities to understand them is exciting — a testimony to "the power of modularity," as Carliss Y. Baldwin and Kim B. Clark, of Harvard Business School, put it in their recent book *Design Rules*. For Baldwin and Clark, the application of the principle of modularity (seen especially as the division of design and production tasks into many separate "modules" governed only by a shared set of "design rules" that ensure ultimate complementarity and fit) "decentralizes" the process of design, increases the number of design options, and "accommodates uncertainty" — that is, allows for the process of design and production to go on in ways that make sense, that are almost certain to produce coherent and useful results, but that are fundamentally unpredictable. In a fully modular environment for the design of a product, or anything else, the precise kind of product that will emerge at the end of the process is not, cannot be, foreseen at the beginning. The people involved must simply trust in the "design rules" to set procedures, but not ensure particular results. Baldwin and Clark call this model "design evolution," for reasons we will discuss a bit later.

Baldwin and Clark are primarily concerned with the ways in which modularity makes good business sense, but the principle of modularity has other and deeper implications. Some of these are explored in Steven Johnson's fascinating new book *Emergence*. For Johnson, modularity (though he does not use that term) makes "emergent systems" possible. But what are "emergent systems"? Johnson begins his book with a concise, lucid explanation of the curious behavior of the slime mold, an exceptionally primitive amoeba-like organism that has the ability, at need, to organize itself into large communities which act as a single organism — and then (also at need) to divide again into smaller units. For many years this behavior puzzled scientists, who could but assume that "slime mold swarms formed at the command of 'pacemaker' cells that ordered the other cells to begin aggregating." But no one could find the pacemaker cells. Johnson points out that scientists had similar difficulty in understanding the behavior of ant colonies, with their remarkable divisions of labor and consequent ability to manage an extraordinarily complex social order: surely the ant "queen" was somehow giving orders that the other ants carried out? But no one could figure out how such "orders" could be given.

In fact, *no one* gives orders in an ant colony, and slime molds have no pacemaker cells. Slime molds and ant colonies are "self-organizing complex systems" — *emergent* systems, in that their behavior simply emerges rather than deriving from some centralized or hierarchical plan. The division of labor in an ant colony (some ants foraging for food, others taking out the trash, still others disposing of the dead) is thoroughly "modular"; the colony's complexity results, surprisingly enough, from the application of a few simple yet immensely productive "design rules" which govern ants' responses to trails of pheromones deposited by other ants. Having long been blinded by our predilection for hierarchical, command-governed, top-down thinking, Johnson argues, we have only recently been able to discern the power of self-organization: we have "unearthed a secret history of decentralized thinking, a history that had been submerged for many years beneath the weight of the pacemaker hypothesis and the traditional boundaries of scientific research."

The prevalence of modularity in computer design and construction, and of "emergent" strategies and techniques in software design, makes my dreams of Morlockian power seem absurdly far-fetched. If the people who design and build the microchips, construct the hardware, and write the software codes don't understand how exactly the whole thing manages to work — or, as is often the case, why it *doesn't* — then shouldn't I just become the most skillful computer *user* I can (a "power user," as the lingo has it) and forget about tinkering under the hood? After all, Johnson argues that, as self-organizing systems become more and more technologically dominant — a development he thinks is inevitable, especially in computer software — the ability to "accommodate uncertainty" (as Baldwin and Clark put it), to accept one's lack of control over the outcome of a given process, will become a cardinal virtue. Johnson already sees this virtue manifesting itself in children who play computer games that rely on strategies and techniques of emergence:

> The conventional wisdom about these kids is that they're more nimble at puzzle solving and more manually dexterous than the TV generation, and while there's certainly some truth to that, I think we lose something important in stressing how talented this generation is with their joysticks. I think they have developed another skill, one that almost looks like patience: they are more tolerant of being out of control, more tolerant of that exploratory phase where the rules don't all make sense, and where few goals have been clearly defined. In other words, they are uniquely equipped to embrace the more oblique control system of emergent software.

If Johnson is right, then the best course for me to take might be to spend some time cultivating this "skill . . . that almost looks like patience." In this light, my desire to become less of an Eloi and more of a Morlock may just indicate an attachment to outdated command-governed models of human behavior.

Perhaps. But something keeps nagging at me: the question of who writes the "design rules," and why. I have already noted the tendency of Baldwin and Clark to talk about "design evolution"; Johnson also likes to employ Darwinian metaphors. It's easy to see why: anytime one establishes a system which, under certain design rules, is allowed to develop without explicit ongoing direction or control, it starts to look like an ecosystem. In the natural world, biochemistry and environmental conditions combine to establish the "rules" under which certain organisms thrive and others fail; biologists call this "natural selection." But any "evolution" that takes place in the world of computer usage isn't "natural" at all, because some human writes the rules — to return to the terms used by Lawrence Lessig, someone constructs (many people construct) a particular architecture that *could* be different.

Take Steve Grand for instance. Grand is an English computer scientist who, some years ago, wrote a computer game called Creatures (since succeeded by Creatures 2 and Creatures 3) that relied on techniques of emergence to produce digital life-forms called Norns. Grand designed Norns to live for about sixteen hours of screen time, but some players of Creatures have developed such skills of nurturing that their Norns have survived for years. Creatures is just a computer game, some may say, but Grand's view of his achievement is, well, more grand: "I am an aspiring latter-day Baron Frankenstein," he writes in his book *Creation: Life and How to Make It*. But as that title and subtitle suggest, Grand's ambitions may exceed Dr. Frankenstein's. "A game it might have been, but if you'll forgive the staggering lack of modesty this implies, Creatures was probably the closest thing there has been to a new form of life on this planet in four billion years." And Grand's plans are not confined to his work with his own Norns:

> I would like to assert that, although the materialist viewpoint is undoubtedly the truth, it is not the whole truth. I am a computer programmer by background, and as familiar as anyone with the means by which apparently abstract ideas can be reduced to simple mechanical steps. But I believe that the computer, if interpreted correctly, can be the saviour of the soul rather than its executioner. It can show us how to transcend mere mechanism, and reinstate a respect for the spiritual domain that materialism has so cruelly (if unintentionally) destroyed.

To create the first new form of life in four billion years, and to save the souls of those non-digital life-forms created by someone or something else — perhaps ambition isn't quite the word for it. What's so troubling, to me anyway, about Grand's vision is his apparently complete lack of concern about his fitness for such tasks. Though he can say, with an ironic smile, "It's tough being a god" (as he did to a *New York Times* reporter), he can't spare much time or worry for the ancient nightmares of technology run amok. The medieval Jewish legend of the Golem, Frankenstein's difficulties with his creation, Arthur C. Clarke's Hal 9000 — these stories take a cautionary tone towards technology, reminding us that our wisdom may not be adequate to our aspirations or our expertise. After all, Rabbi Loew (in one common version of the story, anyway) only made the Golem because he felt compassion for people who had to work too hard, and wished to provide them some assistance. Grand sees nothing to learn from either the rabbi or the scientists as he contemplates designing creatures that, while fully sentient, couldn't possibly go astray in the way that humans have:

> Human beings are not just nasty because we enjoy it. We're nasty because we feel hard done by, because we're doing something we hate and feel trapped by. And we envy other people. When we have intelligent machines, there's no reason at all why these machines will be envious or unhappy, because we will program them to enjoy the things they do.

How simple a solution! One can but wonder why God didn't think of it.

FOR GRAND, the challenge of "making life" can be met by taking the time and trouble to write a few basic design rules, to situate the resulting "creatures" in a digital environment that's complex enough to be interesting to observers, and then let "natural selection" do its work. All we have to do is sit back to see which Norns make it, and for how long.

Steve Grand's conviction that he has created new forms of life, and his plans to create fully intelligent digital life-forms sometime in the near future, constitute an extreme example of what one might call cyber-triumphalism. And it may be that, whatever the results of Grand's work, it will have little relevance to any of us who don't play Creatures. However, in his blue-skies-smiling-at-me view of a future of infinite technological possibility, he's not unusual; many people have invested similar hopes in (for instance) the community-building, information-providing, freedom-enhancing culture of the Internet. But the driving idea behind Lessig's 1999 book *Code* is that when people talk about the "nature" of cyberspace, of the Internet, they are talking nonsense: "If there is any place where nature has no rule, it is in cyberspace. If there is any place that is constructed, cyberspace is." At the time that Lessig wrote that book, many observers were arguing that the Internet is "unregulable"; but Lessig simply responds, "whether the Net is *unregulable* depends, and it depends on its *architecture*." And architecture is determined by code; and code is written by people; people with various beliefs, commitments, motives, and aspirations. Flawed and *fallen* people, like Steve Grand (or like me). And it is used by people of the same moral constitution. One need not be of a paranoid, or even a suspicious, temperament to be concerned about that.

However, concern should not lead immediately to repudiation of this or any technology. If an uncritical embrace of technological possibility is dangerous, it is also true, as David Gelernter has rightly cautioned, that "to hate technology is in the end to hate humanity, to hate yourself, because technology is what human beings do" — perhaps the most eloquent response imaginable to Theodore Kaczynski, otherwise known as the Unabomber, one of whose bombs almost killed Gelernter in his Yale University office in 1993.

One further example may be sufficient to indicate the impossibility of finding simple answers to the problem of control. Roughly a decade ago now a man named Phil Zimmerman wrote PGP (Pretty Good Privacy), a sophisticated suite of data encryption applications. Recent versions of PGP provide the most impenetrable encryption schemes ever devised, but still, as has been the case from the beginning of Zimmerman's project, PGP may be downloaded for free (from www.pgpi.com). Zimmerman is very proud of having provided this robust instrument for safeguarding privacy to anyone who has a computer and a modem, and has often mentioned the emails of thanks he has received from (for instance) Chinese or Burmese dissidents who could not create effective resistance to their tyrannical governments without the protection of PGP's encryption tools. But it is also widely rumored that PGP has been used, for years, by the various cells of the Al-Qaeda network to maintain communication and to receive and transmit commands. I'm not sure we have a moral calculus discriminating enough to say whether PGP has produced a net social gain or loss.

4.

But let's go back to the mundane world of *our* computers. When Lawrence Lessig wrote *Code,* he believed very strongly that the architecture of cyberspace was still up for grabs: in the last words of the book, he wrote, "We are entering a time when our power to muck about with the structures that regulate is at an all-time high. It is imperative, then, that we understand just what to do with this power. And, more important, what not to do." By emphasizing "what not to do" Lessig meant to emphasize especially the dangers of overzealous government regulation; but he was aware that other forces also work to regulate cyberspace. And now, in his new book *The Future of Ideas,* he has come to believe that our window of opportunity to make the most liberating and enriching decisions about the architecture of cyberspace has closed. We had our chance, and, at least for now, we have blown it. But it is not the U.S. government that has closed the window, in Lessig's view: rather, it is the increasing dominance of cyberspace by two businesses:

> These two companies — AOL Time Warner and Microsoft — will define the next five years of the Internet's life. Neither company has committed itself to a neutral and open platform. Hence, the next five years will be radically different from the past ten. Innovation in content and applications will be as these platform owners permit. Additions that benefit either company will be encouraged; additions that don't, won't. We will have re-created the network of old AT&T, but now on the platform of the Internet. Content and access will once again be controlled; the innovation commons will have bed carved up and sold.
>
> This is the future of ideas. It could be different, but my sense is that it won't.

For Lessig, "the irony astounds. We win the political struggle against state control so as to reentrench control in the name of the market." And I'm pretty sure I know what he means, having struggled, over the years, to maintain a largely Microsoft-free computer environment. Now I find that none of the alternative browsers I have tried (Opera, for instance) works quite as smoothly or quickly as Microsoft's Internet Explorer — which came with my Macintosh, pre-selected as the default browser; while I changed the defaults I kept the application, just in case. I was noticing just this morning that ESPN.com was acting rather strangely when displayed by Opera, and even Netscape (which I also try to avoid, now that Netscape is owned by AOL); but all the irregularities disappeared when I viewed it through Internet Explorer. The people at Microsoft would claim that this is simply because they now make a better browser than their competitors, and perhaps this is true. But I notice that, not long ago, ESPN.com became part of MSN, the Microsoft Network, and one wonders how much incentive the site designers at ESPN.com have for making sure that their pages are as compatible with Netscape as with Internet Explorer. And even websites that have no formal connections with Microsoft are perfectly aware that the market share of Internet Explorer now approaches, if it has not already exceeded, ninety percent; if, when coding pages, the web designers find that they look great when previewed in Internet Explorer, well, that covers nine out of ten users. Do they really have time to worry about little quirks that appear only for the one out of ten who hasn't climbed onto the Microsoft bandwagon?

In light of all these dismal reflections, it would appear that this out-of-control feeling that I can't quite get rid of — whether because I lack patience, as Steven Johnson suggests, or for some nobler reason — has two basic sources: first, my ignorance of computer technology, and second, the increasing dominance that a very few organizations have over my experience of using the computer. As I noted earlier, I have tried to avoid the latter problem by minimizing (if not eliminating altogether) my acquaintance with Mr. Gates's products, but insofar as I have stuck with Apple products instead, there's an irony in that. For Apple's history, as Neal Stephenson points out, is that of a "control freak" corporate culture: the bosses of Apple "have been able to plant this image of themselves as creative and rebellious freethinkers," but they have historically insisted on an unbreakable bond between their hardware and their software. Apple has wanted customers to buy the whole package, and has guarded its corporate secrets with great care. The fences the company has historically built around software developers; its refusal to allow the Mac OS to run on other, cheaper hardware except for a brief period in the '90s; its insistence on maintaining a "closed architecture" whose inner workings are all but inaccessible to the ordinary user; its determination to maintain what Stephenson calls a "rigid monopoly" — all these tendencies have made

Apple a thoroughly inappropriate champion of freedom and autonomy for the computer user. (Some of these tendencies may be changing with the introduction, in the spring of 2001, of Macintosh OS X; but that's a matter I will take up in another essay.) Strangely, it is only Apple's failure to achieve the monopoly it desires that has enabled it to continue to market itself as a computer company for those who would "Think Different." That said, I continue to think that Apple's products are cool as all get-out, and I remain a devoted aficionado; but not an idealistic one.

So, if my devotion to Apple does little to dispel the demons of corporate control, and nothing at all to correct my technological ignorance, what hope is there? Some hope, I think, and it comes from an interesting group of people with increasing influence in the world of computers. Collectively they tend to be called the Open Source Software movement, though I prefer to think of them as the Cyber-Amish, for reasons I will explain in my next essay. These people believe that, largely through the resources of the Internet, communities of like-minded hackers can build *all* of the software any computer user could possibly need, from the kernel of the OS all the way to graphics, CD-burning, and video-editing applications — even games — and make that software available to anyone who wants it and has the skill to download, install, and configure it. Richard Stallmann, of the Free Software Foundation, and Linus Torvalds, the inventor of the Linux operating system — these are the heroes of the Open Source world. If any "true Morlocks" exist, these must be the guys. And they (so I am told) have already bought my ticket to *real* empowerment, *real* liberation.

Well. We'll see.

SECOND STAGE

1.

The one unique benefit that was creating this enthusiasm was not
that this stuff was better or faster or cheaper, although many will
argue that it was all three of those things. The one unique benefit
that the customer gets for the first time is control over the technology he's being asked to invest in.

BOB YOUNG
CEO of Red Hat Linux

Sometime around the year 2002 the venerable computer company IBM
started running a series of television commercials featuring — for reasons
not clear to me or, I suspect, to many other viewers — retired professional
basketball players enacting brief allegorical dramas about business computing. George Gervin, a.k.a. the Iceman, is the coach of this team, and
some of his players include Firewall (played convincingly by the now
portly and indeed rather wall-ish Bill Laimbeer, once a Detroit Piston), and
Middleware (Xavier McDaniel, formerly the intimidating X-Man, and
somewhat thicker in the middle himself). But for me the most interesting
member of this team is "acted" by Detlef Schrempf, one of the more recently retired of the bunch — he was playing in the NBA as recently as
2001. As Schrempf's name perhaps indicates, he's no boy from the 'hood,
but rather a German import, one of the first European players to excel in
the NBA. Schrempf, the only player in the commercials who gets to dunk
— perhaps because he's the only one who still can — plays "Linux," and
the commercials identify Linux as the team's new star. This preeminence
is not unrelated to Linux's willingness to work for "peanuts," simply because "he loves the game."

The casting of Shrempf was a witty move by the makers of the commercials, because Linux (the real Linux) is a computer operating system
that originated in Europe — specifically, in Finland. In the last decade it
has risen from a fragmentary set of routines whose existence only a few

dozen hackers knew of, and still fewer cared about, to an increasingly widely-used and widely-discussed alternative to Microsoft's Empire of Windows. And indeed, it still works for peanuts.

(Throughout this essay I will use the term "hackers" to refer to highly skilled people who mess around in the digital innards of computers because they love to, whether they get paid for it or not — that's how they refer to themselves. People who illegally "hack" into systems where they don't belong constitute a subset of this larger group.)

The story needs to be told in some detail, because the rise of Linux has serious implications for the future of computer technology — and, more to the point, the future of human beings' use of computer technology. The story goes beyond Linux itself; it is the story of "open source software," and the open source movement will, in the coming years, have a lot to say about the extent to which we use computer technology, or it uses us.

Linux, or rather the first attempt at producing the "kernel" — the most elementary and universally necessary routines — of what is now Linux, was written in the latter part of 1991 by a student at the University of Helsinki named Linus Torvalds. Torvalds started to write the code in order to test a possible alternative for another OS called Minix, which had been created by a programmer named Andrew Tannenbaum as a teaching tool: along with an accompanying book, Minix helped computer science students understand how an OS works. For this purpose Minix seems to have been excellent, but students who learned Minix often experimented with it to see if they could improve it and make it more functional for a wider variety of purposes. Linus Torvalds was one such student.

But, before we proceed, let's pause to deal with a question: what's with all the X's? Linux and Minix, yes, but investigators of the history of computing will also encounter Ultrix, AIX, HP-UX, and a number of other OS's that don't announce their parentage quite so openly. And indeed it is a matter of parentage, for all these systems derive from one Ur-father: Unix. Unix was written in 1969, primarily by Ken Thompson, a programmer who worked for AT&T's Bell Labs. Thompson and his colleague Dennis Ritchie had been working on an ambitious multi-company project when the whole thing fell apart; but they thought that some of the work they had done on the project could be rescued and adapted for relatively small computers. Thus Unix was born. And very soon Unix began to produce offspring, because the code which Thompson had written was made available to a wide range of programmers and software engineers in a wide range of universities, government agencies, and businesses. Improving Unix became a collective endeavor, and the OS got much better very quickly because of the many minds working on it. This experience would later become a key, perhaps *the* key, principle of the open source software movement: as one of that movement's key theorists, Eric Raymond, wrote, "Given enough eyeballs, all bugs are shallow" — that is, even the most intractable software problem will eventually yield if enough people devote themselves to solving it.

But soon the Unix world became fragmented: versions of Unix proliferated, each tailored to the needs of a particular company or adapted for a particular set of hardware. Unix ceased to be "open" as many of these companies refused to share their versions; a spirit of proprietary ownership replaced the collective, cooperative spirit of Unix's early days. Indeed, throughout the 1970s a conviction began to emerge that the "intellectual property" embodied in a piece of software — its code, the instructions it gives to a piece of hardware, written by persons just as novels are written by persons — had an economic value that previous generations of computer professionals either had not noticed or had not cared about. Such neglect may seem odd to us, knowing as we do the vast fortunes that have been made in software, but in those days computers were used by very few, chiefly in universities and the government. Programmers paid by those institutions could not make more money by keeping the code they write secret, so they freely shared it with others. Only with the great expansion of business computing and the advent of the PC did it become evident that any software that enabled non-experts actually to *use* a computer — a rather forbidding machine, after all — pretty much determined the value of the machine itself. One of the first computer professionals to see this point was a fellow named Bill Gates: in 1976 he wrote an "Open Letter to Hobbyists" to protest unlicensed use of some software (a version of the programming language Basic for the MITS Altair, the first personal computer) written by him and his partners in the young company then known as Micro-Soft.

Fragmentation and proprietorship; these were the enemies for many ambitious programmers in the 1980s. When Andrew Tannenbaum wrote Minix, he employed the basic principles that underlay Unix; the ancestry of his OS was very clear to all knowledgeable observers. But he couldn't use any preexisting Unix code without being in violation of copyright; he had to write Minix from scratch. Linus Torvalds was in the same position when he started coding Linux. (But for all practical purposes both Minix and Linux are versions of Unix; they use very similar commands, and anyone with Unix experience is perfectly at home in Minix, almost so in Linux.) Both programmers made their work available to the community of hackers, seeking affirmation where possible, correction where necessary. But at that point their paths diverged, and the divergence explains why Linus Torvalds and his OS Linux are increasingly famous and influential, while Andrew Tannenbaum is little known outside the circle of computer professionals.

Minix, as I have said, was written for a particular purpose: as a teaching tool. Therefore, when the many hackers who used Minix reported bugs and offered fixes for them, or suggested better ways for certain subroutines to run, or argued for the need to extend Minix so that users could run more kinds of applications on it — do more things with it — Tannenbaum decided which suggestions to follow on the basis of his conception of what Minix could and should be, given the function for which he had designed it. But Torvalds had no such constraints. His sole interest was making Linux a better OS — and a complete, fully functional one, not just a "toy" — so, at first anyway, he eagerly incorporated almost every useful suggestion. For the hackers who sought to participate in the project, this was heady stuff: they were being invited to participate in the making, not of some minor utility or limited application, but of the very operating system itself — the defining structures of a computing environment. In *Rebel Code,* Glyn Moody tells the story of Matt Welsh — later the coauthor of *Running Linux,* but when he discovered the OS a student at Cornell — who installed Linux and almost immediately "got the fever. It was all about doing things yourself, adding new features, and constantly learning more about how computers and operating systems work." (The work of many of these hackers can still be found among the myriad applications and utilities that come with the versions of Linux available today.) Soon there was an entire virtual community, comprised of people from all over the world, investing thousands of hours in the development and improvement of Linux.

As a result, Torvalds started getting far more input than he could handle, but he kept plugging away as best he could, and Linux grew and grew — not only in size, as it incorporated more functions, but also in cleanness and stability. Linux devotees could be heard to brag that they didn't even know how to make their OS crash — even as versions of Windows became ever more "crufty" (that is, in hackerese, infested with extraneous, outdated, and badly written code) and prone to every sort of crash or freeze imaginable. Moreover, early in its development, Linux started incorporating utilities from the BSD (Berkeley Standard Distribution) of Unix — one of the less rigorously proprietary of the Unix variants — and imported applications produced by the GNU Project. The most comprehensive and ambitious single organization in the open-source movement, GNU is directed by MIT's Richard Stallman, a brilliant and obsessive programmer who hates with a prophetic passion the proprietary model of software engineering, and in that cause founded the Free Software Foundation.

For years now Stallman has had to deal with misunderstandings of his use of the term "freedom." He does not mean that software should never be sold, but rather that its source code should be made available to anyone who wants it for improvement and modification. To do otherwise is, in Stallman's view, "immoral," because it violates certain freedoms he thinks vital: thus, the Free Software Foundation. "Free speech, not free beer," as Stallman helpfully encapsulates the distinction. Other programmers, individual and collective, pitched in, and soon Linux boasted an impressive array of applications written or adapted for it. Companies began putting together "distributions" of Linux — the OS and key applications bundled together, to save people the work of assembling a whole system out of the bits and pieces that were floating around the Internet — and programmers started buying them. Fans of Linux, many of whom were also contributors to its cause, started dreaming big dreams: could it be possible that this almost homemade OS could eventually rival Windows itself? A ridiculous notion, akin to imagining that a group of Amish farmers could displace Archer Daniels Midland as a kingpin of American agribusiness — because, in a way, the open source people are the Cyber-Amish. Like the Amish, they aren't Luddites (they don't repudiate technology altogether), but they advocate a certain small-is-beautiful approach to technology that keeps power in the hands of individuals, informal networks, and communities of practitioners. It would seem that, by definition, such folks couldn't be players on the national technological stage.

But certainly the quality was there. Linux was both stable and powerful — that is, it (and its applications) rarely crashed, and it could run quickly and efficiently on machines with far less memory and processor-power than Windows or the Mac OS demanded. For many programmers and systems administrators it was obvious that Linux offered stability and functionality that they couldn't find elsewhere. The stability of Linux was particularly desirable for people in charge of maintaining websites, and as the Internet became a more pervasive part of business culture, Linux — running the Apache web server software — soon became the system of choice for web administrators, first outstripping IBM's server technology and then Windows NT. (Once IBM realized that they couldn't provide service to compare with Apache servers running on Linux, they decided to buy into the Linux alternative — thus the television commercials noted at the beginning of this essay.) Maybe Amish agribusiness isn't such an oxymoron after all.

But something was missing. At this point everything Linux could do it did from the "command line" — that is, the user gave the computer instructions only by typing commands like `mkdir test2` or `chmod go-w test2`. But ordinary users, even those who may have started computers back in the command-line days of DOS or MS-DOS, had long since grown accustomed to a screen dominated by images and icons, and depended on navigating that screen with a mouse or some other pointing device. If it were ever going to make a splash in the world of desktop computing, Linux needed a GUI, a Graphical User Interface. But it wasn't until the late 1990s that it got a workable one — in fact, two: KDE and GNOME (the latter a product of Stallman's GNU Project). In 1996, when the German computer scientist Matthias Ettrich announced plans to develop

KDE, he referred to it as "a GUI for endusers" — "endusers" being people like me, who don't know how to do much, if anything, from the command line, and are therefore wholly locked into the pointing-and-clicking world of the graphical desktop. With the arrival of KDE and GNOME, the Linux world claimed to be ready for me. But was I ready for it?

2.

> Setting up Corel Linux is a snap, but you should be at your mental and physical best.
>
> *Corel Linux for Dummies*

The story of my life with Linux is a comic tale of misadventure, gross error, the occasional ephemeral triumph, and lots of cursing. At least, I'm *trying* to see it as a comic tale — though to this point there have been more tears than laughs. But, since I am writing these words on a computer running Linux, the experiment hasn't been a total failure. (Yet.) Linux is now a regular part of my computing experience; though how central it will be, and how long I will stick with it, are questions still unanswered.

I explained in the first stage of this essay that in recent years I have become increasingly frustrated with my lack of control over the work I do on my computer; control in two senses of the word. First, I don't know much about how my computer actually works: how it carries out my commands, how it does what I want it to do — or (and when this happens my frustration becomes acute) how it does what *it* wants to do. Second, the dominance of two companies — Microsoft and AOL/Time-Warner — over the world of American computing has made it increasingly difficult for computer users to exercise meaningful choice over the way they interact with their computers. I also explained that reading Neal Stephenson's little book *In the Beginning Was the Command Line* — with its distinction between the technologically knowledgeable Morlocks and the technologically inept Eloi — was a catalytic moment for me.

But (and I did not explain this in the previous movement) I think I can remember the very moment I decided I had to extricate myself from the condition of the typical computer user. In a weak moment I had acquired Microsoft Office 2001 for my Macintosh — not for everyday use, but in order to be able to share files more easily with colleagues and friends in the Windows world. But when I tried to work with Microsoft Word I was maddened by its insistence on divining what I wanted to do — maddened because the stupid program kept guessing *wrong:* its skills of divination seemed uncannily inept, and I spent a lot of time working my way through the Preferences screens, trying to disable the more assertive of the program's default settings. This was not difficult, but it was tiresome, and since the more I used the application the more often it would do unexpectedly annoying things, after a while I found myself just allowing Word to make its own decisions: "No," I thought, "that's *not* how I want to format that paragraph, but it's too much trouble to fix it, so I'll leave it as is." At that point I realized that I was becoming the kind of user Microsoft wanted me to be: passive, accepting, ready to accommodate myself to whatever Word chose to do.

Thinking about this experience, I am put in mind of something I read in Glyn Moody's *Rebel Code:* a comment by Bob Young, the president of Red Hat Linux, about the kinds of people he meets at gatherings of Linux users: "I'm going, OK, let's see, my target market is rocket scientists at NASA or it's blue-haired art students in Toronto." The first group, the "rocket scientists," he had presumably expected to find: they were amateur or professional hackers, do-it-yourselfers — the lineal descendants of the "hobbyists" who, a quarter-century ago, had built their own Altair and Heathkit computers. But surely that other group was a surprise to Young. Who would have expected that significant numbers of people would gravitate to Linux not because they were hard-core techno-geeks, but because they wanted to protest against the hegemony of corporate America as embodied in Microsoft and Intel? Well (I thought), if the blue-haired art students can do it, so can I.

So my course was set. But once I decided I was going to try Linux, I needed two things: software and hardware. The software was easy enough: having studied C/net.com to find out which distribution of Linux was right for me, and having decided that (despite its popularity) Red Hat would probably lead me pretty quickly into problems I couldn't solve, I went down to my local Borders and bought *Corel Linux for Dummies,* which included Corel Linux on a CD. And hardware wasn't too much of a problem, either. Since I had no intention of messing with my Mac (even though several distributions of Linux run on Macs), I called Wheaton College's Computing Services department to see if I could borrow something — surely they had an old PC lying around that no one was using. And it could be pretty "old," at least by the rapid evolutionary standards of today's computers: after all, don't Linux aficionados point with pride to its ability to run on machines that the Windows world deems thoroughly outdated? Even a Pentium I processor would do, my Dummies book told me.

I'm not sure what the people in Computing Services thought of my strange request, though the news that an English professor wanted a machine on which to run Linux could scarcely have filled them with joy. But they were, as always, polite and accommodating, and soon Ted Myhre showed up in my office with a cart containing a grubby, dusty old Gateway computer and monitor. I've been using nothing but a laptop for several years now, and I felt as though someone had dropped a rhinoceros on my desk. The thing must have weighed fifty pounds; I managed to move it to a small second desk, which creaked under the weight, and when I pressed the machine's On button it shuddered and heaved like a beast under anesthesia. I inserted the Corel Linux CD and restarted, but it wouldn't boot. I checked the BIOS (the pre-OS utilities on most PCs that control some of the computer's most basic settings) and found that this machine could boot either from the hard drive or the floppy drive, but not a CD. So I found another PC, inserted the CD, and copied the necessary files to a floppy disk. Then I returned to the behemoth, made sure that it was set to boot from the floppy drive, inserted both the CD and the floppy, and restarted. Soon enough I was given the option of wiping the hard disk and installing Linux, which I chose to do, and by the time I went out to get a Coke and came back I had Linux up and running.

Now, I felt pretty good about this. Clearly the reviews I had read on CNET.com that promised that Corel Linux (unlike several other distributions) would easily install were correct; plus, I had been able to solve a problem by myself, though to be sure it was a minor one. As I looked at the screen, however, I wasn't sure exactly what to do next. I opened the File Manager and fooled around with that for a while. I copied some alternative "themes" from the CD so I could try out different looks for the desktop, but still, it wasn't nearly as attractive as the Mac desktop, and I had that dull, sober feeling I always have when I sit down at a machine running Windows. Beyond these matters of mere aesthetics — and I was determined to think of them as "mere" — the substantive problem, I realized, was that I couldn't connect to the Internet, and so couldn't download the many cool and powerful Linux applications I had read were available for free. I played a little Solitaire, drew a little with a drawing application, and wrote a few paragraphs with the Text Editor — pretty much the sort of thing I did when I bought my first Mac in the spring of 1985 and spent quite a while exploring the fun offered by MacWrite and MacPaint. But this time the exploration got boring pretty quickly. I turned back to my PowerBook and answered some email, the beast snoring heavily behind me all the while. I could almost feel warm, moist breath on the back of my neck as I typed.

While at my Mac, I sent an email to Computing Services asking whether I could be hooked up to the campus network, but this plea was not met with the same snappy approval as my request for an old, unwanted PC. Besides, Behemoth had no Ethernet port to connect the machine to our local network; and a prominent magic-markered command on its back pointed to the phone jack and commanded "DO NOT USE." But if I wanted to do more than draw a few pictures and type plain-text files, I needed some software; so a few days later I went to the computer store to scope out their Linux shelf.

The first thing anyone notices about Linux software is how much cheaper it is than similar stuff for Windows or Mac. The various distributions of Linux tend to cost around thirty bucks, and contain not only the OS, but also dozens of applications. Most contain StarOffice (the Sun Microsystems alternative to Microsoft Office), image editing software (including the GIMP, the GNU Project's free alternative to Adobe Photoshop, which many professionals actually prefer), any number of web browsers and email applications, games and other goodies — as well as a raft of applications and utilities widely used in the Unix world. I did some quick, informal comparisons and figured that the average thirty-buck Linux distribution contained software whose Windows-compatible equivalents would cost a couple of thousand dollars. But which distribution of all this stuff did I choose? On CNET.com I had learned that Linux Mandrake gets high marks for ease of installation and use; I grabbed a copy and started for home.

Driving home, one thought occupied me: Behemoth must go. Every time I had walked into the office, since its delivery, I had winced: there it hulked, dominating the desk, blocking the light from the window, leaving me no room to work. I realized, when I considered it, that I hadn't been more persistent in asking for an additional connection to Wheaton's network because I feared that Computing Services would comply — thus leaving me stuck with that horrible machine. I've been working with my PowerBook for too long to be comfortable with computers that size. I've really enjoyed the spaciousness that my laptop provides my desk, plus the opportunity to sit back and put my legs up with the computer in my lap. So I just couldn't bear to use Behemoth anymore. I unplugged it and stacked the pieces in a corner. (I was embarrassed to ask Computing Services to retrieve it — I thought I'd wait a few more weeks, to give the impression I had taken their gift seriously.) But since I wasn't ready to abandon my Linux experiment, I was faced with a simple problem: how to get a laptop that would run Linux.

I won't bore you with the negotiations I conducted with my wife; they were subtle, protracted, and — from my point of view, anyway — ultimately successful. (Unlike the negotiations I was simultaneously conducting with *Books & Culture,* whose staff did not seem to think this series of articles would be successful enough to justify their buying me a computer. In fact, they seemed to want new computers for themselves.) So I ordered a bottom-of-the-line IBM ThinkPad from an online computer store, and kept my fingers crossed that my new Linux Mandrake would run on it.

It wouldn't. I had no luck booting from the CD, but I had been there before with Behemoth, so I tried the boot floppy which, I was pleased to see, had come in the package: "Boot Failed," the screen said. So I went to another computer and made my own boot floppy: "Boot Failed." OK. I could handle this. Back to Corel Linux — it had worked with Behemoth, right? — so I tried that, again from a boot floppy, because CD installation clearly wasn't happening on this machine either. This time things seemed to go better, because it started installing — though in command-line mode, no images — and indeed got all the way to asking for my username before something went astray. No matter what I did I couldn't get past this point.

Now the cursing began in earnest. But I was not ready to give up. Several "compact" distributions of Linux promising ease of installation were available for free download on the Internet. I tried three; none worked. I borrowed a more recent version of Linux Mandrake from a friend. Nope. Finally, in desperation, I went back to the computer store to try one more highly rated distribution, from the German company SuSE (pronounced "Sousa," like the composer). After all, what was thirty more bucks, given the amounts of money and time I had already invested? I brought SuSE Linux home, inserted the CD, and started the computer. It booted up and installed without a hitch. Go figure. But I wasn't asking questions; now I had a Linux laptop stuffed with applications for every purpose. I was primed to rock and roll.

3.

It's vital to refrain from getting frustrated with the system. Nothing is earned by taking an axe — or worse, a powerful electromagnet — to your Linux system in a fit of anger.

Running Linux

Veterans of Linux no doubt smiled, with some mixture of condescension and sympathy, as they read my last paragraph. They know that my troubles were only beginning; it would not be long before I had burned into my brain the comment I found on a Linux website: "Nothing in Linux works the first time."

But initially the sailing was smooth. I perused the dozen or so word-processing applications and text editors newly loaded on my Linux box, found one I liked, and started drafting the first section of this essay. Once I got a thousand words or so, I figured I had better back up my file — but how? The ThinkPad had no internal floppy drive, couldn't write to a CD, and wasn't connected to the Internet. And while I owned both a floppy drive and a Zip drive, my new OS didn't seem to recognize either of them. I was able to find on the Net various "howto" documents from the many websites created by Linux aficionados to assist "newbies" like me, and I pored carefully over the pages of *Running Linux* (an otherwise admirable resource), but I couldn't seem to make much progress with any of my problems — perhaps as a result of slight variations in the Linux distributions. Eventually I called my colleague Jeff Beaird, an experienced and skilled Linux user, to help me get connected to the Wheaton College network (this time with the blessing and assistance of Computing Services), so at least I could email the document to myself. Jeff did this with relative ease — though even he ran into enough unexpected problems to convince me that I could never in ten years have gotten the machine properly configured all by myself. Still, I told him to leave the floppy and Zip drives to me; I was determined to do *something* on my own.

Well, I still haven't gotten those problems solved. My greatest achievement so far came as a result of my shutting down the computer improperly: the next time I turned the computer on, the startup process was interrupted by this message: "UNEXPECTED INCONSISTENCY; RUN fsck MANUALLY." I had no idea what this meant, but I turned to my Mac and found a "howto" document on one of the Linux sites that took me step-by-step through the procedure. Soon I had the computer running normally again, and had lost no data. And I was very, very proud of myself.

But plainly I have a long way to go, and a lot of work to do; and it's not every day that I feel that it's worth it. Since I started pursuing this project, it has become increasingly obvious that the lines between the Open Source world and corporate America are being blurred. IBM's relentlessly televised touting of its alliance with Linux is the most conspicuous example, but Apple's introduction of Macintosh OS X is more intriguing and perhaps more significant. Since I installed OS X on my PowerBook, I have been running what is essentially a version of Unix (the aforementioned BSD) with a visually dynamic interface superimposed on it. The chess program that comes with OS X is actually GNU Chess, which means that it is available to users under the terms of the famous GNU Public License. This fascinating document mandates that Apple (and anybody else distributing the application) make the application's source code — the actual instructions the application sends to the computer; which collectively constitute the "intellectual property" that Bill Gates and others have insisted on the need to preserve — available on request, and denies Apple, and anybody else, the right to *prevent* free access to that source code. (Because this is such a strange use of copyright — not to ensure the owner's control over his or her intellectual property, but to prevent anybody else from exercising such control — Stallman calls it "copyleft.") And, strangest of all to anyone familiar with the whole Macintosh enterprise, OS X includes a "terminal" — a screen that responds only to typed commands — so that many traditional Unix applications, like the text editors Emacs and vi (pronounced "vee-eye"), can be run from the command line. Apple has even made the source code for the kernel of OS X available, and has invited the open source community to collaborate with them in its development.

It all seems too good to be true — and indeed, say many in the open-source world, it is just that. To anyone who remembers or even has read about the sixties, it's a very familiar debate: the old, intractable question of "co-optation." Are the Big Corporate Brothers co-opting the revolutionary work of the open-source hacker community for their own insidious and thoroughly proprietary purposes — just as university presidents once invited student protesters into university governance and thereby domesticated the malcontents? (After all, Apple hasn't given up corporate rule over OS X's source code.) Are the glorious rebel hackers — with the notable exception of Stallman, who won't cooperate with anyone — simply being bought off? Perhaps; but as the literary theorist Gerald Graff once asked, in reference to the sixties version of the co-optation debate, isn't "being co-opted" merely a derogatory description of *success?* Graff suspects that many would-be revolutionaries prefer to *remain* marginal; they seem to fear that if their ideas gained acceptance it would only prove that those ideas weren't revolutionary after all, just as Groucho Marx didn't want to belong to any club that would accept *him* as a member. If Graff's suspicions are right, then for many in the open source community, the developments I have been tracing here — the embrace of Linux by IBM and Unix by Apple, the creation of slick GUIs for Linux, the interest of Eloi like me in the whole open-source endeavor — are clear signs that it's time to move on to something else, something less accessible to the uninitiated.

But whatever *they* choose to do, it seems clear to me that distributions of Linux are going to get easier and easier to install and configure; soon it will be possible even for people less comfortable with computers than me to run this rebel OS. Indeed, one of the most recent distributions of Linux, from a company called Lycoris, claims to be as easy to use as Windows or Mac, a claim that some reviewers have heartily endorsed. But I'm not sure how I feel about the increasing prominence and influence and accessibility of Linux.

It's certainly not a wholly bad thing. Given that there are so many distributions of Linux out there and no possibility of one taking over, anyone running Linux can escape the domination of the Big Two of the computer industry, Microsoft and AOL/Time-Warner. And that's a very big deal, as far as I and the blue-haired art students are concerned. But the do-it-yourself aspect of the Linux experience will continue to be eroded. Neal Stephenson has described the Linux world as "a bunch of RVs, yurts, teepees, and geodesic domes set up in a field and organized by consensus," so that the residents can work together to build state-of-the-art machines — a sixties collectivist revision of my Cyber-Amish metaphor — and even if they continue to build machines of the same quality, something will be lost when the yurts and teepees are replaced by geometrical rows of prefabricated houses. (Indeed, for the real hackers, the transformation of the field into a subdivision was essentially complete when the distributions started coming out: you can hear their prophetic denunciations and demands for a return to purity on the various websites that purport to teach you how to build "Linux from scratch.") There's no doubt that Linux has been "co-opted" at least in this sense (i.e., it has become successful) and as a result the other aspect of control with which I have been concerned — control over one's use of a computer, over one's interactions with it — is being diminished. It's getting harder to tell the difference between Linux and Mac OS X; in both cases the command line lurks there in the background for anyone who happens to notice it, but soon there may be Linux users who (like almost all Mac users) never *do* notice it. And the Mac interface is far prettier.

It may be, then, that for people like me these are the days, the Golden Age of Linux: using Linux today doesn't require impossible-to-master technical skills, but has enough of a learning curve to be a source of instruction and literacy. I have definitely become far more computer literate as a result of my Linux experiment — and will continue to learn, I trust — but at this point I'm wonderng what that literacy and my newfound skills are worth. I've paid a considerable price, more in time and energy than in money, to reach this point: have I spent my resources well? Well, that's a matter that bears more reflection than I have time to give it right now. Because if I don't find my my */etc/rc.config* file — or, perhaps, my */etc/rc.config.d/ hotplug.rc.config* file — I'm never going to get this Zip drive working.

THIRD STAGE

1.

Dr. Gelernter:

People with advanced degrees aren't as smart as they think they are. If you'd had any brains you would have realized that there are a lot of people out there who resent bitterly the way technonerds like you are changing the world and you wouldn't have been dumb enough to open an unexpected package from an unknown source.

In the epilog of your book, "Mirror Worlds," you tried to justify your research by claiming that the developments you describe are inevitable, and that any college person can learn enough about computers to compete in a computer-dominated world. Apparently, people without a college degree don't count. In any case, being informed about computers won't enable anyone to prevent invasion of privacy (through computers), genetic engineering (to which computers make an important contribution), environmental degradation through excessive economic growth (computers make an important contribution to economic growth) and so forth.

As for the inevitability argument, if the developments you describe are inevitable, they are not inevitable in the way that old age and bad weather are inevitable. They are inevitable only because techno-nerds like you make them inevitable. If there were no computer scientists there would be no progress in computer science. If you claim you are justified in pursuing your research because the developments involved are inevitable, then you may as well say that theft is inevitable, therefore we shouldn't blame thieves.

But we do not believe that progress and growth are inevitable. We'll have more to say about that later.

FC

"Dr. Gelernter" is David Gelernter, a computer scientist at Yale University, who received this letter on April 23, 1995. "FC," other documents from the same author explained, stands for Freedom Club — but despite the use of plural pronouns in this letter and many others, one person wrote the message: Theodore Kaczynski, otherwise known as the Unabomber. On June 23, 1993, Gelernter had opened "an unexpected package," which immediately exploded, wounding him severely. In 1998, Theodore Kaczynski pled guilty to the charge of being the "unknown source" of the package that injured Gelernter.

It seemed strange to many that Kaczynski would single out Gelernter, who is distinctive among computer scientists for his aesthetic sensibilities and his lack of enthusiasm for technology as such. Indeed, some of Gelernter's warnings about over-reliance on computers can sound oddly like statements in the Unabomber's notorious Manifesto. (A more likely antagonist would be someone like Ted Nelson, inventor and promoter of "hypertext," who in his 1974 book *Computer Lib/Dream Machines* exhorted, "You can and must understand computers NOW.") But perhaps it was

Gelernter's very humaneness that, to Kaczynski, made him so dangerous: by striving, in several books, to demystify computer technology and usage; by designing hardware and software that would be comfortable, functional, and un-intimidating to ordinary users; by insisting that people with no formal training in computer programming could nevertheless come to understand at least the basics of how computers work, Gelernter might actually do more to solidify the place of computers in our everyday lives than the real "techno-geeks" ever could.

Kaczynski's arguments stand in direct contradiction to the thoughts and concerns that have motivated this series of essays. Like Gelernter, I have assumed that the continuing, indeed the increasing, centrality of computers to our culture is "inevitable." (I suspect that Kaczynski secretly thought so too: he was certainly smart enough to know that the use of computers is not curtailed by the bombing of a computer scientist. If he had had real hopes of lessening our dependence on computers, he would have attacked the machines themselves — or the factories that made them — just as the nineteenth-century Luddites destroyed the knitting machines that were putting them out of work. Kaczynski's resort to mail bombs is really an admission of futility.)

But I do not believe that the inevitability of computers equals the inevitability of theft. Theft is a crime, the computer a technological product; and the problem with technology is always to find a way to put it to proper uses while avoiding putting it to dangerous, destructive, or immoral uses. True, any knowledge *I* gain about computers will do nothing to halt experiments in genetic engineering or slow "excessive economic growth," though I can imagine ways in which computer-literate others might contribute to those causes; I also think it safe to say that my *refraining* from computer literacy, or even computer usage, won't be of any help. But within my own daily sphere of action, I believe that increasing my ability to use computers can be helpful to me. (And it can surely help me to preserve my privacy, though that goal is not high on my list.)

I was encouraged, as I began this project in self-education, to discover the very comment from Gelernter's *Mirror Worlds* that angered Kaczynski. I was likewise emboldened by this statement from the engineer Henry Petroski: "I believe that anyone today is capable of comprehending the essence of, if not of contributing to, even the latest high technology" — though I think I would have felt considerably more emboldened if this sentence had come at the beginning of a 400-page book about computers, instead of a 400-page book called *The Pencil*. (It's a wonderful book, though.) I have tried to record, especially in the second essay in this series, some of the rewards (as well as some of the frustrations) that I have received in my plunge into the world of computer technology, especially my encounter with Linux and the world of open-source software. But I am faced now with certain important questions that I have not even begun to address. For myself, I need to ask whether the rewards have been commensurate with the investment. But more largely, I need to ask whether I can or should recommend such a project to others: do I imagine what I have done to be of such general value that it transcends mere idiosyncrasy of interest? More specifically, I find myself wondering if this whole area of inquiry has implications for the Christian life? To the personal and the larger questions alike, I believe my answers are Yes. But even to begin to explain why, I need to explore the terminology needed to conduct these explorations.

2.

Looking back over the reading I have done in preparing to write this essay, I notice a widespread tendency to speak of the concerns raised by the increasing prevalence of computers as *technological* concerns; the assumption shared by almost all parties is that any "problem" following from the cultural dominance of computers is but a special case of what the philosopher Martin Heidegger famously called "the question concerning technology." Henry Petroski emphasizes the links between pencils and computers: both are technological products. Kaczynski sneers at "techno-nerds"; some years later, as I noted in the first essay in this series, Gelernter would tacitly respond by writing that "to hate technology is in the end to hate humanity, to hate yourself, because technology is what human beings do." (Thus the title of another of Petroski's books: *To Engineer Is Human*.)

But I have become convinced that technology as such is not the issue at all. Theodore Kaczynski certainly made studied use of technology in designing and building his bombs, even to the point of encasing them in carefully wrought wooden boxes. But, as he wrote in his infamous "Manifesto," not all technologies are equal: "We distinguish between two kinds of technology, which we will call small-scale technology and organization-dependent technology." The distinction, however, does not have the force that Kaczynski wants it to have: powerful computers can be built and used by persons no more dependent on "organizations" than was Kaczynski when he bought the materials with which he built his bombs.

We come closer to the heart of the matter when we think of computers in terms of *information* technology. Here the work of the philosopher Albert Borgmann is important. In his seminal book *Holding on to Reality: The Nature of Information at the Turn of the Millennium*, Borgmann identifies three types of information:

1. Information *about* reality. In this category Borgmann includes many forms of "reports and records," from "medicine rings" constructed by the Blackfoot Indians of Montana, and the altar Abram built to the Lord at Hebron, to many forms of the written word.
2. Information *for* reality, or "cultural information." This includes recipes and instructions of all types: "there are plans, scores, and constitutions, information for erecting buildings, making music, and ordering society."
3. Information *as* reality. This is the peculiar province of certain, especially digital, technologies: in it, "the paradigms of report and recipe are succeeded by the paradigm of the recording. The technological information on a compact disc is so detailed and controlled that it addresses us virtually *as* reality."

The power that we have achieved to produce so much of this third type of information, and produce it so skillfully, concerns Borgmann deeply. He believes that throughout most of human history we have managed a degree of balance between "signs and things," but in these last days have achieved a technology of signs so masterful that it "steps forward as a rival of reality."

207

Borgmann's book is excellent in many ways, but in his complaints about the dangers of a world dominated by technologically produced signs he often descends into a metaphorical vagueness — the sort of vagueness that tends to get a writer called a Luddite. For instance, he is somewhat unhappy about the creation of enormous and sophisticated databases of ancient Greek and Roman texts because he believes that, in the use of such databases, "texts get flattened out, and scholars get detached from their work." But what Borgmann means by "flattened" and "detached" never becomes clear, at least to me.

In more anecdotal passages, though, his argument takes on meaningful flesh, and does so in ways that illuminate the issues I am concerned with. Considering Microsoft's virtual version of London's National Gallery (a CD-ROM from the mid-'90s), Borgmann comments,

> No amount of commentary can substitute for the grandly bourgeois and British setting of Trafalgar Square whose center is marked by the monumental column that supports Lord Nelson, one of the protagonists in Britain's rise to world power. But it is not simply a matter of perfecting technological information to the point where users of the *Microsoft Art Gallery* can have an interactive full motion video that furnishes them with the experience of strolling through the museum and ambling out on Trafalgar Square to admire the Nelson column. The highly impoverished quality of such walking aside, virtual reality, however expansive, is finally bounded and connects of itself to nothing while the actual Gallery borders on Trafalgar Square adjoining in turn St. Martin's Church and neighboring Charing Cross and so on in the inexhaustible texture of streets and focal points that is London.

The virtual Gallery necessarily lacks the *surround* of the real (historical and physical) world: it cannot provide the contexts, contrasts, and surprises that that world offers.

To be sure, the virtual world offers contexts, contrasts, and surprises of its own — after all, a virtual Louvre is available for purchase also, which makes it possible to compare the holdings of two great museums without having to take a train through the Chunnel. On the other hand, as long as I am sitting in front of my computer I can't take the trip from London to Paris. I can't experience the important feeling of disorientation, so striking to almost every American (even before trains connected the cities), that derives from experiencing the geographical proximity of these two dramatically different capitals. I can't know the neighborhoods in which the great museums are situated. It would not even be possible for any Londoner or Parisian, no matter how eager they might be, to be rude to me. These experiences would be unavailable because I would be sitting at my desk, looking at my computer, and scanning the images produced by software that I purchased — images that can inform me about, but not allow me to experience, the different sizes of the paintings, or their full dimensionality, since the textures produced by different brush techniques are often invisible even on the highest-resolution monitor. (These particular problems computers share with books, indeed with all forms of mechanical reproduction of the visual arts.)

Of course, I can easily imagine the responses advocates of this technology would make to the points Borgmann and I are making. In fact, I do not need to imagine them: I can simply consult a book like *Multimedia: From Wagner to Virtual Reality,* and find celebrations on almost every page of the immense aesthetic and informational capabilities of computer technology. Scott Fisher: "The possibilities of virtual realities, it appears, are as limitless as the possibilities of reality." Lynn Hershman claims that digital works of art allow people to replace "longing, nostalgia and emptiness with a sense of identity, purpose and hope." Marcos Novak imagines "liquid architectures in cyberspace," in which "the next room is always where I need it to be and what I need it to be."

I do not wish to dispute any of these claims; they are often interesting and sometimes, when fleshed out, compelling. Rather, I merely wish to note that the conflict between Borgmann and the celebrants of *Multimedia* centers on two issues: first, the relative value of different kinds of information, and second, the importance of wide accessibility of information. Borgmann makes a strong case for the depth of the losses incurred when we forsake information *about* and *for* reality in favor of information *as* reality; and he shows how the ready accessibility of an overwhelming range of technological information creates the temptation always to settle for the instantly available. After all, it takes a lot more trouble and money to buy tickets and drive to see the Angeles Quartet than to sample my collection of their CDs — and the inertia can be hard to resist even if I know that the "context" and "surround" of the live performance offer me a quality and quantity of experiential information not available on compact disc.

What Borgmann does *not* adequately address is the compensatory value of technological information for those who do not, and cannot reasonably hope to, have access to the "real thing"; nor does he give judicious assessment of the claim that the marshaling of diverse kinds of information ("multimedia") on a single computer enables the user to produce and control context in a way that has its own distinctive value. And so the argument goes on — indeed, I believe that it is in its early stages, because I believe that as yet we have no conceptual vocabulary adequate to assessing these various and often competing goods.

Therefore, I don't claim that I can even begin to answer the questions raised by the technophiles and their critics. But I do believe that in raising and considering them, I am led back to the unique role of the computer as an information machine — to my claim that the lexicon of "technology" doesn't help us very much as we try to think well about these things. Borgmann has clarified the situation considerably, but to get to the heart of things, we need to consider the intellectual origin of the modern computer, in a paper written by the English mathematician Alan Turing in 1938.

The paper is called "On Computable Numbers," and its chief purpose was to work through a question (called the *Entscheidungsproblem*, or "decision problem") that had been raised a few years earlier by the German mathematician David Hilbert, and had been complicated by the simultaneous work of the Czech Kurt Gödel. I cannot explain this problem, because I do not understand it; but for our purposes here what matters is a thought experiment Turing undertook in his pursuit of the problem: he imagined a certain machine, which he would call a "universal machine," though later it became known as a "Turing machine." He wrote: "It is possible to invent a single machine which can be used to compute any computable sequence," and one could say — indeed, many have said — that in imagining it Turing *did* invent it. He did not build a computer at that time, but he showed that such a machine *could* be built, and that the key to it would be the simplicity of its basic functions: "Let us imagine the operations performed . . . to be split up into 'simple operations' which are so elementary that it is not easy to imagine them further divided." In fact, today's digital computer chips, based as they are on a binary system where the only possibilities are zero or one, on or off, work in a manner *so* simple that it cannot *possibly* be "further divided."

How operations so basic can be multiplied and combined until they produce the extravagantly complex results that we see on our computers today is explained, with wonderful clarity, by W. Daniel Hillis in his book *The Pattern on the Stone*; but what is so extraordinary about Turing's little paper is his ability to intuit, long before our current sciences of chaos and complexity, that the more simple his imagined machine was, the more powerful and indeed universal it could become.* It is the very simplicity of the Turing machine's organizing structure that enables it, as Turing demonstrated, to perfectly imitate any other machine organized on similar principles.

This point takes us to the heart of the matter we have been discussing, because today's computers come remarkably close to being universal machines in practice as well as in theory. My laptop fulfills the functions that, when I was in high school, were fulfilled by the following "machines": typewriter, radio, stereo, television, film projector, calculator, ledger, address book, mailbox, tape recorder, chessboard, games arcade, clock, newspaper, magazine, encyclopedia, dictionary, thesaurus, film projector, slide projector — even library and museum. And that is of course a very incomplete list. This comprehensive ability to *imitate* — what I will call the computer's "mimeticism" — is what makes the computer so different from any other form of technology; it is also what makes the challenge of responding wisely to the machine's enormous promise so formidable.

---

*As vital as this insight was, in order for computers to develop into the powerful machines they have become another fundamental idea was needed, the idea of the "bit" — that is, the fundamental unit of information. That idea was discovered by the American engineer and mathematician Claude Shannon, whose paper "The Mathematical Theory of Information" (published in the *Bell System Technical Journal* in 1948) has an importance equal to that of Turing's "On Computable Numbers." Shannon, whose ratio of importance to obscurity may be as high as anyone's in the twentieth century, died in 2001 at the age of eighty-four.

In daily practice, it seems to me, the most important consequences of the potent mimeticism of the computer are two: the constriction of spatial experience, and the reduction of the play of the human body. When my computer becomes the sole, or at least prime, source for a great deal of information that once I would have sought from many different machines, located in many different places in my house, my community, or beyond, the *meaningful space* of my daily life is more and more often reduced to the size of my screen. As a direct result, sometimes the only parts of my body that receive meaningful employment in my daily labors are my eyes and my fingers — I don't even have to turn my head to find out what time it is, nor, if I wish to listen to music (for example), do I have to get up, cross the room, find a CD, insert it in my CD player, and turn it on. I need do no more than shift my eyeballs and tap a few keys.

Interestingly, fictional dreams of "virtual reality" — starting, perhaps, with Vernor Vinge's 1981 story "True Names" and proceeding through William Gibson's *Neuromancer* (1984) and Neal Stephenson's *Snow Crash* (1992) — imagine realms of purely mental experience: one lives in a digitally generated world, possessing an equally digital "body." One's real, material *corpus* lies motionless at some insignificant point in "meatspace" while one's mind explores the Metaverse (Stephenson) or the Other Plane (Vinge). Such fantasies enact, as many commentators have noted, a classically Gnostic longing for liberation from the body. And even for those of us who have no interest in experiential games of that particular kind, if we feel that our most important work is done at our computers, then our bodies' needs — food, sleep, exercise, urination, defecation — can seem irritatingly distracting or even embarrassing. As though bodily functions were signs of weakness; as though thought alone dignifies us. One of Vinge's characters, an elderly woman, wishes to record her whole being in the bits and bytes of the Other Plane so that, as she puts it, "when this body dies, *I* will still be" — and a more exciting, elegant, and powerful self than her embodied self ever was or could have been. And I find myself guessing that Vinge participates to some considerable degree in this Gnostic fantasy, primarily because his characters spend untold consecutive hours fighting spectacularly powerful and evil forces in the Other Plane without ever having to pause to go take a pee.

3.

Perhaps what I am saying here is little more than a rephrasing of Borgmann's distinction between information about and for reality (which I get by moving physically about in "meatspace") and information as reality (which the computer, by miming so many machines and therefore encouraging me to stay in front of it, wants me to be content with). But I believe I am pointing to something that Borgmann does not address except, perhaps, by implication: the relation between thinking and embodied experience.

In order to elucidate this point, let's revisit that fruitful period of sixty or so years ago during which our computerized world was launched. If the work of Turing and Shannon laid the *theoretical* groundwork for the rise to dominance of the computer, some of the key *imaginative* groundwork was laid by a man named Vannevar Bush, who during the Second World War (while Turing was building computers to break the codes created by the German Enigma machines) was the chief scientific advisor to President Roosevelt. As the combat drew to a close, and as the technological achievements of the war years filtered into civilian life to find new uses, Bush understood that one of the great problems of the coming decades would be the organization of information. He believed that what was needed, and what indeed could be built, was a "memory extender," or a "Memex" for short. Bush's Memex, which he conceived in the form of a large desk with multiple hidden components, would be able to store information of many types, visual and aural — words, plans, drawings, diagrams, voice recordings, music — and would possess an elaborate mechanism to file, classify, and cross-reference all that it contained. In short, Bush imagined a personal computer with an Internet connection (though in his prospectus the Memex was mechanical in a Rube-Goldbergish sort of way, rather than digital and electronic).

What I find especially telling is the title Bush gave to the essay — it appeared in the *Atlantic Monthly* in June 1945 — in which he described the Memex: "As We May Think." Bush's argument is that the technologies of warfare can be converted into technologies of knowledge, and that the conversion will enable us to think differently and better. It strikes me that the hidden, and vital, connection between these two technologies is the principle of *action at a distance.* After the horrific trench warfare of World War I, military minds spent much of the next twenty years engineering combat machines that would enable armies to inflict damage on enemies too far away to be seen, much less fought with hand-to-hand. From the expanded use of hand grenades, to the increase in the range of artillery, to the development of plans for extensive strategic bombing, the methods of warfare during the Second World War sought to act against the enemy from long range. (Of course, all parties to the war developed similar methods and machines, so none got its wish of being able to fight from a position of safety.) Vannevar Bush seems to have translated this principle to the struggle to acquire and organize information: he imagines people of the future conquering their enemies — Ignorance and Disorder — without ever leaving their Memexes. Military technology and information technology, in Bush's vision, turn out to have the same goals: the maximizing of efficiency and the minimizing of both risk and the expense of energy. It is a vision prompted by a belief in the scarcity of resources and the imminence of danger; and it has become the vision of the Information Age.

Because we believe in this vision, because we think (against all the evidence) that we need to conserve our intellectual resources — or, perhaps, simply because we are lazy — we listen eagerly to those who offer us machines that are more and more truly universal; and we become increasingly deaf to the call of other voices from other rooms. In such a climate, one is tempted to believe that what the Universal Machine doesn't offer can't be of such value that it would be worthwhile to get up from one's desk and seek it out. I recall a forecast Jean-François Lyotard made in *The Postmodern Condition,* almost twenty years ago: "We can predict that anything in the constituted body of knowledge that is not translatable in this way will be abandoned and that the direction of new research will be dictated by the possibility of its eventual results being translated into computer language." In nineteenth-century Oxford a little poem circulated featuring as its purported speaker Benjamin Jowett, translator of Plato and Master of Balliol:

First come I, my name is Jowett;
There's no knowledge but I know it.

I am the master of this College;
What I don't know isn't knowledge.

The personal computer is the Jowett of our time: what it doesn't know isn't knowledge.

4.

It was, I now see, an intuited sense of the dangers posed by the Jowettization of the computer that led me to conduct the experiment with Linux that I described in the previous movement of this essay: I was seeking (with apologies to the prophet Isaiah) to make the straight paths crooked and the plain places rough. If David Gelernter — as I noted in the first essay of this series — wants software that will make the computer "transparent" to our desires, I craved opacity. I had become so used to my computer, so disposed to exploit its resources and explore its capabilities, that I had begun to wonder, like one of the travelers in Bunyan's *Pilgrim's Progress*, if perhaps this smooth, broad road were a little *too* inviting, a little *too* easy to traverse; a feeling that intensified at those points when the tiniest of difficulties presented itself and, lo, Bill Gates appeared at my elbow, saying, "Here, let me help you with that."

Some years ago the novelist John Updike wrote this telling reflection on much art, especially visual art, of the twentieth century: "we feel in each act not only a plenitude (ambition, intuition, expertise, delight, etc.) but an absence — a void that belongs to these creative acts. *Nothing is preventing them.*" In contrast, "works like *Madame Bovary* and *Ulysses* glow with the heat of resistance that the will to manipulate meets in banal, heavily actual subjects." Precisely: resistance. The mind needs resistance in order to function properly; it understands itself and its surroundings through encountering boundaries, borders, limits — all that pushes back or refuses to yield. Now, Updike believes that artistic greatness is often achieved by those who *overcome* such resistance; but the resistance must be felt, and forcefully felt, for that overcoming to be artistically productive. I am no artist, of course, and I doubt that Updike would feel plenitude in

215

anything I do; but his notion seems immensely relevant to my condition nonetheless.

A curious feature of this resistance is that it can only happen when each party is exerting pressure on the other; and as my computing life became smoother and more featureless, I became increasingly unable to tell whether this was because my computer was yielding to my desires or I to its. (The more confused and uncomfortable a computer user is, the more enthralled he or she becomes to the computer's preferences; such a user offers little resistance to the "defaults." The issue of resistance is significant for every computer user, though in different ways.) So I plunged into the world of open-source software precisely because, in the words of the aficionado I quoted in my previous essay, "nothing in Linux works the first time." I wanted to be puzzled; I wanted to be at a loss sometimes. I wanted to have to get up and go to the library or bookstore; I wanted to need to call a friend for help. Linux user groups — there are hundreds of them across the country — periodically stage "Installfests," where users bring their computers and software and either help or get help from others. Running Linux, therefore, often involves moving one's body, expanding one's spatial environment, and interacting with other people in a kind of *ad hoc* community. The *resistance* offered by the collaborative and decentered development of Linux, and its consequent lack of immediate "user-friendliness," may create frustrations, but it also encourages the cultivation of certain virtues — patience, humility, teachableness — and opens the user to a range of benefits. I have described this project of mine as a quest for control, but in some ways it would be more accurate to describe it as a quest for a situation in which control is always being negotiated; where the boundaries shift because the forces of resistance wax and wane, on both sides.

However, the Linux experiment, I must admit, is one that I now find hard to sustain. Like most people, I have daily responsibilities that do not allow me to spend an indefinite amount of time fiddling with configuration files, or solving whatever the Linux conundrum of the moment happens to be. Sometimes I have to go back to what I know, whether I want to or not. And in this context the new Unix-based Macintosh OS X begins to feel like a rather insidious temptation: whenever I start to feel a longing for "resistance," I can always fire up the terminal and use old-fashioned text-based applications, like the Lynx web browser, Pine for email, emacs for text editing — though whenever those pleasures ebb I can immediately switch back to the inimitable Mac eye-candy. If using Linux is like moving into a log cabin, using OS X is like visiting a dude ranch: you know that whenever "roughing it" grows tiresome or uncomfortable, all the comforts of capitalist modernity can emerge from their hiding place to meet your needs.

But still, I think, my experiment has reminded me that the ways we use our computers could be *other* — there are alternative models of organizing and deploying information than those which our computers supply by default, out of the box. Even when I set aside my Linux box and return to my Macintosh, I find myself using that computer in a more self-conscious way, with a clearer sense of its capabilities and its limitations. And I find it easier to spend time away from the computer, re-acquainting myself with some of the non-digital ways of thinking and learning and writing with which I grew up. I value my computer as much as, or more than, I ever have; but I feel that in some sense I have put it in its place.

And what is its place? As a tool: an unprecedentedly resourceful and adaptable tool, to be sure, but no more. It lacks purposes of its own; those it appears to have are the purposes of its makers, and these may or may not be *our* purposes; we should ask whether they are. Many years ago Jacques Ellul called us all to "the measuring of technique by other criteria than those of technique itself," and this obligation is all the more vital when the "technique" involved is a universal machine that shapes, or seeks to shape, how we may think. Ellul even goes so far as to call that task of measurement "the search for justice before God." That very formulation of the issue is a challenge, a challenge I have had in mind throughout my exploration of my computerized life and its alternatives. The chief value of my experiment, I have come to believe, is that it has reminded me both of the importance of offering resistance to our computers' preference for their own "default positions," and of the ability of the created order to resist the attempt of the pervasively mimetic machine to substitute for it. God's ways, it turns out, are often not the ways of the computer builders and software designers. The problem of "computer control" is, in the end, the problem of restraining the ever-increasing ambitions of the universal machine's makers, not in order to repudiate those machines, but in order to harness them and employ them in the search for justice before God.

Notes

xi   **"Our ears burn"** Homer, *Odysssey*, trans. Robert Fitzgerald (New York: Farrar, Straus and Giroux, 1998), Book XXI, ll. 363ff.

xii   **"mixture of falsehoods"** Bacon, "Of Truth," *Francis Bacon: A Selection of His Work*, ed. Sidney Warhaft (New York: Bobbs-Merrill, 1965), pp. 47-49.

xiii   **"metaphysicians"** In *Philosophy and the Mirror of Nature* (Princeton: Princeton University Press, 1979) Rorty makes the distinction between "systematic" and "edifying" philosophy; later — for instance, in *Contingency, Irony, and Solidarity* (Cambridge: Cambridge University Press, 1989) — he keeps the idea, but terms the opposing camps "metaphysicians" and "pragmatists."

xiv   **"What we suffer from"** G. K. Chesterton, *Orthodoxy* (New York: Image, 1990), pp. 31-32.

xiv   **"Only those who try"** Lewis, *Mere Christianity* (New York: Macmillan, 1960), p. 124.

xv   **"the search for justice"** Ellul, *The Technological Society*, trans. John Wilkinson (New York: Vintage, 1964), p. 38

3   **"at my birth"** Shakespeare, *I Henry IV*, Act III, Scene 1.

5   **"I sit in one of the dives"** Auden, *Selected Poems*, 2nd ed., ed. Edward Mendelson (New York: Vintage, 1979), pp. 86-89.

7   **"In the deserts of the heart"** *Selected Poems*, p. 83.

8   **"Auden on Bin Laden"** http://slate.msn.com/id/115900.

8   **"the mystery of iniquity"** II Thess. 2:7.

9   **"We must love one another *and* die"** For the history of Auden's revulsion towards his own poem, see Edward Mendelson, *Later Auden* (New York: Farrar, Straus and Giroux, 1999), pp. 477-78.

9   **"of walls, doors, and reticence"** *Selected Poems*, p. 191.

10 **"overrun either by Germany"** quoted in Carl Rollyson, *Rebecca West: A Life* (New York: Scribner, 1996), p. 177. The biographical details in my discussion of West I have gleaned from reading Rollyson's fine book.

11 **"preference for the agreeable"** West, *Black Lamb and Grey Falcon* (London: Penguin, 1994 [1941]), p. 400.

12 **"If this be so"** *Black Lamb,* p. 913.

13 **"Art is not a plaything"** *Black Lamb,* p. 55.

13 **"I had reason"** *Black Lamb,* pp. 775-76.

14 **"Of this battlefield"** *Black Lamb,* p. 773.

15 **"wretched, complicated book"** This quote and the ones that follow, including the comment of West's publisher, come from Rollyson's *Rebecca West,* pp. 206-8.

16 **"Artlessness! You say"** Rollyson, *Rebecca West,* p. 215.

16 **"In the strict sense"** Wilbur, *New and Collected Poems* (San Diego: Harcourt Brace Jovanovich, 1988), p. 9.

17 **"There's a certain grain"** O'Connor, "The Nature and Aim of Fiction," in *Mystery and Manners* (New York: Farrar, Straus and Giroux, 1962), p. 77.

18 **"a poem is a witness"** *The Dyer's Hand* (New York: Random House, 1962), pp. 70-71.

18 **"Soon cool tramontana"** Auden, *Selected Poems,* pp. 225-26.

21 **"Audenesque"** See Valentine Cunningham, *British Writers of the Thirties* (New York: Oxford University Press, 1989), Chapter 2.

22 **"in the presence"** from Auden's essay in *Modern Canterbury Pilgrims,* ed. James A. Pike (London: Mowbray, 1956), p. 41.

22 **"There was no hypocrisy"** Auden in an interview with Alan Levy: "On Audenstrasse: In the Autumn of the Age of Anxiety," *New York Times Magazine,* 8 August 1971, pp. 10+.

24 **"really about the Christian"** Edward Mendelson, *Later Auden* (New York: Farrar, Straus, and Giroux, 1999), p. 205.

24 **"neo-Calvinist"** quoted by Mendelson, p. 151.

24 **"the greatest grandest opera"** *Selected Poems,* p. 172.

25 **". . . we are blessed"** *Selected Poems,* p. 173.

25 **"I never suspected the way"** *Selected Poems,* p. 134.

25 **"the author and giver"** "At the Grave of Henry James," *Selected Poems,* p. 123.

26 **"An illusion can never be"** from *The Point of View for My Work as an Author,* as excerpted in *A Kierkegaaard Anthology,* ed. Robert Bretall (New York: Modern Library, 1946), p. 332.

26 **"The mass and majesty"** *Selected Poems,* p. 199.

27 **"incorporated the significant"** *Later Auden,* p. xiv.

27 **"A robin with no Christian"** *Collected Poems*, rev. ed. (London: Faber, 1991), p. 580.

28 **"like all heretics"** "Second Thoughts on Kierkegaard," *Forewords and Afterwords* (New York: Random House, 1973), p. 191.

28 **"A planetary visitor"** from the essay in *Modern Canterbury Pilgrims*, p. 42.

29 **"A sense of humor"** *The Dyer's Hand*, p. 372.

29 **"began to write"** *Later Auden*, pp. 277-78.

30 **"That singular command"** "Precious Five," in *Collected Poems*, p. 591.

30 **"before God"** Kierkegaard's *Either/Or* concludes with a sermon entitled "The Edifying in the Thought That Against God We Are Always in the Wrong." Trans. Alastair Hannay (London: Penguin, 1992), pp. 595-609.

30 **"Do you know"** quoted in Mendelson, *Later Auden*, p. 108.

30 **"I believe because"** quoted in Mendelson, p. 207.

31 **"occupied [Auden's]"** quoted in Mendelson, p. 308.

31 **"Adam still previous"** *Selected Poems*, p. 217.

31 **"The day in which"** Mendelson, p. 333.

31 **"from fatal memory"** Mendelson, p. 359.

32 **"His religion condemned"** Isherwood, *Christopher and His Kind* (New York: Farrar, Straus and Giroux, 1976), p. 249.

32 **"Though I believe"** quoted in Mendelson, p. 455.

32 **"I am sorry"** "The Love Feast," in *Collected Poems*, p. 614.

33 **"the silliest remark"** Auden, "Squares and Oblongs," in *Poets at Work* (New York: Harcourt, 1948), p. 177.

33 **"Approachable as you"** *Selected Poems*, p. 235.

33 **"a hymn to Our Lady"** quoted in Mendelson, p. 397.

33 **"vocation, for Auden"** Mendelson, p. 348.

34 **"that eye-on-the-object"** *Selected Poems*, p. 219.

34 **"clown of God"** The poem is "The Ballad of Barnaby," in *Collected Poems*, pp. 824-27.

34 **"Now, did He really"** *Selected Poems*, p. 239.

35 **"Can poets"** *Selected Poems*, p. 231.

35 **"fellow-citizens"** quoted in Mendelson, p. 480.

35 **"to do for himself"** *Forewords and Afterwords*, p. 225.

35 **"We can only"** "The Horatians," *Collected Poems*, p. 773.

38 **"I'm getting tired"** quoted in Annie Cohen-Solal, *Sartre: A Life*, trans. Anna Cancogni (New York: Pantheon, 1987), p. 332.

38 **"Tell me, Camus"** quoted in Cohen-Solal, p. 333.

39 **"point to the French"** Camus, *Resistance, Rebellion, and Death*, trans. Justin O'Brien (New York: Knopf, 1960), p. 120.

40 **"being poor and free"** *Resistance, Rebellion, and Death*, p. 119.

40 **"I have always"** Herbert R. Lottman, *Albert Camus: A Biography* (Garden City, N.Y.: Doubleday, 1979), p. 618.

40 **"connected social critic"** Michael Walzer, *The Company of Critics* (New York: Basic, 1998). Chapter 8 is "Albert Camus's Algerian War."

40 **"I believe in justice"** Lottman, p. 618.

40 **"the silence"** Walzer, p. 152.

41 **"The *two* Algerian"** Camus, *The First Man* (New York: Alfred A. Knopf, 1995), p. 315.

41 **"Algeria for the Algerians"** Paul Johnson, *Modern Times: The World from the Twenties to the Eighties* (New York: Harper & Row, 1985), p. 497.

41 **"the only possible"** Johnson, p. 498.

41 **"Camus represented"** quoted in Cohen-Solal, p. 435.

42 **"Between the forces"** *Resistance, Rebellion, and Death*, pp. 73f.

42 **"admittedly paradoxical"** "Preface to *The Stranger*," *Lyrical and Critical Essays*, trans. Ellen Conroy Kennedy (New York: Vintage, 1968), p. 120.

44 **"I want to write"** *The First Man*, p. 310.

45 **"A chapter on the war"** *The First Man*, pp. 312-13.

47 **"the archetypal trimmer"** Said, "An Exchange: *Exodus and Revolution*," *Grand Street* 5:4 (Summer 1986), p. 257.

49 **"comic"** quoted in D. M. Thomas, *Alexander Solzhenitsyn: A Century in His Life* (New York: St. Martin's Press, 1998), p. 524.

49 **"in terms of"** David Remnick, *Resurrection: The Struggle for a New Russia* (New York: Random House, 1997), p. 130.

49 **"passé"** Thomas, p. 528.

49 **"If literature"** Remnick, p. 114.

49 **"fictive experience"** Thomas, p. xvi.

49 **"And may the spirits"** Thomas, p. xviii.

50 **"a rough wooden cross"** Scammell, *Solzhenitsyn: A Biography* (New York: W. W. Norton, 1986), p. 69.

50 **"a crazy old man"** Thomas, p. 61.

52 **"raged"** Thomas, p. 360.

52 **"The question"** Thomas, p. 287.

53 **"had he been"** Thomas, p. 443.

53 **"the 'Ode on a Grecian Urn'"** from Faulkner's famous *Paris Review* interview, in *Writers at Work*, ed. Malcolm Cowley (New York: Viking, 1958).

53 **"a writer rather"** Thomas, p. 299.

55 **"improbable salamander"** *The Gulag Archipelago* (one-volume edition, abridged by Edward E. Ericson, Jr.), trans. Thomas P. Whitney and Harry Willetts (New York: Harper and Row, 1985), p. xvi.

55 **"in the intoxication"** *The Gulag Archipelago*, p. 312-13.

56 **"Can you describe"** Akhmatova, "Requiem," *Selected Poems,* trans. D. M. Thomas (London: Penguin, 1988), p. 87.

56 **"As I ascend the hill"** quoted in Scammell, p. 587.

57 **"In the struggle"** An online version of Solzhenitsyn's Nobel lecture may be found at http://www.columbia.edu/cu/augustine/arch/solzhenitsyn/nobel-lit1970.htm.

57 **"just as it really"** quoted in Thomas, p. 479.

57 **"an artist died"** Thomas, p. 484.

58 **"there is much"** Thomas, p. 487.

58 **"caricature of a patriot"** quoted in Thomas, p. 513.

60 **"Pass Over"** This poem appears in Gregerson's collection *Waterborne* (Boston: Houghton Mifflin, 2002), pp. 34-38.

61 **"Tell all the truth"** *Complete Poems of Emily Dickinson* (Boston: Little, Brown, 1960), #1129.

62 **"If the whole human race"** Though this statement appears in many dictionaries of quotations, I have been unable to trace it to its source.

62 **"In the months"** Peter Abrahams, *Tell Freedom* (London: Faber, 1954), p. 238.

63 **"I took leave"** Abrahams, p. 246.

65 **"peculiar treasure"** Exodus 19:5.

66 **"I knew that you"** Jonah 4:2.

66 **"by their secret arts"** Exodus 7:22.

66 **"Have I any pleasure"** Ezekiel 18:23.

71 **"There's not room"** "Not Dark Yet," from *Time Out of Mind* (Columbia Records, 1997).

71 **"Thus one portion"** *William Blake* (Oxford Authors Series), ed. Michael Mason (Oxford: Oxford University Press, 1988), p. 15.

72 Relevant selections from Jung's *Psychological Types* may be found in *The Portable Jung,* ed. Joseph Campbell (London: Penguin, 1971), pp. 178-272; Auden's view may be found in *The Prolific and the Devourer* (New York: Ecco Press, 1981), *passim.*

74 **"All will be judged"** Auden, *Selected Poems,* p. 123.

74 **"Can poets"** Auden, *Selected Poems,* p. 231.

74 **"Take, eat; this is my body"** Matt. 26:26.

76 **"I don't want"** Mortimer rewrote his screenplay into a novel, also called *Titmuss Regained* (New York: Viking, 1990); this scene is on pages 257-58.

76 **"when she turned"** *Titmuss Regained,* p. 278.

77 **Lyall Watson** *Dark Nature: A Natural History of Evil* (New York: HarperCollins, 1996).

78 **"justify the ways"** *Paradise Lost,* I.26.

79 **"Nature is not"** This great poem was published in *Image* 28 (Fall 2000), pp. 37-38.

82   **"Bless you, prison!"**   see page 59 above.

83   **"is addressed to"**   Kass, *The Beginning of Wisdom: Reading Genesis* (New York: Free Press, 2003), p. 1.

83   **"How does a man"**   Kass, p. xi.

84   **"Public teachers"**   Kass, p. xii.

84   **"a reason to be suspicious"**   Kass, p. 3.

85   **"manner not its manifest"**   Kass, pp. 2-3.

85   **"reading without presuppositions"**   Kass, p. 17.

85   **"to read in the spirit"**   Kass, p. 16.

85   **"suspending disbelief"**   Kass, p. 17.

85   **"the democracy of the dead"**   G. K. Chesterton, *Orthodoxy* (New York: Image, 1990), p. 48.

85   **"attempts to understand"**   Kass, p. 13.

86   **"As were the protagonists"**   Kass, pp. 20-21.

86   **"In short, the first"**   Kass, p. 57.

86   **"A main teaching"**   Kass, pp. 40f.

86   **"to encourage the ambivalent"**   Kass, p. 198.

87   **"three fundamental human types"**   Kass, p. 215.

88   **"rejection of polytheism"**   Kass, p. 27.

89   **"In its presentation"**   Damrosch's essay is in *The Literary Guide to the Bible*, ed. Robert Alter and Frank Kermode (Cambridge: Belknap/Harvard University Press, 1987), p. 76.

89   **"The failure of the city"**   Kass, p. 247.

90   **"fraught with background"**   Auerbach, *Mimesis: The Representation of Reality in Western Literature*, trans. Willard R. Trask (Princeton: Princeton University Press, 1953), p. 12.

90   **"No story in Genesis"**   Kass, p. 333.

91   **"Abraham I do not"**   Kierkegaard, *Fear and Trembling/Repetition*, ed. and trans. Howard V. Hong and Edna H. Hong (Princeton: Princeton University Press, 1983), p. 37.

91   **"teleological suspension"**   *Fear and Trembling*, Problema I, pp. 57ff.

92   **"this awesome and shocking"**   Kass, p. 333.

93   **"The book of Genesis"**   Kass, p. 661.

97   **"Most of us know"**   *Kipling, Auden & Co.* (New York: Farrar, Straus and Giroux, 1980), p. 177.

97   **"glorious Revolution"**   Simon Schama, *Citizens* (New York: Alfred A. Knopf, 1989), p. 561.

98   **"a monumental chariot"**   *Citizens*, pp. 564-65.

99   **"I have received"**   quoted in Maurice Cranston, *Jean-Jacques: The Early Life of Jean-Jacques Rousseau* (Chicago: University of Chicago Press, 1982), p. 306.

100   **"I do not like you"** I have used the translation in Cranston, *The Noble Savage: Jean-Jacques Rousseau, 1754-1762* (Chicago: University of Chicago Press, 1991), pp. 221-22. But Rousseau himself reprinted the letter in the tenth book of his *Confessions*, adding a note affirming that he had never shown the letter to anyone nor spoken of it. "The evil I have had to say of my enemies I have told them in private to their faces; the good, when there is any, I say openly and with a glad heart" (trans. J. M. Cohen [Harmondsworth: Penguin, 1953], p. 501). Rousseau does not attempt to reconcile this claim with the fact of the letter's reproduction in the very public *Confessions*.

100   **"I have abandoned"** quoted in Cranston, *The Noble Savage*, p. 122.

101   **"the devout party"** quoted in Cranston, *The Noble Savage*, p. 30.

101   **"I wanted to philosophize"** quoted in Cranston, *The Noble Savage*, p. 31.

101   **"that fool Rousseau"** quoted in Cranston, *The Solitary Self: Jean-Jacques Rousseau in Exile and Adversity* (Chicago: University of Chicago Press, 1997), p. 7.

102   **"Rousseau's early life"** Cranston, *The Noble Savage*, p. xiii.

104   **"How is it that"** quoted in Cranston, *The Noble Savage*, p. 163.

104   **"Extreme insolence"** quoted in Cranston, *The Noble Savage*, p. 164.

104   **"Oh why did Providence"** quoted in Cranston, *The Solitary Self*, p. 1.

105   **"As for kindnesses"** quoted in Cranston, *The Noble Savage*, p. 86.

105   **"I shall not praise"** quoted in *The Noble Savage*, p. 161.

105   **"there cannot be"** quoted in *The Noble Savage*, p. 130.

105   **"I am made unlike anyone"** Rousseau, *Confessions*, trans. J. M. Cohen (Harmondsworth: Penguin, 1953), p. 17.

106   **"I require from a friend"** as quoted in *The Norton Book of Friendship*, ed. Eudora Welty and Ronald A. Sharp (New York: Norton, 1991), p. 187.

107   **"first began to live"** *Confessions*, Book Nine, p. 375.

107   **"Gothic cottage"** Cranston, *The Noble Savage*, p. 21.

107   **"I could say"** *The Noble Savage*, p. 173.

108   **"one of the strongest proofs"** quoted in Paul Johnson, *Intellectuals* (New York: Harper, 1989), p. 24.

108   **"I contradict myself"** Whitman, "Song of Myself," section 51, in *Leaves of Grass* (1892 edition).

108   **"I publicly and fearlessly"** *Confessions*, Book Ten, p. 606.

108   **"Man is born free"** *The Social Contract*, trans. Maurice Cranston (London: Penguin, 1968), p. 49.

109   **"I have displayed"** *Confessions*, p. 17.

110   **"There must be theatres"** Cranston, *The Noble Savage*, p. 35.

111   **"created virtually from whole cloth"** Cohen, *Freedom's Moment: An Essay on the French Idea of Liberty from Rousseau to Foucault* (Chicago: University of Chicago Press, 1997), pp. 6, 10.

111   **"our master and our brother"**   Levi-Strauss, *Tristes Tropiques* (1955), trans. John and Doreen Weightman (Harmondsworth: Penguin, 1992), p. 391.

111   **"one does not arrest"**   quoted in *Freedom's Moment*, p. 48.

112   **"that melodramatic"**   Gay, *The Enlightenment: An Interpretation, Volume II: The Science of Freedom* (New York: Norton, 1969), p. 530.

114   **"There are only two"**   quoted in *Freedom's Moment*, pp. 23, 73.

114   **"there are not two"**   quoted in *Freedom's Moment*, p. 146.

114   **"terror is harmful"**   quoted in *Citizens*, p. 828.

114   **"I believe patriotism"**   quoted in *Citizens*, p. 842.

115   **"Robespierre guillotining"**   quoted in *Citizens*, p. 850.

117   **"Good represents"**   Murdoch, *Metaphysics as a Guide to Morals* (London: Penguin, 1992), pp. 496, 473.

118   **"the good things"**   *The Good Apprentice* (London: Penguin, 1985), p. 522.

118   **"pictures will as a blend"**   *Metaphysics*, p. 300.

119   **"If it must be a play"**   *Metaphysics*, p. 98.

119   **"the achievement"**   *Metaphysics*, pp. 146-47.

119   **"in the traditional novel"**   *Metaphysics*, p. 97.

120   **"remember Eckhart's"**   Murdoch, *The Green Knight* (London: Penguin, 1993), p. 266.

121   **"The 'demythologisation'"**   *Metaphysics*, p. 460.

121   **"old dogmatic literalistic myths"**   *Metaphysics*, p. 135.

121   **"a Christian who loses"**   *Metaphysics*, p. 376.

121   **"Can one simply decree"**   *Metaphysics*, p. 458.

122   **"parish magazine"**   MacIntyre, *Whose Justice? Which Rationality?* (Notre Dame: Notre Dame University Press, 1988), p. 5.

122   **"our minds are . . ."**   Murdoch, *Metaphysics*, p. 329.

123   **"A mother asks her son"**   *Metaphysics*, p. 338.

123   **"Keats says that"**   *Metaphysics*, p. 506.

124   **"supreme fiction"**   See Stevens's poem "Notes toward a Supreme Fiction," in *The Collected Poems* (New York: Vintage, 1982), pp. 380-408.

124   **"incredulity toward metanarratives"**   Lyotard, *The Postmodern Condition*, trans. Brian Massumi (Minneapolis: University of Minnesota Press, 1985).

125   **"There are, indeed"**   Murdoch, *Metaphysics*, p. 30.

125   **"Should we let"**   *Metaphysics*, p. 327.

125   **"a Christ who"**   *Metaphysics*, p. 419.

126   **"The charm, attraction"**   *Metaphysics*, p. 81.

126   **"are in a sense"**   *Metaphysics*, p. 128.

126   **"however, God sees"**   *Metaphysics*, p. 83.

127   **"foolishness to the Greeks"**   I Cor. 1:23.

127   **"now thou art"**   *King Lear*, Act I, Scene iv.

129	**"marionette theater"** Gates, "Whose Canon Is It, Anyway?" in *Debating P.C.*, ed. Paul Berman (New York: Dell/Laurel, 1992), p. 192.
129	**"confronted by argument"** Milosz, "On Pasternak Soberly," in *Emperor of the Earth: Modes of Eccentric Vision* (Berkeley: University of California Press, 1977), p. 125.
132	**"myths arise from"** Soyinka, *Myth, Literature, and the African World* (Cambridge: Cambridge University Press, 1976), p. 34.
132	**"THE WILL of man"** *Art, Dialogue, and Outrage: Essays on Literature and Culture* (New York: Pantheon, 1994), p. 247.
133	**"the bane of themes"** Soyinka, *Death and the King's Horseman* (New York: Hill and Wang, 1975), "Author's Note."
133	**"All is prepared"** *Death and the King's Horseman*, p. 40.
134	**"condemned to wander"** *Death and the King's Horseman*, p. 71.
134	**"is entitled to whatever"** *Death and the King's Horseman*, p. 53.
135	**"The confrontation"** *Death and the King's Horseman*, "Author's Note."
137	**"Babangida's love"** *The Open Sore of a Continent* (New York: Oxford University Press, 1996), p. 14.
138	**"stood a reasonable chance"** *The Burden of Memory, the Muse of Forgiveness* (New York: Oxford University Press, 1998), p. 4.
138	**"dissociation of sensibility"** Eliot coined this phrase in his early essay "The Metaphysical Poets," which may be found in his *Selected Essays* (New York: Harcourt Brace and World, 1950), p. 247.
138	**"That the very existence"** *Art, Dialogue, and Outrage*, p. 300.
140	**"political animal"** *The Open Sore of a Continent*, pp. 128f.
143	**"his dark materials"** *Paradise Lost*, 2.916.
143	**"Pullman knows"** from an interview conducted in 200, just before the publication of *The Amber Spyglass*: "you can tell from the general thrust of the book that I'm of the devil's party, like Milton." (http://www.avnet.co.uk/home/amaranth/Critic/ivpullman.htm)
144	**"a great destiny"** Pullman, *The Golden Compass* (New York: Knopf, 1995), p. 176.
144	**"Lyra and her daemon"** *The Golden Compass*, p. 3.
145	**"one of the most"** Pullman, "The Dark Side of Narnia," *Guardian* (London), 1 October 1998.
145	**"The Authority"** *The Amber Spyglass* (New York: Alfred A. Knopf, 200), pp. 31-32.
156	**"every church"** *The Subtle Knife* (New York: Scholastic, 1998), p. 45.
146	**"she and the rebel"** *The Amber Spyglass*, p. 479.
146	**"The Christian religion"** *The Amber Spyglass*, p. 441.
146	**"We know no time"** *Paradise Lost*, 5.860ff.

148   **"seek[ing] him out"**   *The Amber Spyglass*, p. 328.

148   **"a round disk"**   *William Blake* (Oxford Authors Series), ed. Michael Mason (Oxford: Oxford University Press, 1988), p. 44.

149   **"a being whose"**   *The Amber Spyglass*, p. 404.

149   **"Killing is not difficult"**   *The Amber Spyglass*, p. 205.

149   **"Pope John Calvin"**   *The Golden Compass*, p. 30.

150   **"atoms of his beloved"**   *The Amber Spyglass*, p. 418.

150   **"vivid little burst"**   *The Amber Spyglass*, p. 364.

151   **"all we can say"**   *The Amber Spyglass*, p. 447.

151   **"Mrs. Coulter"**   *The Amber Spyglass*, pp. 210-11.

152   **"war of every man"**   Hobbes, *Leviathan* (1651), Chapter XII.

152   **"There are only"**   see p. 114 above.

152   **"people are too complicated"**   *The Amber Spyglass*, p. 447.

153   **"the rhetorician would"**   Yeats, "Ego Dominus Tuus," in *Collected Poems*, ed. Richard J. Finneran (New York: MacMillan, 1989), p. 160.

154   **"tenth Muse"**   Anne Carson, *If Not, Winter: Fragments of Sappho* (New York: Knopf, 2002), p. ix.

154   **"most beautiful"**   These hints of biography are quoted by Carson in the "Appendix: Some Exemplary Testimonia," *If Not, Winter*, pp. 393ff.

154   **"a word *beudos*"**   *If Not, Winter*, p. xii.

155   **"]bitter"**   p. 177.

155   **"this would render"**   p. xi.

156   **"having come from"**   *If Not, Winter*, p. 113

156   **"do I still yearn"**   *If Not, Winter*, p. 219

156   **"("Eros the melter"**   *If Not, Winter*, p. 265.

157   **"If you persist"**   Carson, *Autobiography of Red* (New York: Vintage, 1999), p. 12.

157   **"The fragments of"**   *Autobiography of Red*, p. 5.

159   **". . . he will never"**   Murdoch, *The Green Knight*, p. 392.

159   **"sexual relations"**   *The Foucault Reader* (New York: Pantheon, 1984), p. 345.

160   **"sex is boring"**   *The Foucault Reader*, p. 340.

160   **"techniques of the self"**   *The Foucault Reader*, p. 341.

160   **"Eros seemed to Sappho"**   Carson, *Eros the Bittersweet* (Princeton: Princeton University Press, 1986), pp. 3, 4, 6-7.

161   **"No simple map"**   *Eros the Bittersweet*, p. 7.

161   **"Is the pleasure"**   *The Foucault Reader*, p. 346.

162   **"Well he's a taker"**   Carson, *Glass, Irony, and God* (New York: New Directions, 1995), p. 3.

162   **"Loyal to nothing"**   Carson, *The Beauty of the Husband* (New York: Vintage, 2002), p. 9.

164   **"For if she flees"** *If Not, Winter*, p. 5.

165   **"ordinary love song"** Bonhoeffer, *Letters and Papers from Prison*, enlarged edition (New York: Macmillan, 1971), p. 315.

165   **"I will do anything"** Carson, *Plainwater* (New York: Random, 1995), p. 29.

166   **"blest bridegroom"** *If Not, Winter*, p. 229.

169   **"It lets you use"** http://www.retiary.org/ls/.

171   **"All these permutations"** Lanham, *The Electronic Word: Democracy, Technology, and the Arts* (Chicago: University of Chicago Press, 1993), p. 12.

172   **"the linear habits"** Landow, *Hypertext 2.0: The Convergence of Contemporary Critical Theory and Technology* (Baltimore: Johns Hopkins University Press, 1997), p. 98.

174   **"a diary rather"** Steve G. Steinberg, "Lifestreams," *Wired* 5.02 (February 1997): http://www.wired.com/wired/archive/5.02/fflifestreams.html.

174   **"Complexity makes"** David Gelernter, *Machine Beauty: Elegance and the Heart of Technology* (New York: Basic Books, 1998), p. 22.

175   **"Contemporary culture"** Neal Stephenson, *In the Beginning Was the Command Line* (New York: Avon Books, 1999), p. 58.

178   **"Often when a large"** W. Daniel Hillis, *The Pattern on the Stone: The Simple Ideas That Make Computers Work* (New York: Basic Books, 1998), p. 143.

179   **"the power of modularity"** Carliss Y. Baldwin and Kim B. Clark, *Design Rules, Volume 1: The Power of Modularity* (Cambridge: MIT Press, 2000).

179   **"slime mold swarms"** Steven Johnson, *Emergence: The Connected Lives of Ants, Brains, Cities, and Software* (New York: Scribner, 2001), p. 14.

180   **"unearthed a secret"** *Emergence*, p. 17.

181   **"The conventional"** *Emergence*, p. 100.

182   **"I am an aspiring"** Steve Grand, *Creation: Life and How to Make It* (Cambridge: Harvard University Press, 2001), p. 10.

182   **"A game it might"** *Creation*, pp. 8-9.

182   **"I would like"** *Creation*, p. 4.

182   **"It's tough being a god"** Sarah Lyall, "The Man Who Would Be God," *New York Times*, February 2, 2002, B7.

183   **"Human beings"** quoted in Lyall, "The Man Who Would be God."

183   **"If there is any"** Lawrence Lessig, *Code: And Other Laws of Cyberspace* (New York: Basic Books, 1999), p. 25.

184   **"to hate technology"** Gelernter, *Machine Beauty*, p. 135.

185   **"We are entering"** Lessig, *Code*, p. 239.

185   **"These two companies"** Lessig, *The Future of Ideas: The Fate of the Commons in a Connected World* (New York: Random House, 2001), p. 265.

186   **"have been able"** Stephenson, *In the Beginning*, p. 31.

188   **"The one unique benefit"** quoted in Glyn Moody, *Rebel Code: Inside Linux*

and the Open Source Revolution (Cambridge, MA: Perseus Publishing, 2001), p. 225.

190   **"Open Letter to Hobbyists"**   http://www.blinkenlights.com/classiccmp/gateswhine.html.

191   **"got the fever"**   quoted in Moody, *Rebel Code*, p. 57.

192   **"Free speech, not free beer"**   http://www.gnu.org/philosophy/free-sw.html.

194   **"Setting up"**   Stephen E. Harris, with Erwin Zijleman, *Corel Linux for Dummies* (Foster City, CA: IDG Books, 2000), p. 16.

195   **"I'm going, OK"**   quoted in Moody, *Rebel Code*, p. 225.

199   **"It's vital"**   Matt Welsh, Matthias Kalle Dalheimer, and Lar Kaufman, *Running Linux*, 3rd ed. (Sebastopol, CA: O'Reilly, 1999), p. 43.

202   **"a bunch of RVs"**   Stephenson, *In the Beginning*, p. 7.

203   **"Dr. Gelernter"**   Theodore Kaczynski's letter to David Gelernter is available online at (among other places) http://pages.prodigy.com/gvmm68e/letter1.html.

204   from the cover of Nelson's book, as reproduced in Randall Packer and Ken Jordan, eds., *Multimedia: From Wagner to Virtual Reality* (New York: W. W. Norton, 2001), p. 154.

205   **"I believe that anyone"**   Petroski, *The Pencil* (New York: Knopf, 1989), p. ix.

207   **"We distinguish"**   The "Unabomber Manifesto" may be found at, among other sites, http://www.soci.niu.edu/~critcrim/uni/uni.html.

207   **"1. Information about"**   Albert Borgmann, *Holding on to Reality: The Nature of Information at the Turn of the Millennium* (Chicago: University of Chicago Press, 1999). See, for an overview of these points, the opening pages of each of the book's three main sections.

208   **"texts get flattened"**   *Holding on to Reality*, p. 209.

208   **"No amount of"**   *Holding on to Reality*, pp. 199-200.

209   **"The possibilities"**   Fisher, "Virtual Interface Environments," in *Multimedia*, p. 246.

209   **"longing, nostalgia"**   Hershman, "The Fantasy beyond Control," in *Multimedia*, p. 303.

209   **"liquid architectures"**   Novak, "Liquid Architectures in Cyberspace," in *Multimedia*, p. 264.

210   **"It is possible"**   Alan Turing's "On Computable Numbers" was originally published in the *Proceedings of the London Mathematical Society*, 1936-37. It is available online at http://www.abelard.org/turpap2/tp2-ie.asp.

212   **"when this body"**   Vinge's "True Names" is reprinted in *True Names and the Opening of the Cyberspace Frontier*, ed. James Frenkel (New York: Tor Books, 2001); see p. 329.

213 **"As We May Think"** is much reprinted; it may be found in *Multimedia*, pp. 135-53.

214 **"We can predict"** *The Postmodern Condition*, p. 4.

214 **"First come I"** There are several versions of this rhyme, most of which can be found scattered about the Internet. I do not remember where I came across the one I know and cite here.

215 **"we feel in each"** Updike, *Hugging the Shore* (New York: Knopf, 1983), p. 235.

217 **"the measuring of"** Ellul, *The Technological Society*, trans. John Wilkinson (New York: Vintage Books, 1967), p. 38.